AND SO IT HAPPENED

by

ROY GRAY HILL

Published 1997

by

WILTON 65
Flat Top House, Bishop Wilton, York. YO4 1RY

Copyright © Roy Hill

ISBN 0 947828 51 6

Printed and bound by
Antony Rowe Ltd, Chippenham, Wiltshire

CONTENTS

PAGE

Dedication	1
Foreword	2
Chapter 1 - Early Days	7
Chapter 2 - The School	24
Chapter 3 - Early Travels by Rowland	41
Chapter 4 - Separate Ways	53
Chapter 5 - Upcoming Liverpool	79
Chapter 6 - Prestigious Years	110
Chapter 7 - With the Beduins	133
Chapter 8 - Birkbeck's Sons	161
Chapter 9 - Nightmare Scenario	176
Chapter 10 - Sir Norman Hill & The Titanic	184
Chapter 11 - War and Lusitania	205
Chapter 12 - Between The Wars	226
Chapter 13 - Roy Gray Hill - Boyhood	241
Chapter 14 - The Second World War	252
Chapter 15 - Aftermath of War	263
Chapter 16 - A Peaceful Decade	275
Chapter 17 - Victorian Roots	290
Chapter 18 - End of an Era	298
Chapter 19 - So it will happen	312

ILLUSTRATIONS

Between pages

Thomas Wright Hill.	22-23
Kidderminster Home.	22-23
Bruce Castle.	78-79
Sir Rowland Hill	78-79
Perspective view of Liverpool c.1770.	108-109
Britannia at Boston 1847.	108-109
John Gray Hill and Caroline Hill.	116-117
Water Street Liverpool 1864.	116-117
Birkenhead Ferry c 1830.	116-117
George Mabbedy.	132-133
Some of our faithful servants.	132-133
Map of Syria showing routes taken.	132-133
Riding in the desert.	132-133
Ain el Beda. The Howeytat come out of the reeds.	160-161
Walking for a change.	160-161
Sheik Khalil of Keraki and another of his tribe.	160-161
Keraki discussing division of the spoils.	160-161
George Birkbeck Hill and his three sons.	174-175
Sir Maurice J. Hill.	174-175
Sir Norman Hill.	174-175
Sir Leonard Hill.	174-175
Sir John Gray Hill, President of the Law Society.	174-175
The *Titanic* strikes the iceberg.	204-205
New York Times reports sinking of the *Titanic*.	204-205
The sinking of the *Titanic*.	204-205
The *Lusitania*. Taking to the boats.	220-221
The sinking of the *Lusitania*. May 7th 1915.	220-221
Establishing Merchant Navy Officers Pension Fund.	252-253
Martin Spencer Hill.	252-253
Roy Gray Hill joins the Royal Air Force.	252-253
German bomber crew shot down.	262
Roy Gray Hill and Norah Olive Hill. Wedding day.	274-275
Roy Gray Hill.	274-275

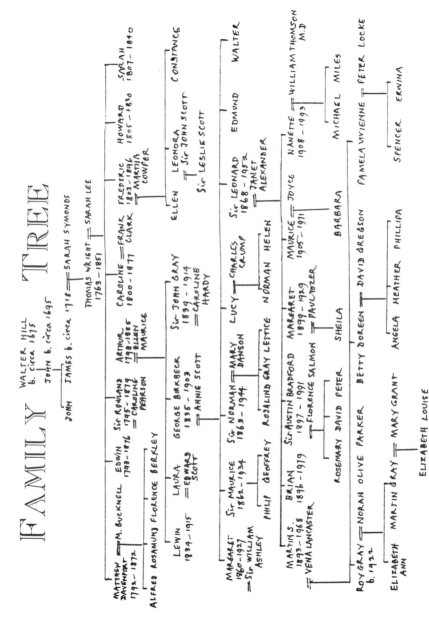

DEDICATION

I dedicate this work to all those who have gone through this world before us and have given us all that we are and have today. As well, to my beloved wife, Norah, in whom throughout life I have placed complete trust and reliance. To my daughter, Elizabeth and my son, Martin, who as the present generation preserve the values of their forebears. To my granddaughter, Elizabeth, to whom falls the task of preserving those values in what will be a rapidly changing world offering much for the future. Finally, to all those who serve at sea and who contributed so much to saving this country in two world wars and their association, Numast.

FOREWORD

I was born into the 1920s at a time when the Great War remained well in mind as the war that was to end all wars. I came into a world that was very different to that of today with few motor cars and fewer aeroplanes and no supermarkets. Much road traffic was still horse drawn as was all agricultural machinery. Wireless was at its beginning, and the British Broadcasting Corporation was still of the future. Few of our modern electrical appliances then existed. In some areas electrical power was not yet available including my wife's family home on the Isle of Wight. Birth took place at home with generally only the district nurse attending. Medical care was minimal compared with what the National Health Service has provided following the second world war.

I was born into a professional family of five generations of which three generations were intimately involved in shipping as marine solicitors practising under the name of Hill Dickinson & Co. As such, they managed various shipping organisations including the then leading Liverpool Steam Shipowners Association. I was to become the fourth generation. Later, my son was to become the fifth generation in a much changing world. In his time, many aspects of practising law have changed, so that today it appears much more of a hard nosed business looking for the maximum profit.

Some years ago, I decided to record the history of Hill Dickinson & Co. in which my family had occupied a unique position in advising British shipping as it prospered and grew. Thus, at the opening into the twentieth century, British shipping comprised just under half the total of world tonnage. For some years after the second world war, British shipping still comprised one quarter. Yet, following the second world war, successive governments allowed that asset to waste away in excessive taxation to subsidise a standard of life that its citizens did not earn. So that today the British fleet barely comprises one half per cent.

Researches into family and firm records and an ending of Hill Dickinson & Co. resulted instead in my chronicling the past three centuries as my forebears and I participated in them. Three centuries of vast change in human affairs, which I believe heralds an evolutionary change of human making going far beyond our present imagination. Yet a minuscule period in cosmic terms, so that human nature and characteristics remain little changed.

Chronicling events over three centuries produces many individual tales within the whole while the whole provides a scenario of changing social condition. A scenario of travel through time and a changing world seen through the eyes and minds of those who were then present.

The scenario opens with the many social problems of living in the 18th century. They include tales of flight from a forced marriage, the horrors of plague, an old woman rescued from drowning as a witch, and the difficulties of the married woman. It continues in the benevolent school of Tom Hill and his sons that so much contrasted with schools generally of the era. Schools that were extremely cruel, vice ridden, and the subject of repeated flogging and appalling bullying.

The scenario changes to the endeavours of Tom's sons to alleviate the social problems of the early 1800s. They included the difficulties faced by Rowland when he introduced penny postage and later came to modernise the Post Office with the aid of his two brothers, Edwin and Frederic. Also, they included the activities of Matthew Hill, barrister and member of Parliament and criminal law reformer, and of Arthur who took over as headmaster of the family school. They further included the prison reforms introduced by Frederick. He was the first appointed prison inspector for Scotland, Northumberland and Durham and a prison reformer of his day.

Especially, Liverpool and its prosperous shipping within an expanding Empire are central to the scenario as, first, the railway replaced the horse drawn coach and the steamship replaced sail. Tom's grandson, John Gray Hill, came to Liverpool in 1864 to practice marine law. Following his appointment as secretary of the Liverpool Steamship Owners Association, he rapidly found himself at the centre of British shipping. He was much involved in the North Atlantic trade and in advising its participants, Cunard, Inman and the White Star Line and many other shipping names of the time. Yet

3

he and his wife, Carrie, led a second life perilously exploring then little explored parts of Syria.

John Gray Hill's nephew, Norman Hill, followed his uncle to Liverpool. He acted for the White Star Line when the *Titanic* was lost and for the Cunard when a German torpedo sunk their luxury liner *Lusitania* during the Great War. Narrated evidence portrays these two tragic losses through the eyes of those on board. Also during the Great War, Norman Hill recommended adoption of the convoy system to overcome the overwhelming shipping losses that they were then sustaining. Furthermore, Norman was an expert in maritime law and served on many government committees dealing with maritime affairs including as chairman of the Merchant Shipping Advisory Committee. His letters following the war reveal social problems of that time.

After demobilisation following the Great War, the author's father, Martin Hill, nephew of Norman and great-nephew of John Gray, came to Liverpool. His earlier years in Liverpool were a continuation of those of Norman Hill. Especially, Britain continued at the head of a great Empire and as such recognised the importance of her shipping. Shipping which provided employment and overseas earnings and formed the fourth arm of defence.

Meanwhile, Geo Birkbeck Hill, John Gray's brother and my great-grandfather, had distinguished himself in the world of literature and specially in editing a new edition of Boswell's Doctor Johnson. He plays his part within the scenario. Not least because of his three sons, each steered by their parents into a chosen professional career in which each received a knighthood for services to his profession.

Thus the eldest son, Maurice, became a barrister and later, after appointment as Queen's Counsel at the Admiralty bar, became the Admiralty judge. The second, Norman, became a solicitor and, as already mentioned, followed his uncle, John Gray Hill, to Liverpool. The third, Leonard, Martin's father and my grandfather, devoted his life to medical research. He added greatly to the knowledge of the respiratory and circulatory systems and of protection of life at sea.

Leonard in turn had four sons who played their part within a changing scenario. As already mentioned, Martin, my father, came to Liverpool following the Great War. Brian was an author of some repute. Perhaps, the best known is Sir Austin Bradford Hill (Tony) who as an epidemiologist discovered the connection between smoking and lung cancer and heart diseases. Maurice went to the bar, but finding this unrewarding became a solicitor and established the well-known shipping and insurance firm Messrs Clydes

Last appearing within the scenario by way of a short autobiography is myself. I who have seen Great Britain as she once was heading a great empire on which they said the sun never set and owning the greatest fleet of all time. Later, I played my part as the nation stood alone against the most evil of regimes when all around expected her to fall. Yet, following victory after six desperate years of war, I have seen, a generation later, the nation collapse morally and financially as empire collapsed. So that today, another generation later, the nation again looks to its future. Yet, our once great fleet and brave seamen are now all but disappeared, and I despair that the remnants may have entirely disappeared before few decades have passed

Sources of the scenario are Geo. Birkbeck Hill's *Life of Sir Rowland Hill* and *History of Penny Postage* published by Thos De La Rue in 1880 that contains original descriptions by Rowland Hill and Geo. Birkbeck Hill. Also early letter books of Hill Dickinson & Co, which contain tissue thick copies much faded by time and difficult of interpretation. After separating out much dross, they deliver up pearls descriptive of social life in the mid-nineteenth century. The private letter books of John Gray Hill are another source of information and, especially, his privately published *With the Beduins* which I have epitomised. Likewise are the private letter books of Norman Hill.

The annual reports and the 1958 Centenary History of the Liverpool Steamship Owners Association are a source of quotation. Unpublished writings of Brian Hill relating to his parent's courtship have proved another useful source of information. I am indebted to Bruce Castle Tottenham who have made various records on the Hill family available to me, and to the Mary Evans Picture Library for the use of pictures. Also, I have gained assistance from an ancient publication *Annals of Liverpool* that itemises events in Liverpool to the end of the nineteenth century.

Finally, I am especially indebted in respect of format and presentation to my publishers for their invaluable assistance and specialist knowledge, and to Andrew Price for expert and detailed work on the photographs as well as for the cover design.

Roy Gray Hill
March 1997

CHAPTER 1

EARLY DAYS

A small stone monument stands on the windswept Freshwater cliffs at the Isle of Wight bearing the poignant inscription:

Erected in remembrance of a most dear and only child who was suddenly removed into eternity by a fall from the adjacent cliff on the rocks beneath

28th August 1846

Reader prepare to meet thy god for thou knowest not what a day may bring forth for in the midst of life we are in death.

Another monument at Kidderminster commemorates Sir Rowland Hill and his introduction in 1840 of penny postage throughout the British Isles. These monuments mirror an age and a people totally different in their manner of life and beliefs to those now facing the twenty first century. Yet they were our forebears of only some six to eight generations ago.

The monument at Freshwater is now only a faint echo of great sadness at the sudden ending of a young life. This at a time when life could be hard and bleak and sickness and death of loved ones were an ever present anxiety. It strikes little chord today, except to those enjoying the tranquillity of the place who suddenly find themselves transported back in time to that tragic event.

The monument to Sir Rowland Hill bears testimony to his contribution to those vast changes in human life that have taken place over the last three centuries. A minuscule period measured against the existence of human life, and the more so when measured against the life of our planet, our solar system and the universe. Yet it was a period that transformed human life from one of little more than bare existence to one of material comfort and well-being.

Other members of the Hill family have contributed to these changes, especially, in education, the law, medicine, and in shipping. An industry in which Britain was once supreme, but squandered away her inheritance during the second half of the twentieth century by profligate government, poor management and appalling labour relations.

The best interpretation of past events comes from those who were present at the time. Such an interpretation avoids the partiality of later generations to interpret the past as if what is has always been. Thus, these pages view the changes that have taken place as seen through the eyes of the Hill family and their contemporaries.

W.T.J. Gun in his *Studies in Heredity* (published by George Allen and Unwin in 1928) wrote of the Hill family:

'From James and Sarah Hill descended one of the most intellectual families that have ever arisen in England. The bright particular star was Sir Rowland Hill famed for his introduction of the now alas defunct penny postage. Others were Matthew Davenport Hill, criminal law reformer; George Birkbeck Hill, writer and critic; Rosamund Davenport Hill, the most prominent member of the old London School Board; and at the present day (1928) Sir Maurice Hill, High Court Judge and Sir Leslie Scott, late Attorney General. Though these were the most prominent, they are far from exhausting the list of members of this family who have shown marked intellectual distinction.'

The writings of Geo. Birkbeck Hill assist in portrayal of these earlier events. Especially, his *Life of Sir Rowland Hill* and *History of Penny Postage* published by Thos de la Rue in 1880. This work comprised two volumes that Birkbeck wrote to the direction of Sir Rowland Hill and included quotations from Rowland's original Journals.

These writings describe the Hill family as originating in the west country and subsequently descending through a wealthy landowner of the seventeenth century. The latter abandoned his children by a first wife largely to fend for themselves. No information is available to explain how he came to part from his first wife, but her early death seems the likeliest cause. A son, Walter Hill, set up business as a hatter in Kidderminster followed by his son, John, as a tailor and his grandson, James, as a baker and corn chandler. The family were puritan in character and of strong Protestant beliefs. It is James to whom Gun refers as the patriarch of the Hill family.

James Hill was born in 1718 into an era still predominantly based on land and agriculture and the old feudal system. The Courts imposed hanging and transportation for quite minor crimes. Whipping posts, stocks and ducking stools were common to most English villages.

During the seventeenth century, the population of England and Wales increased from five and a half million to nine million. The economic and social harmony of Queen Anne's England was giving way to competing interests of town and country and of rich against poor. Uncontrolled individualism and greed in the pursuit of wealth were despoiling the beauty of England with sprawling and overcrowded development and slum housing. Disease was rampant, including plague, cholera and tuberculosis, and was to continue so over the next century and longer.

In our modern civilised world of social protection, comfort and leisure envisaging the lives of our forebears of but a few generations ago is not easy. They would have been much as ourselves, but anxious and despairing as they faced the ever present risk of illness and early death. Reader, imagine yourself without tap water, electricity, gas and sanitation; with the most primitive forms of medical care; with inadequate police and fire protection; and with movement restricted to foot and horse along rough track. That was the best for which our forbears could hope. They looked upon God as a living being to whom they could turn for succour and an eventual life of joy in heaven.

Birkbeck Hill describes how James Hill, the baker, refused his vote at county elections to the local squire. Bakers then heated their ovens with faggots of wood bought from the squire. The squire refused James further faggots. James was an ingenious man. He experimented and found that he could properly heat his ovens by a mixture of faggots and coal. Bakers had not previously used coal, although it was cheap for their ovens. Further experiment enabled James to go on lessening the faggots and increasing the coal. He was so successful that other bakers in the district followed his lead. The squire found himself short of buyers. The position became reversed with the squire seeking orders for faggots from James.

James had a brother John. Those of the times describe John as a searcher after liberty and the Protestant religion. In 1745, he enrolled as a volunteer against the invading Scots who were serving under the leadership of the young Pretender, Bonny Prince Charles. The latter was attempting Stuart restoration to the throne. The Prince first had some success, but finally King George II and his army were victorious.

Another time, John served on a jury at Worcester. They said of him that he alone of the twelve good men and true refused a bribe. The judge hearing of this praised him highly. Whenever on the same circuit, he would ask whether he was to have the pleasure of meeting the honest juror.

John lived to the age of ninety and was well known to Rowland Hill and his brothers to whom he recounted his exploits. In turn, they told them to their nephew and the author's great-grandfather, the writer Geo. Birkeck Hill. Again this emphasises the relative shortness of time between these earlier events and life as it now enters the twenty-first century.

In 1759, James Hill married Sarah Symonds. Her father was John Symonds, a surgeon and apothecary of Shrewsbury, who also carried on business as a dry salter and maker of British wines. It is of James and Sarah that Gun wrote in his *Studies in Hereditary Ability*.

Speaking of John Symonds, Gun further wrote:

'John Symonds continued the family profession, and devoted his spare time to extempore prayer and sermon-making. Would-be suitors for his daughter were conducted into an inner sanctum and examined as to their proficiency in these exercises. James Hill, a baker and dealer in horse corn, passed this test with flying colours. Notwithstanding his apparently lower social position, he was allowed to wed the surgeon's daughter Sarah.'

Gun also considered the common maternal link of John Symonds in both the Hill and Mackenzie family trees that resulted from the marriage of Symond's granddaughter, Elizabeth, to John Mackenzie. Thus, Sarah Hill was the great great-aunt of the

10

Victorian throat specialist, Sir Morell Mackenzie, who attended on the German Crown Prince Frederick William at Potsdam when dying of cancer. She was also the great great-aunt of the author, Sir Compton Mackenzie, and his actress sister, Fay Compton. Over the years, both families have had much in common, especially, in providing leading medical specialists of their day.

A son, Thomas Wright Hill (Tom for short) was born to James and Sarah in 1763. James and Sarah were god fearing and puritanical and their household the subject of a religious but loving discipline. Tom has left a verbatim account of a typical Sunday at his Calvinist home. The reader may be interested to compare this account with his own Sunday.

The day opened with breakfast taken at eight with much gravity. An extempore prayer from 'my father' followed. Two hours of chapel in the morning, a further two hours in the early afternoon, and one and half hours in the evening occupied much of the day. Many in the congregation were unable to read, so that singing of hymns was line by line as each line was first read out by the clerk. Morning service was nine until eleven o'clock.

As recounted by Tom:

'The amen to the final blessing was the most delightful word in the service to myself and I conjecture to others for it was then eleven o'clock. Arrived back home, we changed our coats for morning gowns and gathered for family service of readings and extempore prayers by my father. That brought us near to noon, our Sunday's hour for dinner. The dinner rarely consisted of anything more than a boiled pudding, sometimes made savoury with suet and sometimes with dried currants, and sometimes made of small bread boiled and rendered palatable by a compound sauce. We rarely ate meat on Sundays. If we did, it was always cold. By what salvo they conscientiously got over the Sabbatarian law in boiling the pudding, I never learnt.'

Afternoon service was from one until three, and Tom continued:

'Now we had my mother's company thither and that of her faithful maid, Sarah, who, though honestly religious, was rendered from her labourious life often to pass much of her sitting time in nods and starts. Three o'clock arriving, they pronounced another delightful amen from the pulpit, and again did I get a momentary release from thraldom. At this hour, my father frequently used to entertain my brother and me with scripture stories told in familiar language. The story of Gideon was a great favourite, and ecstatic was the moment when my father came to narrate the breaking of the jugs, the sudden blaze of the lamps and the accompanying shouts of the watchword ..... the sword of the Lord and of Gideon.'

Evening service was at five and continued about an hour and a half, so that they pronounced the third welcome amen at about half past six.

Tom continues:

'On the return home, our good mother took us into her chamber to repeat our catechism and our hymns. An affectionate address followed, this exhorting upon the fulfilment of religious and moral duties. That was by far the most interesting and delightful portion of our Sunday's exercise, which, I doubt not, had on us a most powerful influence as to our future characters. The close was attended with the gift of a piece of plum cake or something of the kind. An almost necessary preparation for what was to follow.

'This was the reading in the family of some long religious extract - often a whole sermon - to be followed by the longest of my father's prayers, all of which were extempore. When the prayer of Sunday night was concluded, my feelings I was used to compare with those of Christian when his burthen was miraculously unstrapped and fell from his back. This conclusion would occur about nine o'clock. The family then took a cheerful supper and thoughts of religion were suspended for a time.'

As further described by his grandson, Geo. Birbeck Hill, under the first chapter of his *Life of Sir Rowland Hill*:

'When he left school in 1777 at the age of fourteen, Thomas Wright Hill expressed a strong wish to be articled or apprenticed to an attorney. However, his good mother was incredulous as to the possibility of a lawyer and an honest man being united in the same person. Instead, they apprenticed him to his uncle who

12

was a brass founder in Birmingham. In this employment, he later considered that he had wasted the best years of his life. Nevertheless, he succeeded in managing a Midlands brass foundry and, in leisure time, lecturing on natural philosophy.'

Tom's mother would never have believed that she was to become the matriarch of a line of eminent lawyers continuing for more than two centuries. Lawyers who were to play a substantial part in the great social changes to come, and whom the Crown was to honour for their services to the nation.

While apprenticed and living in Birmingham, Tom became friendly with the divine and natural philosopher, Dr. Joseph Priestly. Like Tom, Preistley's parents had brought him up in an atmosphere of Calvinism, but he had adopted a more liberal view for his time of religion and politics. Tom became a member of his congregation and attended his classes on natural philosophy. Later, Tom was himself to lecture at the Birmingham Philosophical Institute.

Following upon the French revolution of 1789, the twenty years of war between England and Napoleonic France (1793-1815) with its blockades and counter blockades caused havoc to economic life in England. Later, the American war of independence (1812-1815) caused further havoc. However, this was all in the future when the wedding of Tom Hill and Sarah Lea took place in 1791. Yet it was to have its effect on their married life.

Birkbeck Hill writes of Sarah's grandmother and parents in manner reflecting life in the early eighteenth century:

'Sarah's grandmother had been left an orphan at an early age. She was an heiress to a considerable fortune and brought up by an uncle and aunt. They were severe disciplinarians, even for their time, and tried to force her to marry a man for whom she had no liking. When she refused, they subjected her to close confinement.

'She escaped their house in the habit of a country woman, with a soldier's coat thrown over it. Sarah set out to walk to Birmingham, a distance of some fifteen miles. On the road one of her uncle's servants overtook her on horseback. He asked of her whether a young lady whose appearance he described had passed

13

her. She replied that no such person had passed her. The man rode away leaving her rejoicing at the completeness of her disguise.'

'To her fortune she never laid claim. At the end of two years, she married a working man named Davenport. For thirteen years they lived a happy life. Then a fever broke out in the town, and carried off many people including a neighbour. The alarm was so great that no one would go near the dead man's house. Mrs. Davenport, fearing that his unburied body might spread the pestilence still more widely through the neighbourhood, ordered his coffin, and with her own hands laid him in it. Her devotion cost her life. In a few days, this generous woman was herself swept away by the fever.

'About a year later, her husband also died. They left four children. The eldest, a daughter of thirteen also named Sarah, managed to support herself and her brothers by sewing. When the two boys were old enough to be apprenticed to trades, she went out to service in a farmhouse. She married her master's son whose name was William Lea.

'He had earlier saved a poor old woman from death by drowning, to which a brutal mob had sentenced her on a charge of witchcraft. He saw the unhappy woman struggling for her life in the water. A crowd surrounded her as cruel as it was ignorant hurling abuse at her misery. Forcing his way through the crowd, he plunged into the water and rescued the woman. In defiance of her persecutors, he took her into his own home until she had recovered.'

William and Sarah Lea of this tale were the parents of the bride of Tom Hill also named Sarah. Her father's rescue and support of the woman showed much courage and humanity on his part, especially, when people truly believed in witches and their reputedly evil and magical powers.

Birkbeck Hill describes how, in 1791, Tom had to delay his marriage to Sarah Lea for a short time, because of injuries he received during the Birmingham riots. These riots took place during the years of war with revolutionary and Napoleonic France. A period of such suspicion and reaction that people said it was safer to be a felon than a reformer. The authorities saw Jacobin spies and subversive agitators in any political meeting however small and innocent.

The dissenters and the nonconformists of the day with their unorthodox views on religion and politics were the subject of the greatest suspicion. Brutal Church and King mobs burnt their chapels and many of their houses to the ground. Birkbeck Hill narrates how Tom and several of his companions had offered to defend the house of their revered pastor, Dr. Priestly. He declined their services since, so he said, it was the duty of a Christian priest to submit to persecution.

Next, as described by Tom's eldest son, Matthew:

'My father's companions went away. Perhaps to escort their good pastor and his family, whose lives would not have been secure against the ruffians coming to demolish their home and property. My father barred the doors, closed the shutters, made fast the house as securely as he could against the expected rioters, and then awaited their arrival. He has often described to me how he walked to and fro in the darkened rooms, chafing under the restriction that had been put on him and his friends. He was present when the mob broke in, and he witnessed the plunder and destruction, and the incendiary fire by which the outrage was consummated.

'The magistrates swore in special constables. My father was one of them; and, like his comrades, compendiously armed with half a mop-stick by way of a truncheon. The special constables at first drove all before them, despite the immense disparity of numbers. After a time, they became separated in the melee and sustained a total defeat. The rioters severely bruised some of them, and one died of his injuries. Although my father was not conscious at the time of having received a blow, the next morning he could not raise his arm. He was always of opinion that, if they had a flag or some signal around which they could have rallied, the fortune of the day would have been reversed.'

The blow that Tom Hill received was so severe that he had to postpone his marriage for a fortnight. His bride too had become involved in the riots. As a child's governess, she was driving in an open carriage with her charges, when a gang of rough looking men stopped it. They ordered her to echo their shouts of Church and King. Staunch to her convictions of nonconformity and liberalism, she refused. They made a menacing movement towards the carriage, but the leader of the mob said impatiently:

"Leave her alone! She's a brave young woman."

They allowed the carriage and its occupants to go on its way.

Another instance of her courage came later. Her husband, as foundry manager, had occasion to dismiss a bad worker. The man called that same evening at their home. His surly manner and angry tone of voice alarmed Sarah, and more so when she observed the glint of a pistol barrel in the breast of his jacket. With great presence of mind, she turned to her husband and asked him to run upstairs and see to the baby whom she said was crying. The moment he had gone, she seized the unwelcome visitor by the coat collar. "You villain! You villain!" she cried and ran him the man out of the room and down the passage. She had slammed the front door on him before he had sufficiently recovered his wits to offer any resistance.

However, this was then in the future. For the first four years of their married life, Tom and Sarah lived at Birmingham on an income of no more than twenty one shillings (£1.05) per week. They then inherited the family home at Kidderminster. There Rowland was born. In all they had eight children. Their family table may be of some assistance to the reader as follows:

Thomas Wright Hill, Born 24th April, 1763. Died 13th June, 1851.

Sarah Lee, Born 23rd August, 1765. Died 9th April 1842.
Married, 29th July 1791.

Their children
Matthew Davenport, Born 6th August 1792. Died 7th June 1872.

Edwin, Born 25th November 1793. Died 6th November 1876.

Rowland, Born 3rd December 1795. Died 27th August 1879.

Arthur, Born 27th August 1798. Died 1885.

Caroline, Born 18th August 1800. Died 16thSeptember1877.

Frederic, Born 29th June 1803. Died 1896.

William Howard, Born 26th July 1805. Died 30th November 1830.

Sarah, Born, 9th July 1807. Died 12th June 1840.

Unfortunately, the war with Napoleonic France ruined the manufacture in which Tom was engaged and resulted in the loss of his Kidderminster home. He moved to Wolverhampton. There he found employment and later became manager of a brass foundry. His salary was so small that the family survived only by the severest thrift.

Tom rented an old farmhouse named Horsehills about a mile out of Wolverhampton. It had long been empty and the rent so low that it first excited his suspicion. It was not until he had signed the lease that he learned that ghosts reputedly haunted the house. However, he was much pleased with his low rent and cared nothing about ghosts.

There Rowland, at the age of three or four, nearly died of scarlet fever that then so often proved fatal. He was so ill that, for a short while, his mother and father thought that he had ceased to breathe. The attack left him weak for some years. He had passed his seventh birthday before they taught him his letters.

Though initially backwards in book learning, he showed considerable mechanical ability. At the age of five, he made a small water wheel that worked well in a local stream. More important, he found an aptitude for mental arithmetic and of arithmetical calculation that so distinguished him in later life. Later, Tom and Sarah were to lose both their youngest son and a daughter at early ages through illness. This was not an unusual average for those times.

17

Birkbeck Hill wrote of how, in his eighties, Rowland provided clear recollections of his childhood and early home Horsehills. How they were living there during the terrible dearth of 1880 of which, for many a year, men could hardly talk without a shudder. He recalled how one day, during this famine, a beggar came to their door when they were dining on bread and butter and lettuce. His mother took one slice from the dish and sent it to the man, but he refused it owing to insufficient butter for his liking.

Rowland further recalled the half-starved people plundering the fields for potatoes. How the family dug up and spread their own crop of potatoes over the parlour floor for security. He recalled the bread riots and the violent clamour made against the corn dealers and farmers, for the rioters thought that they created artificial scarcity. How the rioters threatened the farmers and set their barns and ricks on fire.

He recalled how one day a band of rioters came to their farmhouse home believing the occupier to be a farmer.

Next, in his words:

'They entered the house and demanded bread. The poor fellows, hungry as they doubtless were, listened to explanations. Upon one of them saying, Oh, come away. Look at the missus how bad her (she looks), they all quietly withdrew.'

Rowland recalled his father saying so terrible had been the dearth and so painful the memories raised that they had all come to look upon bread as something holy.

Rowland recounted what he described as an adventure of his childhood that impressed itself most deeply on his memory. A tale of special significance to those who now live in more enlightened times, and yet need to protect their children from the worst types of violence.

Rowland's father had gone one day on business to a town some miles off and was very late in returning. His mother became uneasy and set off quite alone to meet her husband. Soon after she had started, he returned but, although he had come by the way along which she had gone, he had not met her. In his turn, he was full of alarm. He sent off the eldest boy, Matthew (then nine years),

18

in one direction. He directed the next two boys, Edwin (eight years) and Rowland (six years), to go by one road to Wolverhampton and to come back by another. Rowland's father took a third way.

The two youngest lads set out, not without fear, but with conviction that the work must be done. They first had to go along a dark lane. Then they came to a spot where underneath the crossways lay buried the body of a lad who had ended his life with his own hand. They knew the place as *Dead Boy's Grave*. They had next to pass near the brink of a gravel pit. 'To us an awful chasm that we shuddered by as best we could.' At length they made their round and reached home not far off midnight.

There to their great joy they found all had returned safely. The mother had been coming back along the lane, when a man sprung up on the other side of the hedge and frightened her. In her terror she had cleared the opposite fence at a bound and had made her way home over the fields. The next day, her husband went with her to the spot. Although he was an active and muscular man, he failed to make in his strength the leap that she had made in her terror.

Rowland recollected how, in the autumn of 1801, his elder brothers had come back with the news that the mail coach had driven into Wolverhampton decked with blue ribbons. Tidings had just arrived of peace with France. The whole country was in a blaze with bonfires and illuminations. The boys joined in this general rejoicing by setting fire to the stump of an old tree. When war broke out again with France, the family was living in Birmingham.

As described by Rowland:
'Old Boney became the terror of all English children. Within half-a-mile of our house, the forging of gun barrels was incessant, beginning before dawn and continuing long after nightfall. The noise of the hammers was drowned ever and anon by the rattle from the proof houses. Our own house each time felt the shock, and the constant jars injured my mother's brewings of beer. Press-gangs now and then came as far as our inland town. I remember the alarm they caused to myself and my brothers. We were fearful, not

so much for ourselves, but that they would enrol our father.'

Rowland well remembered the mingled joy and grief at the great but dearly bought victory at Trafalgar and the following verses of a ballad sung in the streets:

On the nineteenth of October
Eighteen hundred and five,
We took from the French and Spaniards
A most glorious prize.

We fought for full four hours,
With thundering cannons ball;
But the death of gallant Nelson
Was by a musket ball.

Britannia and her heroes
Will long bemoan their loss;
For he was as brave an Admiral,
As e'er the ocean crossed.

Birkbeck Hill continued in his narrative of past events told by Rowland thus:

'Other memories expressed in his latter years carried back those who heard him talk to a state of life that was very unlike the present. The baker who supplied them with bread kept his reckonings by tallies. Their milk-woman had just such another score as that which was presented to Hogarth's Distressed Poet. A travelling tailor used to come his rounds and, by the common custom, live in their house while he was making clothes for the family. In every show of feats of horsemanship, the performance always ended with the burlesque of the Tailor riding to Brentford to vote for John Wilkes.

'The changes that he saw in the currency were very great. In his early childhood, gold pieces - guineas, half guineas and seven shilling bits - were not uncommon, but they began to disappear and before long were scarcely ever seen. About 1813, one of his brothers sold a guinea for a one pound note and eight shillings in silver. As people began to hoard gold, these one-pound notes took their place. Birmingham people looked upon Bank of England notes with suspicion, for forgers more often forged them than provincial notes.'

Birkbeck Hill goes on to tell how one daring and notorious forger in Birmingham, who was named Booth and known on sight to Rowland Hill, had long defied the few police there. His house stood in the midst of an open plain some miles from Birmingham. Booth very strongly barricaded it. The officers had more than once forced an entry. However, so careful had been Booth's watch that, when they broke in, he had destroyed all proof of his crime.

At length he became careless. A messenger sent to the rolling mill with metal had forgotten to bring a pattern. Taking out a three-shilling piece, the man inserted it in one slit after another of the gauge, until he found the one that corresponded exactly with its thickness. This he gave as a guide. That immediately aroused suspicions. They mustered the Birmingham police force and a troop of dragoons from local barracks.

The police brought a ladder, and made an entrance through the tiling of the roof. It seemed as if they were again too late. For, at first, nothing could be found. However, while mounting the ladder, one of the runners observed Booth through an upper window hurriedly thrusting papers into the fire. A hole was broken into the chimney. They found there one whole note and one partly burnt. They arrested Booth. The Court convicted and sentenced him to hanging for what was then a capital offence.

Birkbeck Hill suggests that it was scarcely surprising that criminals openly defied the laws. Birmingham with its seventy thousand inhabitants had a police force of less than twenty men. The usual body of ancient and most quiet watchmen guarded the town at night that, like other towns, was but dimly lit by oil lamps.

Birmingham sent prisoners by stage coach to the Warwick assizes that Rowland recalled they equipped with strong staples to which they fast locked the fetters of prisoners. When still a young lad, he had sat on a coach beside a man thus fettered. The latter had sought to justify his position on grounds that he had only robbed a hen-roost and they could not touch his neck for that.

Tom and Sarah brought up their eight children to love and fight for freedom. Not as occurred in France by revolution and bloodshed, but by working through constitutional means to overcome the evils of oppression.

Birkbeck Hill writes:

'Scarcely any reformers were left in Parliament. The great Whig party was either indifferent or hopeless. Everywhere the Criminal Law was administered with savage severity. The Bishops with the Archbishop of Canterbury at their head were ready to hang a poor wretch for the crime of stealing goods that were worth five shillings. The Royal Dukes fought hard for the slave trade. The Habeas Corpus Act was suspended, and honest men were left to languish in prison.

'Such were the evil days in which Thomas Wright Hill brought up his children, and such were the evil deeds that were ever rousing his fiercest anger. The savageness of the penal code, he hotly denounced.   Slavery and the slave trade and religious oppression of every kind, he utterly loathed and detested. "We were all" said one of his sons "born to a burning hatred of tyranny".'

Tom and Sarah were successful in that five of their eight children contributed much to the social development of their country during the nineteenth century. No mean effort in that two died young and their daughter, Caroline, achieved her aims in marriage. She emigrated with her husband and family friend, Frank Clark, to Adelaide Australia. One of her nieces later unkindly remarked:

"The Clarks? I believe they run about Adelaide like rabbits."

Birkbeck Hill, subsequently describing his grandparents, wrote:

'Thomas Wright Hill was a man of a very unusual character. He had a simplicity, an inventiveness and a disregard for everything that was conventional. His friends used to say of him that he had every sense but common-sense. He was the most guileless of men. He lived four score years and eight, and at the end of his long life he trusted his fellow-men as much as he had at the beginning. Sarah, his wife, though the inferior of her husband in quick intelligence and originality, was his superior in shrewd common sense and in firmness

22

Thomas Wright Hill

Kidderminster Home

of purpose. She was as practical as he was theoretical and as cautious as he was rash.'

CHAPTER 2

THE SCHOOL

Birkbeck Hill describes a vast change that took place in the family life of Thomas Wright Hill in 1801 when he was nearing forty and Rowland Hill was seven.

Sarah Hill always believed that her husband could make better use of his intellectual powers. Also, she wished to obtain for her children a better education than any that they could then afford. A friend wished to dispose of his school in Birmingham. Sarah persuaded her husband to give up his business in Wolverhampton and to buy the school. They transferred it to a convenient house called Hilltop on the outskirts of Birmingham. There, without experience, Thomas Wright Hill pioneered a highly unconventional system of education for his time.

As expressed in his address to parents:

'T. Hill, sensible of the severe responsibility attached to the office of a public preceptor, resolves, if entrusted with that charge, to devote himself to the duties of it with assiduity, perseverance and concentrated attention as indispensable to reputation and success. To ensure the cooperation of his students, he will make it his study to excite their reasoning powers and to induce in them habits of voluntary application. For this purpose, he will vary the ordinary course of instruction and, as occasion shall offer, point out subjects more particularly fitted to interest their feelings. He will always endeavour by kindness, patience, firmness and impartiality to secure for himself their affection and esteem.'

This was in stark contrast with the then harsh oppression of the public schools. These schools were notorious for their lack of discipline, bullying, vice, drunkenness, savage bouts of fisticuffs and repeated flogging of pupils. Conditions that caused the poet Shelley (born 1792) to describe his days at Eton as hell on earth.

Tom Hill's unusual form of address does not appear to have

24

deterred the hard headed inhabitants of the Midlands from sending their sons to Hilltop. No doubt the moderate level of fees, even for those days, played its part. They were only four or five guineas a year for day scholars and twenty or twenty-five guineas for boarders according to age. Rowland and his brothers were placed within the school and, at the age of seven, Rowland began his formal education.

Birkbeck Hill tells an amusing tale of how, one Good Friday morning, Rowland and his brother Matthew were sent with a basket to buy hot cross buns for the household.

Birkbeck Hill continues:

'As they went along the street, vendors were calling out after the Birmingham fashion

Hot cross buns! Hot cross buns!
One a penny, two a penny, hot cross buns!
Sugar 'em, and butter 'em, and clap 'em in your muns.

'The two lads, as they came home, began in jest to mimic the cry. To their surprise they found themselves beset with purchasers. Not having face enough to reject the demands that they had provoked, they soon emptied their basket. They had to return for more. However, they considered themselves well recompensed for their additional trouble by the profit made on the difference between their buying and selling price.'

As told by Birbeck Hill, the family were extremely poor and their troubles only worsened following the opening of the school. They grew worse and worse as the French war continued.

'Never,' wrote Thomas Wright Hill, 'was a time when debts were collected with more difficulty or left uncollected with more danger.' His wife tried more than one plan to add to the earnings of the family, and every plan she would talk over with Rowland while a mere child. She had a hatred of debt that became shared by her children.

Rowland wrote:

'I early saw the terrible inconvenience of being poor. My mother used to talk to me more than to all the others together of our difficulties, and they were very grievous. She used to burst into tears as she talked about them. One day she told me that she had

25

not a shilling in the house. She was afraid lest the postman might bring a letter, while she had no money to pay the postage.'

In those days the recipient and not the sender had to pay the postage. The amount was substantial and varied according to weight and distance. For a working man, it could amount to a day's pay.

Tom Hill appointed his sons as pupil teachers at ages which today would be considered quite unsuitable. He simply could not otherwise afford to pay for assistance in the classrooms. Rowland was only eleven when called upon to help his father. His elder brothers, Matthew and Edwin, were respectively fourteen and thirteen when similarly called. By the age of twelve, Rowland was much more a teacher than a pupil. No sooner did he learn something new than he himself set about teaching it. He received the best part of his own education from his father, not in class hours but in family discussion and debate.

Additionally, all the family took their part in the cleaning of the house including the chimneys, which was was done by the simple expedient of setting fire to them.

As Rowland later wrote:

'The family called upon me at a very early age to perform many offices that, in richer families, servants discharge exclusively. These included going on errands, helping in cleaning, arranging and even repairing, and, in short, doing any sort of work that lay within my power. By this means, I gradually acquired a feeling of responsibility, habits of business, dispatch, punctuality and independence that have proved invaluable to me through life.'

This was demonstrated in 1807 when their father fell ill. Rowland (then aged 12) and his two elder brothers, Matthew (aged 15) and Edwin (aged 14), carried on the school single handed for a week.

As the years passed and the brothers grew to adult years, so they became more ambitious in their plans for the school. The eldest brother, Matthew, set about improving the teaching, while Rowland took on responsibility for the organisation of the school and the management of the accounts. By the time he was seventeen (1812), Rowland had taken over the preparation of the school accounts.

Ably and gradually, he succeeded in discharging an accumulation of debts and improving the school's monetary affairs.

In 1815, Thomas Wright Hill was giving lectures on electricity to the Birmingham Philosophical Society of which he was a member. Rowland helped his father with models and designs made by himself to illustrate each lecture. Once he showed the model of a church that was complete with a lightning conductor. An imitation thunder cloud passed over the building without effect. Then they removed the lightning conductor. Again the thunder cloud passed over, the lightning struck, and the spire fell shattered. Another time, Rowland produced a mimic volcano.

On a third occasion, his father gave a lecture on astronomy. A model provided electric sparks that pinpointed the heavenly constellations. This proved an exciting experience.Afterwards, Thomas Hill was bringing some scientific friends back home to supper. Continuing in his dissertation, he invited their further contemplation of the stars and in the dark led his guests directly into a horse pond.

Today, such experiments are simple, but they were not so in those days of a rudimentary knowledge of electricity. Few then appreciated its true significance and what it was to mean for mankind. This is well illustrated in an epigram written in all sincerity by a friend of the Hill family:

> *And what did Watt accomplish for mankind? -*
> *What was the produce of his powerful mind?*
> *He found machinery a deadly curse;*
> *And what did Watt? He left it ten times worse.*

Unlike his friend, Thomas Hill was a progressive political and economic thinker. He scorned all social objections to the use of machinery, and he foresaw the benefits that such use would bestow upon mankind. He strongly condemned the judge-made law of the time that treated a profit share or dividend paid on subscribed capital as giving rise to partnership liabilities. Unlike the judges, he foresaw the benefits that enterprise would gain from limited liability that later followed in the limited company.

Matthew and Rowland were then writing a treatise based on their own experiences and setting forth their own ideas on the education of boys in large numbers. A work that Rowland was anxious to see published. However, in 1815 at the age of twenty-three, Matthew decided to give up teaching to read for the Bar and to qualify as a barrister. He thus sought to fulfil the ambition that his grandmother's aversion to lawyers had denied to his father. To keep himself, he became a reporter of the debates in the House of Commons. The second brother, Edwin, was a mechanic of considerable ability. He had also given up teaching and had articled himself to the proprietor of a Birmingham rolling mill. He was later to become its manager.

Following their departure, Rowland became the principal manager of the school helped by his younger brothers and, especially, Arthur.

To quote from Rowland's *Journal*:

'Arthur has made himself master of Latin by very intense application, which is a considerable relief to my mind. As Matthew was a good classical scholar, I thought that he would continue that department of instruction. I had pursued mathematics, which is a study better suited to my taste than any other.

'Matthew's entry as a student at Lincoln's Inn disarranged all my plans. Lately, I decided to pursue the study of language, for I consider a classical knowledge as absolutely necessary to the master of a school. Now that Arthur has taken that department and as I have no doubt he will manage it well, I shall pursue my mathematical studies with increased vigour.'

The following year 1816, Rowland introduced a new constitution into the school. This gave the pupils a large say in the government of the school and in school courts dispensing justice. Corporal punishment was abolished.

Rowland narrated under his *Journal*:

'Soon after Midsummer, I established a Court of Justice in the school. The judge, with the sheriff and the keeper of the records, are chosen monthly by the Boys. I appoint the attorney and the Solicitor-General. The judge appoints the inferior officers such as the clerk and the crier of the court and the constables, etc.

'The jury consists of six boys chosen by ballot from among those who have not for the past month disgraced themselves. The court hears all evidence including that of the parties. We hold the assizes once a week. It sometimes happens that there are no offenders. The sheriff keeps a book in which he enters all the sentences. These are generally the forfeiture of premial marks, a certain number of which entitle a boy to a holiday. If a boy cannot pay the marks, we imprison him in a large wooden cage for one hour for five marks.

'The greatest number of offences is leaving school without permission and before tasks are completed. If a boy pleads guilty (as most of them do), his punishment is always lessened one-sixth. The sheriff always presents his book to me for my signature to each sentence, and I have the power of mitigating and pardoning. I never yet have had cause to find fault with a single verdict of a jury or sentence of a judge. I have found that these trials have very considerably lessened offences, besides saving my father and myself a deal of trouble in deciding disputes and investigating offences.

'Soon after Christmas 1816, with my father's approbation, I drew up a scheme for appointing a committee of boys for the school management. They have the direction of everything except the school hours and the quantity of work to be done. They appoint the officers of the Court of Justice, who were before appointed by the whole school.

'The committee is chosen monthly by nomination and ballot. I attend the meetings of the committee, which we require to meet at least once a week. After a bill has passed the committee, it is presented to my father for his approbation without which it is not considered law. My father has never yet found it necessary to refuse his approbation.

'The best effect of this mode of governing is upon the morals of the scholars. They feel themselves under some obligation not to break those laws, which they themselves have assisted in enacting. They cannot complain that the laws are too severe because, either in their own proper persons or in those of their representatives, they

29

must have assisted in passing them.'

The procedures for nomination to the Committee were such as to give the senior scholars a greater say in the nomination. Thus, the head boy of the school was entitled to make a nomination. The next two boys in order of seniority were jointly entitled to make a second nomination. The next three boys jointly were entitled to make a third nomination and so on down the school to the most junior boys.

Rowland also introduced a system of voluntary labour. Favourite activities included working the school printing press; penmanship of various kinds; drawing, etching and painting; surveying and constructing maps; reading books; studying music; and constructing machines. Rowland further introduced a school currency in the form of counters earned by meritorious work and behaviour. Fines imposed by the school courts for misbehaviour lost that currency.

Rowland wrote under his treatise on education:

'The great feature of the object that we have in view is the establishment of a system of legislation and jurisprudence. A system in which the power of the master is bounded by general rules and the duties of the scholar accurately defined. The boys themselves examine and decide upon the conduct of their fellows. Thus, we provide a course of instruction in the great code of morality, which is likely to produce far more powerful and lasting effects than any quantity of mere precept.'

Rowland further described how over the years the number of pupils attending Hilltop school gradually increased. By 1818, it was upwards of seventy boys. The family decided that bigger premises must be found. Under Rowland's guidance, they purchased a site at Edgbaston then a country village. Rowland drew up the plans for the new school house having then added architecture to his other studies.

Rowland described thus how he acted as the architect and clerk of works for the new building:

'As duty of an architect devolved entirely on me, I had fallen to drawing plans, designing elevations, &c. After much labour - for I believe I drew at least twenty plans in all - my work being in a sufficiently forward state, we applied to a builder for an estimate. The amount he named being too large for our means, I had gone to work a second time. I formed, after many attempts at economy, an entirely new set of plans that considerably lowered the estimate. On the more moderate expense we resolved to venture.

'It was in the summer of 1818 that the building began. Besides being the Architect, I found myself compelled to act as clerk of the works. As without sharp daily inspection ..... hourly would have been better if I could have spared the time ..... constant departures from the contract occurred. Some of these would have proved very injurious to the building. As I had the main responsibility of the school most of the time and no vehicle at command, the two miles and back had always to be by foot. Thus, the work was very heavy, though probably the exercise was beneficial. In July 1819, the house being finished to which we gave the name of Hazelwood, the school was removed thither. Our larger and more commodious premises enabled us to make various improvements previously impracticable.'

He wrote to his eldest brother Matthew:

'We find that comfort we expected from the superior convenience of the house. Everyone who visits it is delighted with its plan. It is so seldom one finds a house built purposely for a school that it has been the object of considerable interest. At present, we have every reason to be satisfied with our determination to remove from Hill Top.'

Unhappily the following year, on the morning of Wednesday 23rd August 1820, fire cut short that early promise. The cause was combustion in a bundle of carpets stored in a closet under the roof. The fire soon cut off the attics and put the building in peril of total destruction. In those days, the equipment used in fire fighting consisted of a horse draw cart or a manhandled trolley fitted with hand operated pumps and pipes known as the engine. The occupier needed to provide or find a water supply.

The following is but a short extract of the events as narrated by Rowland:

'At about half past five, two or three boys awakened me with the alarming information that the rooms in the roof were on fire. In a moment, I was in the roof rooms with my brothers.

'These rooms were even then so full of smoke that to discern objects near to us was difficult. We found the fire to be in a closet opening into one of these rooms. Flames appeared through the crevices of the door. The first impulse was to endeavour to open the door and to throw in water, but in this we did not succeed. After a moment's reflection, we judged it best to confine the flames as much as possible. For, had the door been opened, the fire would have burst upon us in such a manner as to have driven us from the room.

'The whole family had now caught the alarm. This plunged them into the most active and distressing employment. The first anxiety was for the safety of the boys but, as the fire was over their heads, alarm on that account soon subsided. As soon as the boys had arisen, they began to throw their bedding out at the windows and to remove the other furniture of the rooms. Even in the midst of all the bustle and anxiety, I could not but admire the activity and presence of mind of the boys. We are indebted to them more than any other individuals that the loss, though very great, was not still more ruinous.

'I was at the front of the house giving directions for procuring water. I there learnt alarming news about a poor woman who had come the day before to do some sewing. She was sleeping with a servant girl in a bed in one of the roof rooms. It had been found that only the girl had escaped.

'Immediately, I ran upstairs and rushed through the room that was on fire into the next. Taking the woman from the bed on which she lay in a fainting fit, I carried her in my arms to the top of the stairs. I could do no more. Although the whole was but the work of a minute, such was the effect of the alarm and the dense smoke I had breathed that I loosed her. Those who stood upon the stairs caught her. I myself staggered down one or two steps. I should have fallen had those who stood about not caught me. A few minutes were sufficient for me to recover my strength. How the woman revived I do not know, but I saw her soon after apparently well watching the furniture at the front of the house.

'It afterwards appeared that the girl was awakened by the smoke, called her companion, and ran downstairs. The woman, instead of following her actuated by one of those motives that sometimes influence the conduct of the uneducated, remained in the room very deliberately dressing herself. I learned afterwards that, when I carried her out of the room, she had very regularly laced her stays.

'The poor woman's obstinacy cost her life. She was not in the least burnt, yet such was the effect of the smoke upon her lungs together with the alarm that the next day she became exceedingly ill. Although we procured for her the best medical advice the town afforded, she died in a few days. The surgeon who attended her said that she died of a disease to which she had long been subject, namely an enlarged heart unable to withstand the smoke and alarm.

'The engines arrived shortly after my rescue of the woman. I had provided water in large tubs in front of the house. One of our pumps was undergoing repairs at the time, so that it did not afford us any water. The other very soon became dry, but we found an excellent supply from a pit. Five men for the promise of five shillings each stood in the water to fill the buckets. Such was the rapidity of the supply that not one engine was for an instant without water.

'To throw the water immediately upon the fire, we raised a ladder that we had made a few months before to be in readiness in case of such an accident. Up this ladder the firemen carried their pipes, and played almost directly upon the flames.

'Among the firemen on the crumbling roof, directing and aiding them, was my newly wed brother Edwin. He observed that one man had difficulty in reaching a place where the flames remained unsubdued. He seized one of the largest slates and so held it as to deflect the stream. All this was done while his bride stood in anxiety below.

'The firemen carried another pipe up the stairs. They threw

33

its water upon the fire through an opening over the back stairs. This engine was very effective, till a scoundrel stamped upon the pipe and burst it. Several scoundrels were about who were taking advantage of the confusion to plunder the house. The scoundrel who burst the pipe intended to add to that confusion. A fireman who saw this took a short staff out of his pocket and gave the fellow a blow on his head. This sent him completely downstairs. About the hour of eight, the engines ceased to play. The fire was out.'

Damage was considerable. The fire had destroyed the whole of the roof, which was open to the sky excepting that part over the school room. It had largely destroyed the garret ceilings and floors. Water also had much damaged the walls and ceilings of the lower rooms.

The family arranged for restoration as quickly as possible. A friend made his nearby empty house available. The brothers sent out printed circular-letters stating the intention to reopen the school on the following Thursday. That was only eight days after the fire. Happily, the fire had not damaged the schoolroom and the chamber over, so that the school did reassemble on that day. The boys slept in the house at Tenant Street until the repairs to the roof were completed. They later occupied the chambers of the house with part of the family sleeping away from home. It took until Christmas fully to reinstate the school and restore normality.

The reader will recall the treatise on Public Education on which Matthew and Rowland were engaged before Matthew left to study as a barrister. This work was completed and published in 1822 under the title *Plans for the Government and Liberal Instruction of Boys in Large Numbers*. Birkbeck Hill describes the plans as mostly the ideas of Rowland and the composition mostly that of Matthew. The treatise set forth a complete scheme for the management of a large school. It embraced everything from the best method of cultivating heart and head of the boys down to the pettiest detail of management and administration.

Before publication of their treatise, Rowland and his brothers had tried to bring the school to a high level of excellence.

Rowland was writing:

'I am perfectly aware that much must be done before our school is fully prepared to stand the minute and, perhaps, often invidious inspection that will take place. That is a consequence of our inviting attention.'

These anxieties proved ill founded. Rowland acknowledged that they had every reason to be pleased with the reception that their book received. He referred to the highest praise contained in the Monthly Magazine and to the general commendation contained in several newspapers.

Thus, Thomas Wright Hill and his sons were singular in the comfort, education and happiness they gave to their pupils in an era of cruel and unhappy schools. Especially, the public schools where the masters met brutal and undisciplined behaviour of pupils with harsh oppression. Vice and drunkenness were common and bullying rife. Lack of discipline led to savage bouts of fisticuffs, and even to riots and mutinies that the police had to quell.

Treatment equally savage contained such behaviour. Flogging of boys was the order of the day. Keate, the headmaster of Eton, birched eighty boys in a day. Parr, the headmaster of Colchester and Norwich grammar schools, considered himself humane because he never flogged the same boy twice during a lesson. When Thomas Arnold later took over as headmaster of Rugby school, he introduced his so called muscular Christianity which improved this appalling state of affairs.

Birkbeck Hill in his *Life of Rowland Hill* asks his readers to recall our schools in the days of our fathers by reading Tom Brown and to consider Rugby even after Dr. Arnold. Then, after expressing his view that Dr. Arnold himself would have been the greater man had he thought a little more of suffering and a little less of sin, he continued:

'At the time that Rowland Hill began his reforms, Arnold was still at Oxford. Rugby did not appoint him till six years after Matthew and Rowland Hill brought out their work on Public Education.

'Little sign then appeared of any improvement in our schools.

Many still exposed a gentle and timid child to savage ignorant cruelty. These ancient foundations boast and with justice of the famous men whom they have reared. They are proud of their traditions. Yet I can never visit one of these old schools without seeing rise before my mind a long line of unhappy children. Young boys who were too gentle and too delicately wrought for the rough and brutal world into which they were suddenly thrown. Whose little hearts were well nigh broken by the cruelty of an unfeeling herd of masters and boys.'

In the year 1821, Southey wrote of a childhood playmate

'They took the eldest son from the Charter House because the devilish cruelty of the boys there literally killed him. They used to lay him before the fire till they scorched him, and shut him up in a trunk with sawdust till he had nearly expired with suffocation. The Charter House then was a sort of hell upon earth for the under boys.'

As Rowland had envisaged, publication of their work *Plans for the Government* and *Liberal Instruction of Boys in Large Numbers* brought fame to Hazelwood. The new school house had opened in 1819 with sixty-six pupils. During the next seven years, numbers steadily rose until by 1826 pupils numbered one hundred and fifty. Rugby then did not number so many.

The *Edinburgh Review* of January 1825 contained a lively description of the school by our very intelligent friend, Captain Basil Hall, who lately inspected the whole establishment. Opening in saying that generally the scheme worked admirably in practice, he continued:

'The most striking circumstance, perhaps, is the universal cheerfulness and the lively terms that the boys are on with the masters. Also the air of hearty attention to their business is something I never experienced in any other school. I observed no languor, no yawning, but all was activity and abstraction from everything but the lesson. They all seemed to go about their work like persons who knew their business and had no doubts about its success. The frequent changes from topic to topic kept this degree of animation always afloat.

'The music consists of a band of twelve boys. Their instruments are the same as those used by military bands. They play extremely well. Study of music, of drawing, of fencing, and of several other accomplishments is quite voluntary. The boys occupy their play hours partly in mere play but chiefly in objects having some useful end in view. They have a printing press of their own. They publish a monthly magazine embellished with etchings on copper and lithographic prints. All executed by the boys. They report their trials at length, they canvass school discipline, they draw up accounts of the expenditure of their funds in a businesslike manner. In short the whole system is a curious epitome of real life.

'They are still boys, but boys with head and hands fully employed on topics they like. They are all very neatly dressed and remarkably clean and tidy. All are rosy and healthy looking and merry as any children could be at home. The house is thoroughly ventilated. The library is well arranged and catalogued, and the boys exclusively manage it like everything else. They allow any boy to propose any book for purchase. He submits the name of the book to the Committee who decide.'

Thus, Hazelwood School provided a truly benevolent education during the early years of the nineteenth century that contrasted most starkly with so many schools of the day. It continued to do so throughout the century in a way that, perhaps, still offers some novel ideas at the opening into the twenty first century.

Yet, the school did not receive universal acclaim. Some criticised it because they said it transformed boys into little men. That it sacrificed the thoughtlessness, the spring, and the elation of childhood for precocious but imitated maturity and the making of a prig. Perhaps, those critics regarded the public school and its cruel ways as character building those destined for national leadership in an era of aristocracy, army and expanding empire.

By 1826, the number of pupils at Hazelwood had increased to 150. Men of rank and learning were sending their children for education there. For a time, so great was the eagerness to get boys into Hazelwood that strangers sought the assistance of a common friend in the hope of securing a place. The youngest brothers, Frederic and Howard, joined their elder brothers in the teaching.

The family decided to open a second school near London.

Rowland undertook the search for a suitable house and it was a long one. In March 1826, he was writing, that 'Excepting a small district that I am just going to explore and a part of Essex, I have examined every great road from London.' Yet shortly afterwards, the discovery of an old mansion house named Bruce Castle fulfilled his search. It was within a beautiful fragment of what once had been a wide park in the then scenic area of Tottenham.

Rowland enjoyed scenery and antiquity. At Bruce Castle, he found both happily combined. The park was small. Yet the foliage of the stately trees was so thick and the undergrowth of shrubberies so luxuriant that its boundaries failed to catch the eye. An ancient tower stood close to the main building from the time when Queen Elizabeth visited the mansion and when Henry VIII met his sister, Queen Margaret of Scotland, there. The house took its name from a former manor owned by the father of King Bruce of Scotland.

Here Rowland brought his bride and childhood sweetheart, Caroline, whom he married in the summer of leaving Hazelwood. They had known each other since the family lived at Horsehills. Caroline's father, Joseph Pearson, was a manufacturer at Wolverhampton, leader of the Liberal party there, and a life long family friend. Rowland recounts their early companionship in a delightfully whimsical way:

'Mr. Pearson's visit led to intimacy between the families, especially regarding the children. As his eldest daughter had attained the age of five while I was no more advanced than six, we found ourselves naturally thrown much together. In fact, we took the first step towards intimacy and affection that marriage cemented some twenty-five years later.

'Under the high road in the part nearest to my father's house ran what is in the midland counties called a culver. That is a long low arc. It was placed there for the passage of the rivulet that turned my little water wheel. Into this culver my brother and I occasionally crept by way of adventure, and at times to hear the noise of a wagon as it rumbled slowly overhead. Into this 'cool grot and mossy cell' I once led my new companion both of us necessarily bending almost double. I cannot but look back upon the proceeding as probably our earliest instance of close association and mutual confidence. Many years later, we revisited the spot together, but found the passage completely silted up and inaccessible to future wooers, however diminutive.'

As for the new school, the family resolved to manage the two schools as one business. Thomas Wright Hill and his wife Sarah retired. The family persuaded the second son, Edwin, and his wife to abandon an industrial career and to take their parent's place. They joined Rowland at Bruce Castle. They took over the business side of the school, while Rowland and the youngest brother, Howard, carried on the teaching. Nevertheless in coming years, the family group was to break up and the participants to go their own separate ways in chosen new careers.

Rowland Hill for long had suffered from ill health brought on by overwork of up to eighteen hours a day. It was in vain that his father and elder brother, Matthew, urged him to spare himself. Whatever he put his hand to he must do with all his might, and yet always be striving to better that which he had done well.

By these endeavours, he brought himself to such a state of nervous exhaustion that he suffered from continuous headaches, body fatigue and low spirits. Such conditions were relieved during the school holidays by walking and other holiday activities, but would return on resumption of his labours. He forever feared a relapse into that 'maddening state of mind from which I have but lately escaped.' He clearly overworked himself to such an extent that he was frequently on the verge of a nervous breakdown.

The youngest brother, Howard, died of tuberculosis in 1830 when only twenty years of age. At the time, he was planning to establish a commune of abandoned children aged two years and upwards supported by charitable contribution. This loss exacerbated Rowland's own problems. For an awful void was left within a devoted family group at a time when he was already bearing the managerial responsibility for the two schools.

Rowland's health was worsening, and he feared that he might suffer some permanent injury. He recognised that periods of rest alone would not suffice while his mind remained active with the affairs of the school and the anxieties of his position. He longed for the greater freedom offered outside school mastering, and began seriously to consider whether he required a complete change of work both physically and mentally.

The brothers met. They resolved upon the sale of Hazelwood and to continue only at Bruce Castle. They appointed Arthur with his scholastic abilities as headmaster. This released Rowland to pursue other activities. The final move from Birmingham took place in 1833. From then on the careers of the brothers diverged. Nevertheless, they continued to act and think very much as a group and, especially, consulting each other on all important matters.

Their mother, Sarah, died on the 9th April 1842 aged seventy-seven. Their father, Thomas Wright Hill, survived her by nine years. A few years after her death, the old man, then eighty-four, was missing from his customary place at home. He had walked ten miles there and ten miles back to visit his wife's grave. He was to follow her there peacefully on the 13th June 1851 aged eighty-eight.

The *Spectator* in an obituary to Thomas Wright Hill wrote:

'His sons by a sort of confederacy of talent, accordance of opinions and unity of sentiment, strengthened each other in their various departments.'

Birkbeck Hill under his *Life of Rowland Hill* wrote:

'Had he not had such a father, he would not have devised his plan for Penny Postage. Had he not had such a mother, he would not have succeeded in making what seemed the scheme of an enthusiast a complete and acknowledged success.'

CHAPTER 3

EARLY TRAVELS BY ROWLAND

Birkbeck Hill describes how from early boyhood Rowland Hill delighted in long walks. He would go many miles to view either fine scenery or an old building. He journeyed in an age confined to foot whether of man or horse or horse drawn vehicle or on water by sail.

When Rowland was a lad of eleven years, his parents took him and his brothers, Matthew and Edwin, on a visit to Shrewsbury.

He reveals under a later account how deeply all that he saw impressed him:

'Those who have travelled along the same road will remember the fine view which bursts upon the sight from the top of a hill a little beyond Shifnal. They may imagine the delight felt thereat by three lads accustomed to little but the plains of Warwickshire.'

He was no less charmed with his first sight of the river Severn:

'Those who have lived from infancy where some river flows can have no conception of its attraction to those who at a later age see it for the first time. The motion of the water, the breadth of the stream, the barges on its surface with their sails sometimes unfurled to the wind, and the lofty bridges with their series of arches were never-ending charms. We could not understand how anyone could regard them with indifference.'

It was assize time at Shrewsbury, and they took him to see a criminal trial:

'Of all that passed before our eyes or occupied our thoughts during this ever-to-be-remembered visit, incomparably the most striking and impressive scene was a criminal trial. I watched absorbed the spacious court, the crowded benches, the barristers in their robes and the servitors with their javelins. Then the awful presence of the judge when he entered amid the sound of the trumpet and took his seat on the lofty bench. All prepared our minds for the solemn inquiry about to begin.

'The case was one of burglary attended with violence. The cottage of an aged couple had been entered and robbed. One of three offenders had beaten the old man. All three had been subsequently apprehended. One whose part in the proceeding had gone no further than keeping watch at the door had, while in prison on another charge, given the information that enabled justice to lay hands on the others. He had consequently been admitted as King's evidence. I need not say that we felt towards him the dislike and contempt with which an appover (informer) is generally regarded.

'His fellows in crime, particularly the chief offender, took their places at the bar. This with a demeanour that astonished us, so completely did it differ from all that we had expected. Doubtless they were seeking to cover their real trepidation with an appearance of unconcern, but this we could not then understand. They taboured on the front of the dock with their fingers, looked about defiantly, and nodded in various directions as if in recognition of acquaintances. Counsel who defended them pleaded, first, that the offence was not one of burglary because they did not commit it by night. The hour was no later than nine on a summer's evening. Second, that, as the door was on the latch, the prosecution could not say that the house was broken open. Points made in desperation, and very summarily dealt with by the judge.

'The only further attempt was to discredit the evidence of the approver, whom they severely cross-examined, though the following short passage is all that I now remember of the process. "How came you to think of informing?" "Because my conscience told me I had done wrong." "And why didn't your conscience tell you had done wrang before you got into prison for stealing the pig?"

'The evidence was too strong to be shaken, and they convicted both prisoners. Of course, when a host of minor offences were capital, so grave a crime was on the fatal list. We heard the judge, after putting on the black cap, pronounce the terrible sentence of death. Both prisoners still maintained their first defiant look. The judge, after warning the more ruffianly of the two that he could not

42

hold out to him any hope of mercy, addressed his companion. He told him that, as he had abstained from violence, his life would be spared. The latter at once broke down, falling upon his knees, while he poured out his thanks and promises of amendment. Shortly afterwards, they executed the sentence passed on the other. Somewhat beyond the fatal hour, while going on an errand, I unfortunately and most unintentionally caught a distant sight of the hanging body.'

For many years Rowland's excursions were chiefly by foot. Though of delicate health due to scarlet fever at a tender age, he was active and capable of great endurance. As a boy, he was one of the quickest runners and best jumpers in the family school, and he became a strong swimmer. Perhaps, because of him, the family school was more interested in teaching the individual sports of athletics and swimming than the more usual school team games. The author subscribes to that view.

Rowland recounted many of his early walks and travels in his Journal. He walked to Stourbridge once a week to give a lesson there without the least fatigue. Because it was distant only twelve miles and he often walked upwards of thirty miles in one day.

Rowland also recounted how, in the year 1813 when aged eighteen, he accompanied his mother to Margate for the benefit of his health. He saw for the first time London and the sea.

'We could see the coast of France. My mother was uneasy at being so near to the French. I walked over to Dover and began to sketch the castle and town. Some soldiers told me that, a day or two before, they had put a man in prison for drawing there. I could not believe them and went on with my drawing. However, in a little time, a file of soldiers came out of the castle with fixed bayonets. They told me that, if I did not go away directly, they would take me into custody. I now thought it time to be gone. So I walked to our lodgings with no wish to stop in a town where the inhabitants were under a military government.'

The following year England made peace with France.

An entry under Rowland's *Journal* read:

'June 3rd, 1814 At about three o'clock this morning, the

glorious news of the signature of the preliminaries for peace arrived in Birmingham. I was up at four o'clock for the purpose of going to Hagley, to which place I had the pleasure of taking the news. I never saw so many pleasant faces in my life.'

In the summer of 1815, Rowland and his brother, Matthew, were eager to repeat their visit to Margate and to see again London and the sea. They raised the money to pay for their holiday by lectures they gave at Stourbridge. Matthew was the speaker and Rowland managed the experiments. They earned sufficient profit to cover their journey. They left Birmingham for London at half past six o'clock in the evening of 23rd June.

Rowland continued under his *Journal*:

'At three o'clock in the afternoon of the next day, we entered London amidst the thunder of carriages and the buzz of people. In the afternoon, I went to see the paintings at Somerset House. Of the landscape, Turner pleased me most. One, a most beautiful painting, he called ' The Rebuilding of Carthage'. Turner is almost the only man who attempts to paint the sun. It is done in this picture with great success. It quite dazzled my eyes to look at it. The reflection of the sun upon the water was remarkably fine. The Exhibition closed this evening for the season. I stopped as long as I could. That same evening, I walked about the streets to see the illuminations for the late victory at Waterloo.'

He recorded while at Margate:

'Margate, July 3rd, 1815. We went to see the steamboat come in from London. Two wheels work it. They resemble water wheels. One is placed each side of the vessel and about a-half sunk in the water. The steamboat comes from London and returns three times in each week. It generally performs the voyage in about twelve hours. In the best cabin is a handsome library, draughtboard &c. It is surprising to see how most people are prejudiced against this packet. Some say that it cannot sail against the wind if it is high. However, when it entered the harbour, the wind and tide were both against it, and the former rather rough, yet I saw it stem both. A

44

great crowd was present and much enthusiasm, though carpers predicted failure, and sneered at smoke jacks.' Perhaps an early portent of what was later to become the family participation in the affairs of shipping.

On their journey home, they visited Canterbury. On seeing the destruction of Thomas a Becket's tomb, Rowland wrote:

'There are, indeed, few monuments that were erected prior to the Reformation but what are defaced in some way or other. It is surprising that people should be so bigoted against bigotry.'

In the summer holidays of the next year (1816), Rowland made a tour of Derbyshire with some companions. He thus described two views that he saw:

'The views in this valley varying at every step are extremely beautiful. Sometimes the river is pent between the surrounding hills, and the eye is at a loss to discover the passage by which it enters or leaves the valley. Go a little further, and the spectator is enchanted with the long perspective of woody hills and barren rocks between which the rapid Derwent pours its foaming waters.

'As we sat with the window open to enjoy the freshness of the air, we just distinguished the massive outline of the opposite rocks through the gloom of the night. Only the low murmur occasioned by a fall in the river broke the silence of the evening. This created very pleasing sensations in our minds. It was a kind of silence hearable if I may be allowed to use a parody.'

They went to see a great chasm in the earth called Eden Hole enclosed by a wall of which he wrote:

'The woman who keeps the key went with us. On the road we discussed the right of the land owner to lock up the place, which debate we interspersed with many learned remarks respecting the equality of birthright &c. When we came to the hole, we were unanimous in agreeing that it was for the good of the neighbourhood that they should securely fence it. We threw several large stones down the hole. At first, they made a very loud noise. This then ceased, as though the stone had lodged on some projecting rock, but directly continued less loud to become an unequal moan which perceptibly died away.'

45

On their way home, Rowland and one of his companions walked in a day from Ashbourne to Birmingham, a distance of some forty-three miles. For many days, heavy rains had fallen, and the River Dove had overflowed its banks. Rowland recounted under his *Journal*:

'We came to a turn in the road about a furlong from the bridge. We were surprised to find the road and the fields on each side, as far as the eye could reach, covered with water. The top of the bridge was the only dry spot we could see. It was a distressing sight. They had mowed most of the fields but a few days before. We could just see the top of the haycocks above the water. A great number of men were employed in carrying away as much of the hay as they could save from the flood.

'Whilst we were waiting undetermined what steps to take, two men came up who had ridden through the flood on horseback. They told us that the road was inundated for a mile and a-half and that in some places the water was deep and rising fast. We enquired if there was any other road by which we could reach Lichfield (the next town on our road). They informed us that there was none but what it was most probable would be in the same situation.

'Our alternatives were either to go back to Sudbury, and perhaps remain there two or three days, or to wade through the flood. As we were both able to swim should it be necessary, we determined to proceed. We reached the bridge by going out of the road and along a field, but could proceed no further in that way.

'We now sat down, took off the lower parts of our dresses and made bundles of them. These with our folios we fastened upon our backs, that our arms might be at liberty if we should find it necessary to swim. We waded through the water, but did not find it so deep as we expected. By keeping to the highest part of the road, we never found the water more than three feet in depth.'

They reached Lichfield at five in the afternoon. They stopped to bathe in the canal only to see the Birmingham coach go by. Rowland continued:

'After bathing, I found that my heel, in consequence of the continual rubbing of my shoe, had become very painful. So much so

46

that it was with the greatest difficulty that I could walk at all. However, I managed to double the heel of my shoe under my foot and tie on the shoe with strings. I could then walk very well.

'The next coach passed us when we were within about eight miles of Birmingham, and we determined then to walk the whole of the way. Before this, it began to rain and did not cease till we reached home, which was at about eleven o'clock. Having walked forty-three miles, we were not ashamed to own ourselves tolerably well tired.'

In the Easter holidays of 1817, he set out on another tour.

'April 4th, 1817. After we had breakfasted, we set out on foot at a quarter after three in the morning. We reached Wolverhampton at a little before seven. We dined at Shifnal at a baker's shop on bread and butter. Our dinner cost us not quite fourpence. At Shrewsbury we found much competition among the coach proprietors, and that they had reduced the fare to Liverpool to four shillings. As such an opportunity might never occur again, we determined upon setting out the next morning.'

At Chester he had time to see the Cathedral:

'I do not know whether, as this was Easter Sunday, they had provided a better choir than usual. I never heard any singing that pleased me so much. They played the organ, a fine toned instrument, with great skill. The effect was one of heavenly harmony.'

From Liverpool Rowland Hill and his companions walked to Bootle then a small village but now an industrial area. They looked about for an inn to stay the night:

'The only inn in the village is the Bootle Hotel. We were afraid of that word Hotel. Learning that there was another inn to be found a little further on, we proceeded. However, this we found as much too mean as the other was too grand for us. We went on and soon came to a third inn. Here we were more frightened than before for the sign was The Royal Waterloo Hotel.'

In June 1817, Rowland went again to London and then on to the Isle of Wight with his father:

'I left London at six in the evening for Southampton. The road lay through Brentford and Staines. Near to the latter place, in a field, I saw the place where King John signed the Magna Carta. A sundial marks the spot. I was glad to hear some passengers give it as their opinion that something of the kind was wanting now.

'As soon as it became light (the reader should be aware that the horse drawn coach was travelling overnight), we enjoyed the most delightful views of a richly wooded county. The trees in Hampshire are the largest I ever saw, and the county is almost covered with what we consider large woods. There is not a finer sight in the world than to be elevated above an extensive wood. One sees the trees extending as far as the eye can reach, till they become scarcely distinguishable from the sky.'

Crossing over to the Isle of Wight, he passed through the village of Freshwater. 'Wishing to know the etymology of the name Freshwater, I asked the sailors if the water in the bay was not so salt as sea water generally.' "Oh yes," they replied, "it's all alike." "What then is the reason of the names Freshwater town and Freshwater Bay," I enquired. "Why, they are in the Freshwater Parish to be sure" was the reply.'

On his way home, he saw Stonehenge and recorded:

'It is certain that great numbers of stones have been carried off (I suppose in pieces) and afterwards used in building. Inigo Jones has mentioned this as occurring between his two visits to the Temple. I cannot guess the feelings of those who could, for the value of the stones as building materials, disturb and destroy so venerable and interesting a monument of antiquity. I think it would be well if the government of the country would purchase this and every other valuable antiquity of the island. They should preserve them as much as possible from injury.'

Later, in old age, he was to describe his last visit to Stonehenge thus:

'We also went to see Stonehenge for about the tenth time in my life. I never failed to take advantage of a chance to visit this most interesting and much controverted antiquity. However, this, my last visit, was a very different affair from my first visit in 1817.'

'Forty-three years before, I had set out for Stonehenge in company with my father. We had breakfasted on the way at a small

48

inn a mile or two from the place. While my father rested, I went sketch book in hand to the so-called Druid temple. Not a creature, human or animal, was in sight, not even the Shepherd of Salisbury Plain himself. I was alone with the wonderful stone monument, and nothing but the sky and the vast downs was in sight. By-and-by came a shepherd, chatty and communicative, with fifteen hundred sheep. Thus only, was my solitude broken.

'Yet today (1860) what a change! Easy communication and love of locomotion had vulgarised even Stonehenge. We found a crowd of people making noisy the place and rudely shattering my early peaceful associations.'

The age of the railway had come.

In the summer of 1821, Rowland Hill and his brother, Arthur, crossed to Ireland to inspect the Edgeworth-Town Assisting School. On their way they passed through Manchester. For the first time they saw there a whole town lighted by gas.

Rowland recounts that 'steamboats ran between Liverpool and Dublin during the summer months. However, the steamers charged high fares - a guinea and a half for the passage, while the sailing packets charged but seven shillings. On landing they had to undergo Custom House examination as import duties were still kept up between the two Islands.' Rowland describes two packets arriving at almost the same time. Yet only one officer was available to examine all the baggage. They had to pay customs dues. The difference that still subsisted between English and Irish money rendered an overcharge by the officer easy .

During their stay in Dublin, they drove out with an Irish barrister to see the Dargle. Arthur described their visit thus:

'We found a line of bushes laid across the road into the grounds. Men working on the spot told us that we could not pass as the place was under preparation for the King's visit. Had we been alone, we should have either turned back or tried the power of a bribe. Our Irish friend knew better. After one or two cajoling phrases that moved not very much, he went on to damn the King. The effect was complete and a gap was at once made through which we passed. As we did so, one of the men remarked that others had applied

49

speaking of the King in high terms, but they had turned all those back.'

One evening Rowland and Arthur watched the general departure of the mails for the provinces. They expected to find the guard of each coach, as in England, armed with a blunderbuss. However, they found that he carried also a sword and pistols, while some coaches had two guard and others even three. They left Dublin for Edgeworth-Town on a Sunday morning. Rowland entered in his *Journal*:

'On the road to Edgeworth, we were struck with the miserable state of the poor Irish. Many live in huts without either window or chimney. The door serves every purpose of ingress and egress. The poor women and children were generally without shoes and stockings. However, the men wear both. Even in the midst of summer they appear dressed in great coats. Though Sunday, we saw many parties dancing in the roads and fields, the men in their great coats. Carts and wagons passed along apparently as much as on any other day. Every time the coach stopped beggars surrounded it. They appeared in the lowest possible state of misery.

'With a few exceptions, everything appeared neglected. The land appears miserably cultivated and worse fenced. The houses are apparently falling into ruins. One sees gates with one hinge and no fastenings tied up by means of ropes or haybands. They have reduced windows from a proper size to a single pane of glass. The remainder of the window, as it was broken, they have stopped up with a flat stone, a piece of wood, plaster, or a turf. In many places, half the houses are in a state of ruin and quite uninhabitable. We learned that many had been reduced to this state at the time of the riots.'

The brothers disembarked from the coach at Edgeworth-Town, where they met with Mr Edgeworth for a week's stay at his school. Rowland recounted under his *Journal*:

'The school consists of about 160 boys of all classes from beggars to the most wealthy. The school classes them without any distinction but that of merit. To destroy every difference in appearance, all the boys wore pinafores as a kind of uniform.

However, the school makes some distinction outside school hours. Sons of gentlemen and respectable tradesmen have a separate playground, and the school divides the boarders among two or three houses according to rank. About three-fourths of the boys had neither shoes nor stockings, but they all appeared clean, happy and contented.

'Every boy pays a little for his education-viz, from one penny to five pence per week according to circumstances. The school allows the poor boys to work in the school nursery of four or five acres. In that manner, the school enables the poor boys to pay for their education and for the washing of their pinafores &c.

'The school has two salaried masters. One has the general superintendence of the school in the absence of Mr Edgeworth. The other teaches the classics. Weekly payments of the boys defray every expense of the establishment, except the rent, within about a hundred a year. Boarders pay the masters of the houses at which they lodge for all the expenses attending their maintenance. The boys, as far as we could learn, are exceedingly orderly, attentive and well behaved. Mr Edgeworth states that he finds the children of the peasantry much more docile than those of gentlemen, and the English more tractable than the Irish.'

On their return home, the brothers took the steam packet from Dublin to Holyhead. The Captain told them that his company intended to attempt running the steamer throughout the next winter. He cautiously remarked that in a storm a steamer might even have some advantage over a sailing vessel.

In the summer of the following year (1822), Rowland Hill, accompanied by his younger brothers, Arthur and Frederic, again visited the Isle of Wight. He recounted:

'While on the Isle of Wight, I visited a cave in the side of an immensely high cliff called the Hermit's Hole. The only approach is along a narrow path leading from the cliff top about twenty yards in length. This path is steep and narrow and the descent is somewhat dangerous. A slip would inevitably precipitate a person down the seven hundred feet high cliff into the sea which roars below. Travellers in the Isle of Wight speak in strange terms of this cave. One says that the mere thought of visiting the cave is enough to shake the strongest nerve. He recommends no one to venture as the path is so narrow that turning round is impossible. Consequently, a person who sets out must go all the way.

'Arthur would not venture to the edge of the cliff. After taking off my coat, I went down the path followed by Frederic. At first rock on the sea side protects the path, but after a few yards there is no protection at all. I found the path better than I had expected, but it is very steep and narrow. Several loose stones upon the path made the danger so much the greater. Some of these on the least touch fell into the sea. It was with some difficulty that I overcame an involuntary feeling of the necessity of leaping after them.

'The cave has nothing to repay the danger of reaching it. The whole pleasure consists in danger overcome. Despite the accounts given by travellers, I turned back two or three times to see for Frederic. He ventured the greater part the way. However, when he came to a place where the path turned round a projecting part of the cliff, his courage failed him and he hurried back. I must confess that he accomplished more than I could have done at his age.'

CHAPTER 4

SEPARATE WAYS

Matthew Davenport Hill (1792 - 1872) was the eldest son of Thomas Wright Hill. In 1815 at the age of twenty-three, he gave up teaching in the family school, and entered Lincoln's Inn to read for the Bar and to qualify as a barrister. He thus sought to fulfil the ambition denied to his father because of his grandmother's distrust of lawyers. To support himself while he qualified and ate his dinners and, like Charles Dickens a few years later, he became a reporter of debates in the House of Commons. He also made an uncertain income from freelance journalism.

Also, during this period, Matthew with two friends obtained control of a small newspaper called the Sunday Review. By this means, they attacked abuses and exposed injustices and advocated radical reform of the social and political conditions of the early 19th century. They condemned what they described as the darkest days of the long Tory rule and the most oppressive government since the Stuarts. After proclaiming his views on London to his father, he received a reply not totally archaic to modern times:

'Your account of London is appalling. Yet the land, the sunshine, the rain and our planet are as ever. Why then despair? The political heavens lower, but who shall say of what force the storm shall be and of what duration. Who shall predict ravages too great for compensation by succeeding seasons of calm? Let us not fear for ourselves. Little is needful for life. Let us fear for our beloved country. Let each do his utmost to trim the bark to avoid the rocks of anarchy on the one hand and the equally fatal though less conspicuous shoals of despotism on the other. The time is coming, I apprehend, when none that carries a conscience will be able to remain neutral.'

Matthew qualified and was called to the Bar in 1819. He was the first man from Birmingham to achieve that distinction. At first, briefs were slow in coming his way. Then he appeared increasingly in the defence of men who held similar political views to his own and whom the government was seeking to suppress. He gained the reputation of being a friend to the liberties of his country. That reputation may at first have stood in his way, but later his abilities became generally recognised. While awaiting briefs, Matthew helped his brother Rowland in the completion and publication of their joint work on Public Education.

In later years, Matthew defended Rebecca's rioters of South Wales. They were men who disguised themselves on their forays in women's clothes. The leader called himself Rebecca and his gang Rebecca's daughters. Exploits which the poet and writer Dylan Thomas immortalised with much poetic licence in his romantic screen play for the cinema. When, at the conclusion of the trial, Matthew had spoken in mitigation of punishment, the Attorney General responsible for the prosecution passed him a note. It read:

'You have just delivered one of the most appropriate, eloquent and feeling addresses I have ever heard. I dared not, could not, add a word.'

Praise could go no higher.

Those of the time tell a good story of when Matthew defended a certain Dr. Snaith on a political charge. The jury retired and found that they were eleven to one for a verdict of guilty. In those days, the Court locked the jury in the jury room without food until they reached their verdict.

The foreman told the dissenting juror: 'I have been a soldier and have passed twenty-four hours without food in a ditch, so you had better give way at once. The dissenter replied: 'I have been a sailor. I once passed three days and three nights on a plank with only a crust on the first day and nothing the other two. So I suppose I can hold out as well as any other.'

The prospect of three days and nights without food locked in the jury room so scared the foreman that he sent out a message to his doctor. The latter obligingly gave a certificate that the Court would endanger his patient's life if they kept him long without food. The jury had to be dismissed, resulting in an acquittal for Matthew's fortunate client.

In 1826, Matthew participated in the setting up of the Society for the Diffusion of Useful Knowledge and so did his brother Rowland. The Society defined its objects as importing useful information to all classes of the community. Especially those who were unable to avail themselves of experienced teachers or might prefer learning by themselves. The Society sought to achieve its aims by the periodic publication of booklets intended for those already in the habit of reading but lacking proper means of instruction. The idea was to make good an absence of education in a society that lacked any general schooling.

The first booklet published was by Henry Brougham, the future liberal Lord Chancellor, and was entitled, A Discourse on the Objects, Advantages and Pleasures of Science. It sold thirty-nine thousand copies at six pence a copy. This was a large number for the time and secured both the success of the Society and the intended publication of a Library of Useful Knowledge.

Subjects later covered ranged from algebra and astronomy to political economy, from law to the history of great men, and from mechanics to dying and bleaching. The Society called upon each of the three Hill brothers, Matthew, Edwin and Rowland and on occasions old Thomas Wright Hill to edit various Society's booklets before publication.

The Society subsequently extended its work to booklets for farmers and later to picture books for children published under the management of Edwin Hill. Continued success led to the publication of a Library of Entertaining Knowledge under the chairmanship of Matthew Hill. A series intended to persuade people to read by offering them useful knowledge in an amusing form. The Society also published periodicals. The Penny Magazine proposed by Matthew enjoyed a huge circulation as did The Penny Cyclopaedia and The Workman's Companion. All were forerunners of today's D.I.Y.magazines.

By 1846, the Society had achieved its main object of creating a general desire to read and learn. The Chamber brothers of Edinburgh and like publishers were then meeting a popular demand for a good class of literature at a modest cost. Thus, its purpose fulfilled, the members dissolved the Society.

Another of Matthew's many interests in which he was associated with his friend, Henry Brougham, was the promotion of University College in Bloomsbury. The initial promotion was by a committee of donors and shareholders. They raised the sum of £150,000, chose the site in Bloomsbury, and saw to the laying of the first stone in 1827. They conceived it as a university for London, but this met with political objections to the grant of a Charter. Nevertheless, it later developed into the London University. The new college was distinctive in that it sought no religious qualification for admittance. All creeds were equally welcome.

In 1832, in furtherance of his own political and social thinking, Matthew stood as parliamentary liberal candidate for a Hull constituency. He advocated municipal reform, opposition to monopolies, and repeal of taxes on learning such as excise duty on paper and stamp duty on newspapers. He sought to extend the ballot to women as they have the same interest in politics as men. A novel premise in those days, and one which the ladies did not see realised until the following century.

Matthew was elected. During the next three years, the House of Commons heard his voice in any debate relating to social reform. He supported a petition to the House asking for the removal of civil disabilities endured by Jews because of their religion. He refused to support a movement to do away with bull baiting and bear fighting. That was 'unless this House takes equal measures against hunting, shooting and other blood sports of the wealthy.' He spoke against any interference with the innocent Sunday recreations of the poorer classes. Matthew was well ahead of public opinion, and especially of his grandparents, in his religious views and his broad-minded outlook on Sunday observance. Thus he argued:

'We should put Sunday better to account as a day of leisure free from the restraints that superstition has affixed to its enjoyment. Restraints, I will venture to say, not sanctioned by any precept of religion.'

However, three years later the country's first enthusiasm for

56

reform had ebbed away. Matthew lost his seat. He did not seek another constituency, but concentrated on his legal work. He was appointed King's Counsel in 1834. Five years later, he became the first Recorder of Birmingham or, to the uninitiated, Chief Magistrate. He sought reform in the criminal law. Especially, he advocated the prevention of crime by the twin penal methods of incapacitation and reformation. In his words, 'begin to reform the criminal the moment you get hold of him and keep hold of him until you have reformed him.' Those were novel views for the middle of the 19th century, but, perhaps, they begged the question of when reformation takes place.

Other novel proposals included the regular inspection of prisons. He advocated offering a friendly hand to discharged prisoners as a guard against recurrence. Because, so he said, 'the moment of departure from gaol is the most dangerous crisis of their lives.' Matthew was much interested in the rehabilitation and education of juvenile offenders. He advocated the opening of ragged schools, which would educate free the children of the poor. He further sought proper facilities for recreation, so that working people could usefully employ their leisure time.

On his retirement as Recorder in 1866, the Magistrates of the Borough in a farewell address recorded:

'Whenever the history of the criminal law and of the treatment of crime shall be written, your name will be honourably conspicuous on the record.'

Another of Matthew's legal appointments was that of Commissioner of Bankruptcy for the Bristol district. There he became known for the soundness of his judgements. Once an Appeal Judge remarked to him:

'I don't know how it is Hill, we can't manage to upset any of your decisions.' Matthew responded:

'Nevertheless I do my best to give you a chance - I always try to be right.'

Two other of Matthew's chance remarks are equally apt today:

'Fallacies like abuses are immortal. Like the seven sleepers, they retire to a cave out of sight for a few years, and then awake as fresh as ever.

'No advance on the road to Democracy admits of retrogression. The wheel has a ratchet behind it and will only move one way. It, therefore, behoves us to proceed step by step assuring ourselves of the safety of each before making another.'

Of his family, Matthew married Margaret (nee Bucknell). They had two sons and three daughters. One son, Alfred, followed his father into the law and became the Registrar of the Birmingham Court of Bankruptcy. The youngest son, Berkeley, became Professor of clinical surgery at the University College, London, which his father had helped to found.

However, the three daughters are the most interesting in an era when the family expected daughters to look to marriage and domesticity for fulfilment. This was not so for Matthew's three daughters, who were active in educational work, in the treatment of juvenile offenders and in poor law reform. Rosamund, the best known of them, earned a place in the Dictionary of National Biography. This she achieved as the first woman to sit on the London School Board on which she served for eighteen years.

At a lunch party at Matthew's home that included the author, William Thackeray, discussion centred on the new novel, Jane Eyre. Rosamund thought the author to be a woman. Not so Thackeray, who argued with all due deference to the sex, it shows a grasp of reasoning beyond that of a woman. Unfortunately, Rosamund's response has not been preserved for posterity, and so must be left for conjecture by the female reader.

In 1872, Matthew Hill died at his Bristol home at the age of eighty. His bust stands in the public library at Birmingham.

Edwin Hill (1793-1876), the second son of Thomas Wright Hill, is described as a mechanician of considerable ability. The mechanical labour saving devices within his own home would not be out of place at the end of the twentieth century apart from the absence of electricity. A complex system of pulleys extended like a spider's web across the bedroom ceiling. That system enabled him from the comfort of his bed to open and close the window shutters or to adjust the weight of the blankets over the bed.

Edwin was the first to break away from the family school while still in his teens. He became articled to the proprietor of a rolling mill in Birmingham, and rose to become manager of the mill. However, in 1827, he gave up his industrial career to help his brothers, Rowland and Arthur, in starting the new school at Bruce Castle Tottenham. He remained there until 1840, when he received a further appeal for his assistance from his brother Rowland. The latter was then engaged in the huge task of reorganising the Post Office.

The Treasury appointed Edwin Supervisor of Stamps at Somerset House. In that department, he completely remodelled the machinery in use, and thus saved the nation many thousands of pounds a year. With the assistance of Warren De La Rue, the well-known family of printers, he invented a machine for folding envelopes. This he displayed at the first International Exhibition held in the Crystal Palace as an example of Britain's industrial enterprise. He was also responsible for procuring machines for perforating stamps, for embossing the Queen's head on postal envelopes, and for stamping excise duty on the individual pages of newspapers.

In 1871, an article in the Daily News described the behind-the-scenes working of Somerset House thus:

'It is as if we were in the care of an amiable magician. Doors open of their own accord. A wave of the hand creates stamps of fabulous value out of wastepaper. Unseen agencies move wooden arms and limbs and classify documents with inconceivable rapidity and unfailing exactitude. Bundles of valuable deeds walk gravely into the room unaided and present themselves for stamping. Other mysterious contrivances for lessening human labour abound - ingenious inventions of the Comptroller of the Stamping Department.'

The following year, on Edwin's retirement, a minute of the Board of Commissioners of Inland Revenue paid tribute to his inventive mechanical skills and the many contrivances he had introduced to ease the work of his department:

'We can scarcely overestimate the saving of time, labour and expense that have accrued to the public benefit by means of these appliances. We have undoubtedly attained these important results at the cost of much independent thought and labour by Mr. Hill, while he himself has derived no personal benefit from them.'

Edwin, like his brothers, enjoyed longevity. He died shortly before his eighty-third birthday. He and his wife had the customary large Victorian family of ten children of whom seven survived him.

Rowland Hill (1795-1879), the third son of Thomas Wright Hill, was first schooled and then taught at the family school. He and his brothers established an eminent reputation for the school at Hazelwood and later at Bruce Castle.

In 1832, aged thirty-seven, Rowland was still teaching at Bruce Castle. He was suffering ill-health and looking for a new career to satisfy his ceaseless energies. The family decided that Rowland would retire from teaching; that they would sell the Midlands school, Hazelwood; and that Edwin and Arthur would carry on the teaching at Bruce Castle.

During his final months at Bruce Castle, Rowland was considering a variety of possible schemes for his employment. They included transmission of coal gas compressed along narrow gauge pipes to distant places; propelling steam boats by screw; road making by machinery; and a plan for checking the speed of stage coaches. These were all very novel ideas for his time. He also looked to improving the conditions of service of the common soldier. His thinking included an end to pressing men into military service, abolition of savage punishments such as flogging, and the setting up of libraries and educational facilities.

In the summer of 1883, after leaving Bruce Castle, Rowland went abroad for the benefit of his health. Subsequently, in his words:

'I had spent some weeks in France without though having gone further than Orleans (travelling was slow in those days), when I received an invitation. This was to join in a scheme as Secretary in England for the colonisation of the then unoccupied territory now called South Australasia. I was very unwilling to cut my holiday so short. Yet I feared that, if I missed this opportunity, I might not soon find another equally promising. I determined on accepting the offer and went forthwith to my work.

'The main principles of the Scheme were, first, that the colony should from its very establishment be self supporting (a condition hitherto unheard of). Secondly, that the colonists should be kept from that dispersion which had so often produced grievous suffering and fearful mortality. Thirdly, that no convicts should be admitted into the colony. Fourthly, that there should be immigration of a sufficient number of free labourers. Lastly, that in the selection of these the number of sexes should be kept equal.'

The Colonisation Commissioners for South Australia formally named Rowland Hill as their secretary in May 1835, which position he then held for the next four years. During that period, in 1837, Rowland produced and submitted to Government his first pamphlet on postal reform. The main proposal was a single uniform rate for letters payable by the sender that was to replace a charge that varied with distance and was payable by the recipient.

Rowland drew attention under his pamphlet to the substantial expenditure that the Post Office was then incurring under three separate heads. First, it priced each individual letter by determining the correct postage and then marking it on the letter for payment on delivery. Secondly, it credited and debited postmasters with payments collected and expenditure incurred by each of them. Thirdly, it received and checked payments collected by carriers from the various recipients of mail. He explained that the cost of conveyance of each individual letter was tiny and bore little reference to distance. It depended much more upon the volume of mail carried by each particular stage coach.

Accordingly, he recommended that a single prepaid rate of one penny replace the practice of fixing the price of postage by reference to distance. Further that the Post Office could achieve this without loss of revenue. He recorded under his *Journal*:

'In urging the various benefits that they could anticipate from cheap and easy postal conveyance, I did not fail to dwell on its aid to education. This had at length become regarded as a matter of national interest and national duty, albeit grievously clogged by sectarian prejudice and political animosities.'

A Parliamentary Committee of enquiry into the Post Office was then sitting and summoned Rowland before it. For purposes of prepayment he proposed 'a bit of paper just large enough to bear the stamp and covered at the back with a glutinous wash.' The Committee agreed to recommend a uniform rate of postage only upon the casting vote of the Chairman. The Committee rejected both the proposed penny rate and a three-halfpenny rate, but agreed to a twopenny rate again only upon the Chairman's casting vote.

As described by the historian G.M.Trevelyan, Rowland fought all the way against the indifference of statesmen and the obstruction of the unreformed Civil Service to achieve his penny postage. For example, the Post-Master General (The Earl of Litchfield) said during parliamentary debate:

'With respect to the plan set forth by Mr. Hill of all the wild and visionary schemes that I have ever heard or read of, it was the most extraordinary.'

Many other personages spoke in a similar hostile manner. However, much support came from the more progressive in public life and from the people themselves. The Society for the diffusion of Useful Knowledge asserted under a memorial to the Treasury that existing high postal charges were a great hindrance to literary research and authorship. The Corporation of the City of London and the inhabitants of towns all over the country supported the plan and petitioned Parliament.

A deputation including about one hundred and fifty members of Parliament, mostly government supporters, confronted the Prime Minister. They urged upon him the introduction of penny postage as a measure that liberals had a right to expect from a liberal administration. Thus, conscious that the Government would gain much popularity by the measure, the Cabinet decided to adopt it.

Rowland Hill gives the following amusing account of his subsequent interview with the Liberal Prime Minister, Lord

Melbourne, a conversation that shows how politicians court popularity, but so often fail to understand that which they court. It is first necessary to explain that Mr. Warburton was a Liberal Member of Parliament and a strong supporter of penny postage. Further that the era was one of outrageous class division and oppression of the poor, which the more progressive in society were trying to alleviate.

After saying that Lord Melbourne received him in his dressing gown, Rowland continued:

'In conversation I had occasion to speak of Mr. Warburton, when Lord Melbourne interrupted me with 'Warburton! Warburton! He's one of your moral-force men, isn't he?' I replied that I certainly believed Mr. Warburton's hopes of improvement did rest more on moral than physical force.

'Well,' he rejoined, 'I can understand your physical-force men, but as to your moral-forcemen I'll be damned if I know what they mean.' Later in the interview, Lord Melbourne said ruefully, 'I can't think why a man can't talk of penny postage without going into a passion.' He was referring to Lord Litchfield, the Post-Master General.

In 1839, the bill for penny postage came before Parliament. The majority in favour of the reform was 102: the ayes being 215 and the noes 112. Parliament extended the Act to the whole of the United Kingdom on 10th January 1840. The first postage stamp was the Penny Black. It bore the profile of the young Queen Victoria and the words *Postage One Penny* but not the name of the country. Great Britain did not need it. For on first issue of the stamp, it was the only postage stamp in the world. Today, following that tradition, the stamps of Great Britain do not show the country of origin. The head of the reigning sovereign remains sufficient identity.

Nevertheless, the struggles of Rowland Hill to carry out his reforms in the face of ineptitude had only begun. The Government offered him an engagement within the Post Office at an equivalent salary to that which he was receiving from the Colonisation Commission: namely five hundred pounds per annum. Rowland fairly regarded this offer as insulting. Apart from the uncertainty of the future, it would place him in a very inferior position to the post

63

office officials with whom he would be dealing. They had already shown that they opposed his ideas. Especially, the permanent secretary to the Post Office was a prime opponent with his habitual prediction of failure and delaying tactics.

Eventually, Rowland accepted an engagement within the Treasury at a salary of twelve hundred pounds a year for a term of two years with a year's extension if needed. In Rowland's words:

'If Government ever supposed that they could establish the whole plan within my two-year engagement, they must have held unfounded expectations as to Post Office cooperation. Alternatively, they must have accredited me with such energy and powers of convincing, persuading and over riding vouchsafed to few.'

Worse was to follow. At the end of the three-year engagement, the Tories were back in power. They informed Rowland that they no longer needed his services. He recounted:

'They denied my right to complete my own plan and withheld all opportunity for my doing so. They intended to hand over the measure to men who had opposed it stage by stage. Men who had pledged their reputation to its failure, and had unquestionably been caballing to obtain my expulsion from office.'

During the next three years, Rowland served first as a director and then as Chairman of the then lately formed Brighton Railway Company. He was elected to the Board of the company with only one dissentient. The latter feared that the new broom would prove too sweeping. "We want no Rowland Hills here to interfere with everything and even perhaps to introduce penny fares in all directions." What the new broom did, was to introduce express and excursion trains to the popular seaside resort. The express train travelled at the then startling speed of thirty-four miles an hour.

Rowland's banishment proved short lived. For in 1846, the electorate returned the Liberals to power. The new Government immediately offered Rowland the position of Secretary to the Postmaster General at his former salary of one thousand two-hundred pounds per annum. Though still subordinate to his adversary the Permanent Secretary, Colonel Maberley, he accepted the position. In 1854, the Government transferred Maberley to the Board of Audit.

They appointed Rowland as Permanent Secretary in his place. Thus, the way was open for Rowland to introduce his own ideas for modernising the Post Office.

As narrated, following his first appointment to the Treasury, Rowland had persuaded his elder brother, Edwin, to join him there as Supervisor of Stamps. Also, in 1851, Rowland persuaded his younger brother, Frederic, to join him as Assistant Secretary at the Post Office. For the next ten years following the departure of Colonel Maberley, the three brothers pooled their ideas for modernising the Post Office. They made substantial progress under the benign influence of various Postmaster's General. Nevertheless, Rowland had his enemies within the Department apart from those who caballed against change.

Thus, in the words of Rowland:

'During this time, content prevailed at the Post Office and reports from all quarters spoke highly of the general conduct of those employed in its service. Nevertheless, it was inevitable that among so large a body of men discontent should arise somewhere or other. Promotion by merit, however satisfactory to the deserving, did little to gratify those who had no merit to show. It was yet more distasteful to any whose conduct positively shrunk from examination. Men who found themselves deprived of extra pay long received but never earned doubtless felt even less gratification. Nay, accorded where, instead of additional service, they had remitted even ordinary duty to such an extent as to become little more than nominal.'

By the end of the decade, Rowland was reporting that the Department worked well and that the various improvements produced very good results. Especially, he mentioned continuing improvement in the postal services to the public and increased postal revenue. He referred to the many improvements relating to the health, comfort and remuneration of the staff and promotion based on merit alone. These he described as securing vigorous and harmonious action within the Post Office. Shortly afterwards, he was writing:

'I well remember the satisfaction that Mr Tilley, the Senior

Assistant Secretary, expressed at the general state of the service, so different from what he had once known. He remarked that now everyone seemed to do his duty as a matter of course. I did not then foresee how so serious a change was at hand. Of this, however, I shall speak but very briefly.'

He then referred to that serious illness, of which he had more than once spoken, as coming upon him again in February 1860. An illness that he described as starting with some forty-eight hours of nearly continuous insensibility and that confined him to his house and prostrated his bodily strength. Far worse, which rendered him for a long time quite incapable of mental activity and compelled his absence from work for several months.

Continuing his account:

'Fondly believing that the peaceful state just spoken of would endure, I did not anticipate any very serious positive consequences from my absence. Though, of course, I knew it must delay the progress of improvement.

'Circumstances, however, proved untoward. A breath from without fanned lurking discontent into a flame. As this occurred during my disability and I believe by no accidental coincidence, it gave opportunity for the revival of those cabals higher up in the office. Those who had so frequently interfered with good order and had made improvement difficult.

'At this critical period, the office of Postmaster-General unfortunately became vacant by the appointment of Lord Elgin to direct our expedition to China. When, at length, they appointed Lord Stanley of Alderley, I had not the good fortune to obtain from him that confidence and support, which I had enjoyed with his predecessors.'

Rowland Hill continued that he then had to oppose a fourth cabal at a time of temporary weakness on his part. That he became involved in disputes of increasing severity but without the support of the Postmaster General. Disputes that he no longer had the strength to maintain. It seems that these arose out of Rowland's insistence that promotion should be based on merit alone. After a series of fruitless efforts, his health became so seriously effected as to compel him seriously to consider final retirement; 'Retirement from that important and absorbing task in which I had so long been engaged.'

William Gladstone, then Chancellor of the Exchequer and later Prime Minister, fully recognised all that Rowland had done for the Post Office and wrote to him:

'I have read your completed minute. Though I am to see you tomorrow, I must without waiting say I have read it with a deep sense of pain and some of shame in reviewing what has happened. If you are at present under odium for the gallant stand you make on behalf of the public interests, at a period too when chivalry of that kind by no means pays, I believe that I have and I hope still to have the honour of sharing it with you. I am very thankful that you are once more at your post.'

The following year, 1861, William Gladstone was writing to the Prime Minister, Lord Palmerston:

'At my suggestion and with the knowledge of Lord Stanley, Sir Rowland Hill will call upon you to explain to you his present position in the Post Office. I am afraid we are in danger of losing him. I desire not to be responsible in any degree for bringing so great a misfortune on the public service.'

The Prime Minister was unsympathetic. He replied that the substance of the complaint was that Lord Stanley acted upon his own opinions and not those of Sir Rowland. Asserting that Sir Rowland misunderstood the relative positions of Secretary and Head of a Department, he continued:

'I told Sir Rowland that I considered Stanley quite right in the matter. Rowland Hill had, no doubt, the great merit of suggesting the Penny Postage, but he seemed to me the Spoilt Child of the Post Office. He ought either to make up his mind to be what he really is, a subordinate officer. Otherwise to retire from a post which his own notions of his personal importance make it unpleasant for him to hold. As to Leave of Absence, if I were Stanley, I would give it to him sine die.'

For the purposes of his Biographer, Rowland subsequently

67

wrote:

'I return to the year 1864 and to my personal narrative. The necessity for my withdrawal was the more disappointing, because I knew that I had the full confidence and even sympathy of the Head of that Department (the Treasury) to which the Post Office is subordinate. This confidence, however, was not sufficiently near for my support, and in my immediate department the ground was slipping from beneath my feet.

'The chief point I was striving to maintain was that of promotion at once by absolute merit. The rules by which the Department maintained this had to an important extent been of late set aside, all my resistance to the change being overborne. As the Treasury had made my appointment, I had thought myself justified in appealing to that higher authority. I now learnt for the first time (6th February, 1864) that the Postmaster-General had condemned such appeal. Also, he had denied in general terms my alleged appointment by the Treasury. He maintained that the Postmaster-General alone makes all appointments in the Post Office.

'I had even gone so far (on the suggestion of Mr. Gladstone) as twice to solicit and obtain an interview with the Premier, Lord Palmerston. On the first occasion, he received me in the most friendly manner and listened with great patience. I even obtained some little support. However, on the second interview, I became convinced that I had no hope of effectual aid from that quarter. In short, matters had ere this come into such a state that it was in effect impracticable for me to retain my actual position.My strength was already exhausted.'

Rowland took six months leave of absence. He hoped that his health might sufficiently improve to enable him to hold on in anticipation of better times, but this was not to be. At the end of this period, his doctors most strongly advised him not to return to the Post Office. Moreover, he received confidential information of changes at the Post Office that could only add to his difficulties if he decided to ignore medical advice and return. He called first upon the Chancellor of the Exchequer to let him know of his intended resignation.

He recorded the interview in his *Journal* thus:

'Gladstone greatly regrets my determination to resign. He presses upon me an offer to arrange for another six months' absence. That on the clear understanding I do not return to the Post Office while Lord Stanley of Alderney is there. At his urgent request, promised to consider the question.'

Nevertheless, Rowland remained determined to go. He saw Mr. Gladstone again to expand on the reasons for his going. Additionally, he warned Mr. Gladstone of the evils that must follow from the changes then taking place. Under his Journal, he expressed some comfort from knowing that there remained behind colleagues of tried zeal and ability. Including, as he put it, a few on whom he could rely to support his plans and who would have the strength to endure until the return of better times.

At the time of his going in 1865, Rowland had reanimated every branch of the postal service. He had cut down expenses, decreased the hours of work, raised wages, reduced postal rates, speeded up deliveries of mail, and extended the services offered to the public. As a result, the annual number of chargeable letters increased between 1838 and 1864 from seventy-six million to six hundred and forty-two million. Over the same period, the gross annual revenue increased from £2,346,000 to £3,870,000 and net from £1,660,000 to £1,790,000.

In the subsequent words of the Chancellor of the Exchequer, William Gladstone:

'Rowland Hill's lot was one peculiarly happy even as among public benefactors. For his great plan ran like a wildfire through the civilised world. Never, perhaps, was there a local invention (for such it was) and improvement applied during the author's lifetime to the advantage of so many fellow creatures.'

Rowland recounts how gifts and awards attended his retirement. In 1860, the Crown created him a Knight Commander of the Bath. The Royal Society elected him a Fellow. The Post Office retired him on full salary, and, as well, he received a parliamentary grant of £20,000. Continuing his narrative:

'Amidst these transactions, some events occurred of no small interest to myself. I had the gratification of receiving from the University of Oxford the honorary degree of DCL. A valuable presentation of pictures followed an address voted at a town's meeting at Liverpool. The town of Longton presented me with two fine china vases, specimens of its manufacture. I had the honour to receive the Albert Gold Medal of the Society of Arts presented by the Prince of Wales.'

Thus, Rowland retired in his seventieth year, only upon realisation that he no longer had the time nor the strength to thwart those who conspired against his reforms. He recognised that he must look to those who followed him to preserve what he had achieved. In these circumstances, he enjoyed fifteen years of retirement. Birkbeck Hill writes of his closing years:

'The old family group began to grow thin before his eyes. His two elder brothers went first. His only surviving sister followed them before long. However, they had all reached a ripe age. In the death of his eldest daughter and of more than one of his grandchildren, he felt far deeper sorrow. The sorrow that comes on the old, when they see the young gathered to the grave before them. Outside his own circle, Death, while it so long passed him by, was very busy. Old friends, men eminent in science or in public life, he saw pass away before him.

'Fresh honours were done to him. Birmingham, the town in which he had spent his youth and early manhood, set up his statue. A short time before he died, he heard that Kidderminster, his birth place, was going to pay him a like honour. At the very close of his life, the City of London granted him its Freedom. He was far too weak to attend at the Guildhall. He received it in his bed chamber on the 6th June, 1879, less than three months before his death.'

In presentation the City Chamberlain said:

'We congratulate you that, notwithstanding the labour and sorrow inevitable to the weight of eighty-three years, you have been spared to witness the complete triumph of your postal principles and to receive acknowledgements from the State and honours from your Sovereign. Detractors and obstructors you have outlived, or they only survive to swell the ranks of those who applaud.'

70

'Before leaving the house, I went once more up to his room and through the open door gazed at the man whom I had so much honoured. I did not venture to break on his repose by going in. He had on his face a look of great peacefulness. I never saw him again.

'He died on the 27th August 1879 with his wife beside him holding his beloved hand in hers. His last sign of life was to feel for her wedding ring, that ring which he had put round her finger more than fifty years before. Finding it, with one final gentle pressure he showed that the love he had always borne her from the beginning, he bore her to the end.'

The nation awarded Rowland that final great honour, which the English render to their famous dead of burial in Westminster Abbey. His final resting place is close to the memorial of that other inventor who bestowed great benefits on humanity, James Watt.

Perhaps, his best epitaph is the words spoken to him in life by his brother, Matthew:

"When you go to heaven, I foresee that you will stop at the gate and enquire of St. Peter how many deliveries they have per day and how they defray the expense of postal communication between heaven and other places."

Frederic Hill (1803-1896), the youngest son of Thomas Wright Hill to survive to adult years, was the longest lived. Born in 1803, the year after the abortive peace of Amiens, he died in November 1896. He lived to see two royal jubilees, namely those of King George III in 1810 and Queen Victoria in 1887. An early memory was that of seeing two criminals in the pillory at the Birmingham marketplace.

The author's father was born in Frederic's lifetime and Frederic was born in the lifetime of John Hill. The latter had fought against Bonny Prince Charles in 1745. An illustration of the shortness of time between then and now during which human life has transformed beyond the wildest visions of those earlier generations.

Frederic's great ambition was to obtain an important post under Government as he confessed to his eldest brother, Matthew, while still in his teens and a pupil-teacher at Hazelwood. Matthew

71

replied scornfully, "You remind me of the boy who wished to be apprenticed to a Bishop."

In his youth, Frederic, like the rest of the family, was an enthusiastic worker for parliamentary reform and a relaxation of the harsh laws of the country. Like Matthew, he qualified as a barrister and fulfilled for the second time the ambition denied to his father. After qualifying, he obtained a position as parliamentary secretary to Sergeant Wilde, who was a Whig member of parliament and a distinguished barrister. Frederic's success in this position led to the Home Secretary, Lord John Russell, offering him the newly created office of HM Inspector of Prisons for Scotland, Northumberland and Durham. In doing so he remarked: "There is much work to be done there and I know you will do it."

Thus Frederic achieved his ambition of a position under Government. He was among the first to hold this new office created under the Prisons Act of 1835 to which he brought all his passion for reform. He held the office for sixteen years, during which his reports on prison life and administration advocated many changes for the betterment of the convicts.

For the Home Secretary had been right. Frederic found the prisons under his inspectorate in an appalling state. They were cold and verminous and provided little or no segregation of men and women convicts, who were ill fed if not half-starved. The prisons provided no work of useful occupation but only that of treadmills and hand cranks

In 1835, Frederic's prison work and experiences led him to publish a book *Crime, its Amount, Causes and Remedies*, which followed an earlier book on national education and its prospects. His wife, Martha, nee Cowper, was also interested in educational matters. She was responsible for publication of *The Parents Cabinet of Amusement and Instruction*. This was popular among the Victorians with their large families and the need to entertain their children.

The Home Office invited Frederic to frame a Parliamentary Bill for remodelling the system of prison government in Scotland. Many of his suggested reforms met with great opposition both from local magistrates and from politicians. Especially, he faced opposition from the Home Secretary of that same Tory government under Sir Robert Peel that dismissed Rowland from the Post Office. Nevertheless, he succeeded in getting many of his suggestions carried out. When he ultimately came to leave Scotland, he reported to the Home Office with a great sense of accomplishment that:

1. All the prison buildings were well adapted for their purpose, and they had set up a separate system of prisoner from prisoner.

2. No prison had a single bad officer.

3. Every prison provided industrial occupation mostly of a productive order to the exclusion of all artificial labour. They had abolished the use of treadmills and cranks.

4. Every prisoner who did more than his allotted task was allowed the value of his overwork. This provided a means to the industrious on leaving gaol to make a fresh start in an honest career.

5. The general conduct of the prisoners was good, although they had entirely abolished flogging.

6. The cost per head of the prisoners was comparatively small. To take the last complete year of my superintendence as a guide, the average cost was £16, whilst in England it exceeded £25.

Frederic had shown that good prison arrangements could result in prisoners of ordinary health and strength defraying the entire cost of their maintenance and custody whatever the committal period.

Frederic was the first to recommend the use of the indeterminate sentence. A sentence under which the offender would be detained until he showed a reasonable prospect of his living an honest and peaceable life. Another of Frederic's suggestions was the setting up of a large hostel to house juvenile offenders on their discharge from prison. A place where they could live until suitable employment was found for them.

In his early days as a prison inspector, Frederic met the great Quaker, Mrs. Elizabeth Fry. They discussed much about the state of the prisons and the need for reforms. In discussing the execution of women, he asked her what she found the chief preoccupation of a woman in the days before her execution. "I grieve to say," replied Mrs. Fry, "that commonly the chief thought relates to her appearance

73

on the scaffold, the dress in which she shall be hanged."

Frederic was a keen supporter of the Law Amendment Society. Especially, he worked for the promotion of the Married Womens' Property Bill. A measure aimed at giving married women rights over their own property at a time when marriage resulted in the wife's property becoming vested in her husband. Frederic also sought the general distribution of educative material on political economy. For he hoped that a greater understanding of the subject by employers and employees might lead to fewer strikes.

In 1851, Frederic resigned from the Prison Inspectorate upon the Post Office offering him the position of Assistant Secretary. This was actually a step down for him, but his brother Rowland was fighting a hard battle and needed his help. In the quite extraordinary way in which the Hill brothers rallied round each other, Frederic was obedient to the call. He moved his family south. They settled in Hampstead from where they enjoyed a view over London as far as the Surrey hills. Matthew and Rowland were already there.

On joining the Post Office, Frederic initiated substantial reforms including the expansion of female employment throughout the Post Office. He improved the transmarine postal services and the negotiation of contracts for the carriage of mail by sea. He promulgated rules for regulating the promotion and salaries of rural sub-postmasters according to their performance. They then numbered about six thousand. He took over the management of the money order department.

Frederic also initiated annual reports within the Post Office similar to those that he had maintained during sixteen years as an Inspector of Prisons. He also introduced a series of postal guides edited by himself. Under his direction, the Post Office reorganised its central office with increased efficiency in the use of space, ventilation and fire protection.

The family of Frederic and Martha Hill comprised three daughters. The second, Leonora Edgeworth, married a cousin who, as Sir John Scott, became Judicial Adviser to the Khedive and reorganised the Egyptian legal system. Her son, Leslie, served for many years as Conservative Member of Parliament and, in 1922, became Solicitor General and, subsequently, a Lord Justice of Appeal.

The other two daughters, Ellen and Constance, were unmarried. Ellen studied in Paris and became a talented artist. She exhibited portrait studies from time to time at the Royal Academy. Constance became a writer on various aspects of the eighteenth century literary and social scene. The two sisters lived together to a great age in a charming eighteenth-century cottage in Hampstead.

Arthur Hill (1798-1885), the fourth son of Thomas Wright Hill (and the author's great great-grandfather), devoted his life to Bruce Castle and the headmastership of the family school there.

"I have never known anyone who had a greater devotion to duty than Arthur" said his father. That duty led Arthur, while still a young man who had already taught himself Latin, to study Greek and so extend his qualification as a teacher. He did so with such intensity that he permanently impaired his eyesight by pouring over small print in a poor light. To quote from Rowland's *Journal*:

'June17th 1820: This and last evening some of our boys performed (in Latin) the whole of Plautus's Captives. They were astonishingly perfect.'

'July 20th 1820: In Arthur I find a most able ally in the executive part of the business. His application is almost incessant, and I am sorry to say it has materially injured his eyesight. Under his care the boys have made wonderful progress in the classics. We have found that frequent exercise in Latin dialogue has been of the greatest use in the acquirement of that language.

'For this purpose, the boys learn and perform an act of a Latin play every month. At the same time, other boys are engaged in shorter Latin dialogues, in Greek recitation, and performing scenes from the works of the French dramatists. The very frequent rehearsals that are necessary engaged in a real conversation, frequently speaking of real and tangible objects, familiarizes them wonderfully with the language they are using. It is, I believe, the nearest approach that they can make to the mode in which we learn our native language.'

A week or two earlier their father had written:

'Rowland and Arthur are most laborious and successful fellows. I hope that they are building a reputation that may make them comfortable in their fortunes. Nevertheless, all that be human is precarious. Time and chance must happen to them as to all. A good conscience is the only treasure insured against all risks, and this is a treasure that I trust my dear children will never feel the want.'

Thomas Hill had in his mind the ever present dread of illness and plague. This was a frequent cause of early death in a time of inadequate sanitation and water and rudimentary medical knowledge.

When Rowland finally moved away from the life of the school, the mantle of headmaster fell naturally on Arthur's shoulders. He spent the rest of his working life at Bruce Castle and brought up his family there. His marriage introduced a Welsh strain for his wife, Ellen Maurice, was a sister to the well-known preacher and social worker Denison Maurice. Through her mother, whose name was Bache, she claimed Huguenot descent. The musicians, Edward and Walter Bache, were her kinsmen.

Arthur and Ellen had four children, Lewin, Laura, George Birkbeck and John Gray. In 1839, while the children were still in the nursery, the mother died aged only thirty-two. Arthur was left with four small children to bring up and the school on his hands. His wife's sister, Theodosia, came to the rescue. She made her home with him and mothered the children. Still, any thought of marriage to her brother-in-law was out of the question as then prohibited by law.

Reading was largely forbidden to Arthur by reason of his poor eyesight. He listened a good deal to works read aloud. This led him to cultivate his memory until he could learn and recite with great dramatic power whole plays of Shakespeare. When he finally came to retire as headmaster of the school, he lessened idle hours by translating Horace's *Ars Poetica* into English verse. Knowing the Latin text by heart, he could work out a translation during wakeful hours of the night and dictate it the next morning.

Arthur was a popular headmaster. On his retirement in 1868, the boys subscribed a memorial amounting to £472. He used this sum to set up a trust that provided an Exhibition or Scholarship at Bruce Castle as an award to those showing moral excellence. The trust was to continue while the Hill family maintained its system of education directed to cultivating moral character in preferment to intellectual development. Afterwards, the trustees were to use the sum in the building or purchase of a lifeboat that they were to call the *Arthur Hill Lifeboat.*

Rowland has described how his brother, Arthur, helped him to prepare letters and minutes in support of his scheme for postal reform:

'To me the device and elaborations of plans were incomparably easier than their exposition or advocacy. With my brother, Arthur, the case was the reverse. This leads me to the frequent employment of his pen. What neither of us could have effected separately, joint action made easy.'

Thus, Rowland would sketch out his proposals. Then the two brothers would sit down together. Arthur would dictate and Rowland would write and both would amend until fully satisfied with the results. Seeing the great hostility with which some in public office received Rowland's proposals, it is questionable whether they would have gained acceptance without the exposition and advocacy so elegantly expressed by Arthur.

Like all the family, Arthur believed in regular exercise and long early morning walks and dreaded the fastidious or luxuriant. Perhaps, this was the reason for their longevity. When more than eighty and prescribed an occasional glass of brandy as a stimulant, Arthur refused to have sugar added lest I should grow to like it.

Thus, the sons of Thomas Wright Hill contributed much to the social development of the 19th century. Later generations of the family were to do likewise in their contribution to law and medical science. Arthur's younger sons, George Birkbeck (or Birkbeck as he preferred) and John Gray, were to distinguish themselves by their contribution to the second half of the nineteenth century.

Especially, John Gray and later Birkbeck's son, Arthur

Norman, were to play a leading part in the development of shipping and in the maritime affairs of Liverpool. A city and a port that for over a century was at the centre of a great empire then suddenly collapsed as empire collapsed. First, we shall look at the upcoming of Liverpool during the first half of the nineteenth century. As they recorded the events in the books of the legal practice that John Gray Hill later made so prestigious in maritime affairs.

Bruce Castle

Sir Rowland Hill

CHAPTER 5

UPCOMING LIVERPOOL

1. The Emergence of Liverpool

The emergence of Liverpool as a dark and gloomy pool known as Lyrpwl or Lyppole was inauspicious. For many centuries, it remained an isolated corner of a desolate and savage county where a sparse population eked out a bare living from land and river. By the mid-sixteenth century, Liverpool comprised 138 cottages occupied by 690 inhabitants. These inhabitants, like those of Lancashire as a whole, were poor, uncouth and aggressive with a reputation for disorder, depravity and destitution.

Liverpool was then a thoroughly dangerous place. Justice to all intents and purposes was nonexistent. Punishment deserved or otherwise was cruel in the extreme. Whipping, branding and even plucking out the eyes were common penalties in early days. The whipping posts, stocks and ducking stools were common to Liverpool as to most English villages. In the sixteenth century, a court punished the theft of a purse of gold and jewels by having the offender nailed to a post and whipped out of Liverpool. Until the 19th century, the courts continued to impose hanging and transportation for quite minor crimes.

Disease took its toll, including black death, bubonic plague, cholera and other pestilence. Survival was a continuous struggle against both the forces of nature and the cruelty of man. The inhabitants would have been much as ourselves, but uncouth in habit and anxious and despairing as they faced the ever present risk of illness and early death. They would have enjoyed summer days and the peace of sky, land and water about them and those beautiful local sunsets later painted by Turner. That was when not wholly occupied with survival and the fears for tomorrow and the savagery of winter.

In its early days, Liverpool was subsidiary to and a creek in

79

the port of Chester. Its inhabitants would have regarded life as unchanging for them and for generations to come. However, they were mistaken. Great change was to come at much cost in human deprivation, suffering and degradation.

As the river Dee silted up, Chester's former sea trade came to Liverpool. Thus, between the mid-seventeenth and the mid-eighteenth century, the number of vessels trading out of Liverpool doubled. Yet the real spur to Liverpool came in the late seventeenth century with expanding trade to the American colonies and the West Indies. By the end of the century, Liverpool owned a fleet of some seventy vessels. At the beginning of the eighteenth century, Liverpool led the world in opening the first wet dock. From then on, growth in Liverpool shipping was rapid and continuous and, as the number of ships increased, so did docks, trade and population

The American trade especially in slaves was passing through Liverpool. The Liverpool slavers carried cargoes of finished Lancashire cotton goods to Africa. There the slavers exchanged these cargoes for Negro slaves. They transported the slaves across the Atlantic and returned to Liverpool with cargoes of raw cotton, sugar and tobacco. In 1771, when Thomas Wright Hill was eight years old, 58 slavers sailed from London, 23 from Bristol and 107 from Liverpool. Between them that year, they carried 50,000 slaves under the most appalling conditions of congestion and cruelty. They were also selling slaves directly in Liverpool as appears from the following advertisements of 1776:

'To be sold the 23rd August the hull of the *Molly*.
Also, three young men slaves to be sold at the same time.'

'One Negro man and two boys for sale: Mr. Robinson's office 1st December.'

The 19th century was a time of British Empire coming to occupy one quarter of the world's surface and policing the world. Liverpool, as the gateway into that Empire and into the emergent new world of America, became increasingly prosperous. As the Empire expanded, so did the shipping trade in and out of Liverpool. Shipowners were building finer and larger vessels. Yet, during the first half of the century, most vessels continued powered by wind and sail and constructed of wood.

Liverpool was becoming a place of extremes in wealth and poverty and, in the words of Disraeli, a place of two nations. A place of desolation, humiliation and degradation to those who came to a boom town, which was greedy for their labour but was indifferent to their needs. A town in which tens of thousands were to become hundreds of thousands that would have the most appalling consequences for shelter, food, and drink, and consequently health. An exciting place and time for those fired with ambition, who came to a town where they might gain or lose fortunes overnight. Yet all was creating a depth of antagonism and bitterness that would continue over the next two centuries.

This was a time when Liverpool was building docks, ships, waterworks and buildings of every type, aesthetic and ugly, and later railways and steamship. The beginning of evolutionary change and control by man over his own environment and destiny. A change that was to make the unimaginable to one generation the norm and need of later generations.

Yet it was still a time of duels, of plague, of cholera and other virulent diseases and of travel by horse and coach over poorly constructed roads. It was a time when the express coach to London took more than thirty hours to complete its journey. It left Liverpool at 6.15 am, took a short stop at Birmingham twelve hours later, and arrived at the Bull Inn Leadenhall Street at 1.00 p.m. the following day. In 1814, a severe frost resulted in the London mail coach being delayed four days on the road.

Hours of work were long and arduous. Mercantile offices were open from 8.00 to 8.00 six days a week. Offices were small and, especially, those of the clerks, and windows were shuttered. Heating and lighting was poor, and after dark lighting was by tallow candles or oil lamps.

The life of the law clerk was not an easy one confined to his desk all day except for short intervals allowed for refreshment. He wrote hour after hour with quill pen and handmade black engrossing ink copying deeds and letters from drafts in the hand of his principal. Legal apprentices worked even later hours, but had the satisfaction of spending much of their time out of the office. Both had good reason to complain that they had little time for study to advance themselves in their profession. Principals took refreshment in a glass of Madeira. The more fortunate clerks took a glass of ale. For others a glass of buttermilk sufficed.

Many mercantile offices were situated to the south of the town close to the river and the southern docks. Streets there were long, dirty and narrow with open sewers running down the centre. An ever increasing population overcrowded tenements, which had no sanitation and were hard up one against another so providing poor light and air. Carts delivered water. Still, this was a good commercial centre from which to practice law in a rapidly expanding maritime city.

2. Social problems of the First Half of the 19th Century .

Early copy letter books of the mercantile solicitors joined by Gray Hill in 1865 reflect social problems of living in the first half of the 19th Century. These books comprise copies of several thousand letters made on the thinnest paper in the hand of the clerk faded and many spoiled by damp and age. Reading them is to be placed back into the early and mid 19th Century, when cholera was rife in Liverpool with its resultant high mortality. Not surprisingly with many poverty-stricken inhabitants crowded into insanitary tenements and cellars on an inadequate diet and with no proper water supply.

For those on inadequate means, life must have plunged the very depths of misery and despair in the day to day struggle to live under such awful conditions. A life escaped only with the greatest difficulty. Yet, once escaped by success in commerce or trade, a new and affluent way of life was opened to the escapee and his heirs.

Reading these books is further to realise how little the working of our minds has changed over the intervening years. That is despite the vast changes that have taken place in our material circumstances. To read the advice that they gave in the affairs of men and women now dead for near two hundred years is poignant. One feels great affinity with them and in all for which they were striving. Their success has been our inheritance.

Social conditions are well documented in these letter books. Expanding legal work included the private and family affairs of the new and emergent class of entrepreneur, who were engaged in the ever expanding trade, commerce and business of Liverpool. They sought investment of their newly acquired wealth in property and in stocks and loans of the many expanding businesses and undertakings. Especially, the new railway companies were to prove a popular form of investment.

These entrepreneurs were finding homes by their purchase or leasing in the charming squares of Liverpool and Birkenhead and in the outlying pretty countryside. They were introducing sons and nephews into their businesses to secure succession, and making financial provision for other members of the family. Life insurance was increasing. They were making elaborate marriage and other settlements and wills for the protection of the female members of their family and their children.

The latter protection was necessary to overcome the law of the time that the wife's property became that of her husband. Otherwise, she could find herself deprived of it at his whim or on his indebtedness or death. Vesting the property in trustees avoided such misfortune by obligating the trustees to pay the income to the wife and after her death to vest the property in her children. Thus, they precluded the property from passing into the hands of the husband and his creditors.

The following advice shows the insecurity of the married woman unless she received that form of protection:

'The personal estate or moveables of a woman are vested in her husband as his own property. Whatever personal estate may come to or devolve upon her during the marriage, the husband has the right to receive it and give a discharge for it without her concurrence. Nevertheless, this law is subject that the husband receives the estate or does some act equivalent to reducing it into his possession. Otherwise, if the wife survives him, she becomes entitled to the estate just as she would if she had never been married.'

In the particular case, the husband had not reduced the wife's property into his own possession. It remained her property, and did not pass to the husband's heirs on his death as otherwise would have happened.

An example of creditors attempting to seize a wife's inheritance appears under the following enquiry:

'Clients have instructed us to find out whether Mr. Nicholson, a bankrupt, has in respect of his wife or otherwise any interest under the will of the late Colonel Patrick McNight.'

Thus, if the wife had any such interest unprotected by appropriate trusts, the husband's creditors could have seized it as part of his property. The wife could then have been left destitute.

The counterpart rule of law was that the husband was responsible for his wife's debts. That is unless he had notified the creditors before his wife incurred the debt that he declined to accept such responsibility. Thus, the following endorsement of a claim on a writ of action will not have pleased the husband:

'The claim is for £94. 3. 4d for millinery and other goods furnished to the Defendant's wife between March and July 1841.'

The lot of the debtor and bankrupt was indefinite imprisonment as Charles Dickens so aptly described under his novels. A device of the time to avoid that catastrophe was an arrangement of the debtor's affairs. Family and friends agreed with the creditors to subscribe a specified amount or percentage dividend per £ of debt.

This could prove a labourious task. The family and friends needed both to raise the required monies and to obtain the agreement of all creditors to accept the proposed dividend. If one creditor disagreed, then the attempted arrangement was likely to fail. The spur to the creditors was some payment in place of none or of a trifling amount. Thus, in a bankruptcy case of 1840 designated Stephen V. Ward:

'Defendant's Estate will not pay more than 4/- or 5/- in the pound. The Defendant's uncle became security for him to Mr. Cairns who lent him £300. Twelve months ago they called upon his uncle to pay £100 part of the £300. The Defendant then gave his uncle a warrant of Attorney to secure the £100. About three weeks' ago, the uncle issued execution and swept away Defendant's stock and received the proceeds amounting to £72. The only property that remains is some bank debts. We have made every enquiry as to the probability of any of his friends coming forward and releasing the Defendant if they took him to gaol. We find not the faintest hope of their doing so.'

A further advice of 1842 relating to enforcement of a debt reads:

'The sheriff has written us saying that he has in custody a person named Thomas Brown who lived at Rochdale, is by a trade a travelling scotchman and is about 20 or 30 years of age. Now we wish to know whether this person is the same man who is indebted to you. So that he may be kept in prison if really the person or released if not. You will note that he is not in prison upon your account, but for another case. Also observe that the Sheriff states that the place of residence was Rochdale and the trade different from that you described. He denies that he is the person indebted to you. Please send as full a description as possible of your debtor, naming his place of residence, trade, age etc. We will then write to the Keeper of Lancaster Castle so that he may satisfy himself as to the identity.'

The sensibilities and social niceties of the era are well shown by letters of 1840 relating to the Marshall family and young Lucy Marshall. Those letters might have formed the basis of a novel by Charles Dickens or Jane Austin. Lucy's father had settled annuities for life of £150 on each of Lucy and her sister, Sarah, in circumstances where both girls were born outside marriage and were thus illegitimate. That was a severe social stigma of the day as respects both the mother and the illegitimate children, and something that needed to be kept hidden from society. Thus, the father appointed trustee guardians of the two girls, whom the guardians lodged with a Reverend Hepworth, and the girls attended private schooling. The Reverend Hepworth was a strong disciplinarian and most strict in their upbringing.'

Lucy in her late 'teens formed an attachment with a young man, R.W. Phelps of Tewkesbury. He sought marriage with her,

85

but he did not appear an appropriate suitor. The solicitor trustee advised that, if they began a suit in Chancery for making Lucy and Sarah wards in Chancery, the father would need be a party as settlor. The sisters' illegitimacy might then appear. Instead, he suggested a limited relationship. After some previous correspondence, he wrote to Lucy on the 16th July 1840:

'I am much grieved at what you mention with regard to Mr. Phelps. Entertaining as I do a sincere interest in your happiness, I cannot contemplate your union with him without forebodings of much unhappiness and wretchedness. I do not allude to his character of which I know nothing. Opining it to be good, he appears from his own account of himself to be quite unsuitable for you, at least for some time to come.

'He is, I understand, a young man about 18 years old without any property and in no way of business. I understand a clerk in the office of his father, who has recently sustained very heavy losses that have deprived him of all his property. I would therefore strongly recommend you, if you have any regard for my opinion, to give up all thoughts of such a union at all events for the present. Thereafter, if he should get into any business sufficient to support you, for your annuity would not be enough, you would not be prevented from acting as you might think proper. This advice will not be palatable, but I could give you no other advice if you were my own daughter.'

Lucy replied:

'It was never my wish to enter into a union with Mr. Phelps until he was admitted and settled in a profession such as would enable him to support me comfortably and creditably. I am sure it was not Mr. Phelps' wish either. All I desire is to see Mr. Phelps occasionally. Then I should be willing to wait any time until his affairs were in that state as perfectly to justify him in making me his wife.'

That same day, the Trustee wrote to his fellow Trustee quoting Lucy's remarks and continuing:

'My own view is that the most judicious action would be not absolutely to debar these two young people from all intercourses. Because, with the sentiments that she appears to entertain towards him, if entirely forbidden to see him, she would be more likely to go

86

off with him. She has shown spirit on several occasions for instance escaping from her guardian's house. Whereas, if we permit reasonable intercourse on the undertaking that there is to be no engagement at present, they will probably both tire of each other. At all events, if he is really an unsuitable partner for her. It is I confess a difficult question what is best to be done. I only think that he masters the enquiry as he is her betrothed.

'I had a letter from Lucy herself a few days since. She stated that Mr. Hepworth had treated Mr. Phelps shamefully, and had got police officers to put him out of the house. In consequence, she had accompanied Mr. Phelps to a friend's house at Crosby, where she passed the night with Miss Simmons, Mr. Phelps having left her. Mr. Hepworth brought her home again, but she did not mean to remain with him. She rather thought that we had so vested her annuity as to allow of her choosing her own home. She adds that she does not wish to become Mr. Phelps' partner at present unless circumstances drive her to it. I shall answer her strongly dissuading her from the proposed union, for I quite agree with you that it is very far from an eligible one.'

The trustees decided to move Lucy and place her under the care of a Reverend W.W. Duncan and his sister at Cleish. They anticipated that she would be constant and happy there on being allowed to correspond with young Phelps. However, the following year, she left Cleish of her own volition and joined her sister, Sarah, to board with her uncle at Worcester. On the 25th November 1841, the solicitor trustee was writing to her that he considered the terms of her board reasonable and continuing:

'Given your hint that you will not trouble me long, I infer that you are going to be married. If so, I sincerely wish you may find it for your happiness not only here but the event may be blessed to your eternal good. Remember to have the annuity settled upon yourself. If not, it would go to your husband's creditors in case of misfortune, which would be worse for both of you.'

No further reference is to be found to Lucy Marshall. We may, perhaps, deduce that her story ended happily in the marriage of her choice.

87

Another tale is that of Silvester Thornton. When he was aged fourteen, the criminal court had convicted and sentenced him to transportation for life. He had served sixteen years of his sentence and was seeking a pardon. The same solicitor who had advised about Lucy Marshall was again concerned as the son of the party injured by the crime. On the 4th March 1841, he was writing to Lord John Ansell at the Colonial Office:

'I beg to transmit to your Lordship the enclosed petition from Silvester Thornton. He is a convict holding a ticket of leave now in New South Wales praying for an absolute pardon. In 1824, he was convicted for wilfully setting fire to a warehouse belonging to my late father and was transported for life.

'I am not sure whether the petition is properly drawn up. If it should have come through the Governor of the Colony, I trust that it may be referred to him for his consideration. I draw attention to the very strong recommendations attached to the petition; the uniform good conduct apparently maintained by the petitioner during the sixteen years of his punishment; and that he was only fourteen years of age when the offence was committed. My only object in now addressing your Lordship is to testify my own conviction that, opining the statements in the certificates attached to the petition to be true, which I have no reason to doubt, he is a fit object for the exercise of the Royal mercy. I do so as the son of the person injured by the crime of which Thornton was convicted.'

Only the one letter appears relating to Silvester Thornton, so we cannot say whether they granted him a pardon.

In 1843, an advice given to the merchant house Brown Shipley related to slavery in the Southern states of America. Slavery remained lawful there until the American civil war of 1860. It had been outlawed in the United Kingdom early in the nineteenth century. An opinion of the Attorney General accompanied the advice. It stated that, while a mortgage of slaves was illegal in the United Kingdom, nevertheless the Courts would enforce a judgment for debt by ordering a seizure and sale of slaves overseas. In the words of the Attorney General:

'It is not necessary that the debtor should have defended the action in which a creditor obtains such a judgment. If a debtor voluntarily confers a judgment to provide security for his creditor's just demand, a seizure and sale of slaves under execution of that judgment would not violate the Slave Trade Suppression Act.'

During the nineteenth century, those unable or neglecting to meet their obligations faced imprisoment. Apart from the common debtor, others could find themselves jailed for quite minor transgressions of the law. Hence, in 1840, the solicitors enlisted the help of the Liverpool Member of Parliament to present a case to the Treasury for merciful consideration of a ship's master already imprisoned and facing further imprisoment.

'Captain McArthur was the master of a small vessel employed in the coasting trade. The Owners then sent him on a voyage to Tobago and back to Liverpool. On his return, they had sold the vessel and appointed him to a new vessel. He landed the surplus stores to have them transferred to the new vessel, which he expected would be ready in three or four weeks. However, not being accustomed to any but the coasting trade, he was ignorant of the necessity for any entry or form at the Custom House. This being unfortunately omitted, the Magistrates had no alternative but to convict him in the penalty of £100.

'Captain McArthur had no means of paying the amount since his wages amount only to about £70 a year. Out of this, he has to support himself and three children under eight years of age. He was committed and remained three weeks in Gaol. His Owners required his services in superintending the completion of the new vessel and advanced the £100 for him. The Collector and Comptroller promised to hold it whilst he applied for mitigation.'

'Captain McArthur had previously petitioned the Commissioners of Customs. Mr. Rushton, the Magistrate, certified that it appeared that the articles were surplus stores and that there was reason to believe that he intended them for another Vessel. Moreover, he did not attempt concealment in the unshipment that took place in the daytime.

'Nevertheless, the Commissioners refused to mitigate the penalty in consequence, as we think, of offences of this kind having become very frequent. Yet, if as I think the circumstances show and as I firmly believe, this poor fellow erred through ignorance, it is hard that they should make him an example. I trust that Government may view it as a fit case for mercy. Otherwise it will prove his ruin as he has only his wages to support himself and his family.'

An enquiry of 1840 sought to decide the vesting of a property on a past death in the absence a will. Under the law of the day, freehold property passed on death to the eldest son or, if none, to the eldest daughter. Personal property including a lease was divisible among all the deceased's children:

'The daughter of a person named Joseph Richardson has consulted us. He was formerly of Hull. He sailed as a midshipman under Lord Cochrane about twenty-five years since. Two to three years after he sailed from London, a shipmate called on his family in Hull and informed them that Richardson had died of a fever. Our client was his only child and remembers going into mourning for him when she was about seven or eight years of age.

'His mother and his four sisters survived him. At the time of his death, they occupied a house that his father had built. The mother (our client's grandmother) died about eighteen years since and one sister about twelve years since. The other three sisters still occupy the house. Our client is not able to say what the tenure is. If freehold of inheritance, it belongs to her as heir of her father who was the only son of her grandfather who built it. However, if leasehold, she is entitled to one fourth.'

A report to trustees seeking five children entitled to an inheritance conjures up sad echoes from the past. Disgraceful in the lack of compassion shown by those of the time, we are left with the thought whether their inheritance provided a new and happier style of life:

'At his death, James Cowan had five children living. Of these two, Thomas and Catherine, have been dead some three or four years. Of the three survivors, Charlotte is at present in Gaol here. They convicted her last month for stealing several articles from the workhouse, her previous home.

90

'James, another of the children, is somewhere in this Town, as we understand, and we might probably discover his residence. William Henry, the other child, is living with Mr. George Scott in Hope Lane near Newcastle-under-Lyme. We think you may assume that the infant James may be traded out. They said that he was in the workhouse but he is not there. We shall make further enquiry.'

The following advertisement sought information of those entitled to a legacy:

£2 REWARD

Enquiry for Walter Carlyle formerly of the Parish of Dalton Dumfrieshire Scotland who emigrated to British America and was at Philadelphia in 1833 or 1834. Whosoever will give proof of the death of Walter Carlyle with the time and place of it or, if he is still living, state where he now resides shall receive the above award.

A letter addressed to the daughter-in-law of a Mr. Alston and her reply conjures up much past misery caused by her husband's detention in a lunatic asylum:

'Application has been made to Mr. Alston to increase the allowance to you for the support of yourself and family. He is willing to entertain this on conditions. First, that you do nothing by residence in Northampton or otherwise to keep up excitement in his son's mind. Especially, that you will do nothing to defeat the plan now adopted for his security and ultimate recovery. Secondly, that you do all in your power by industry, economy and personal exertion to educate and support yourself and your family.'

The reply reads:

'I have to say that I do all in my power by industry, economy and personal exertion etc. for the welfare of our family. If Mr. Alston will have the kindness to inform me in what way I have not done so, I shall then see the necessity of binding myself to his wishes. If he wishes to put me in business for the welfare of his son and the education of our children, I will do all in my power in that capacity. With respect to residing in Northampton, I have no wish to do anything that would be likely to excite my husband so to prevent his

91

recovery. During my husband's lucid intervals being anxious about his family is natural for him and to wish to know the state of our affairs. In such a case, I must satisfy him on the subject. If Mr. Alston senior has a wish to do that which is right to his son's family, there will be no cause for unnecessary excitement.'

In 1840, the solicitors made a request to the Liverpool Town Clerk to confine the name of Hood Street to the street off Whitechapel. That is as at today, but in 1840 the name continued along the street now known as Brythen Street. The request illustrates the social problems of 1840 Liverpool with its cosmopolitan influx seeking gratification of sexual and other desires and the many ready to provide for that gratification:

'Please give a new name to the street that is unfortunately too well known as a place of residence of disorderly people. Mrs. Jones is a very respectable woman and the widow of a merchant lost on his passage from Sierra Leone. She has actually lost two to three lodgers in consequence of her street bearing the same name as the street near Whitechapel.'

Other correspondence reveals the charms of Toxteth during the middle of the nineteenth century. The new class of wealthy merchants of Liverpool were seeking houses there and paying high prices. They were also seeking homes in that most fashionable of squares, Hamilton Square Birkenhead, and in Liscard. They described the latter as a village opposite Liverpool on the other side of the River Mersey where many gentlemen live whose place of business is in Liverpool.

In 1844, a move from Rodney Street to Edge Lane was presumably to enjoy a country district in what is now suburbia at its worst. The occupier rented the house under a most peculiar lease for a term of three lives and after that twenty-one years. As further explained:

'The three lives in the lease of my house are all living. Two of them are between sixty and seventy years of age and the other about forty. After the death of all of them, I have it for twenty-one years more.'

Building Societies were making an appearance and adding to

the growth in housing. However, mortgages were generally provided privately. Thus:

'We now require £2000 for a respectable client upon the security of his residence situate at West Derby four miles from the Town Hall. He has recently purchased the residence for £2950, which he considered cheap. It was valued at £3339 just before the sale. The property consists of a large villa, extensive gardens and hot houses. The fair annual rental would be £150. Our client has improved the property, and it is increasing in value. He would give £5 per cent. The tenure is copyhold of inheritance of the Manor of West Derby.'

The following demand shows the risks entailed in a mortgage of one's home, which was often determinable on a mere three months notice. That explains the more common practice of leasing:

'Our client has requested us to remind you that the three months are now up and he cannot wait longer than next week for his money. If not then paid, he has made up his mind to sell the property, and he will insert a Notice in the Albion of Monday week.'

A Mr. Jones of Woodhouse Farm failed to meet commitments under a mortgage of his farm to trustees. He attempted to remove timber from the farm, which the trustees stopped. The trustees took steps to sell the farm. They said: "Mr.Jones has several executions against him and went to Chester goal where he now is."

A letter to Whitchurch solicitors shows monetary problems of the time. It displays both the need to complete property transactions in cash and the criminal practice of chipping or shaving gold coins:

'Out of the parcel of gold that we received from you on Saturday, one hundred of the sovereigns were light and six were chipped. The Bank demanded a commission of five pence each. You can have either the light money back, or we will retain it upon receiving a Post Office Order for £2.11.6d, the amount of the commission.'

Advice on a loan and the effect of usury (excessive interest) on that loan reads:

'Concerning usury, I think you need not feel uneasy. You ask

93

what is the penalty for usury supposing the borrower went against you? The penalty is forfeiture of treble of the amount of the monies lent, but this penalty must be sued for within twelve months after the offence. Besides the penalty, the Act (2 Ann St2C Herp) declares all contracts for more than £5% interest on a loan wholly void.

'However, I think the borrower could not establish usury, at least if I understand the facts. To pay it is not enough. A contract to pay more than the legal rate of interest must subsist. I assume no original bargain or agreement subsists to pay more than 5%, though he afterwards made a payment at a higher rate. The rule is that, if no contract for usurious interest subsists, taking usurious interest does not invalidate the security. I have no fear of the debt on grounds of usury. My only doubt is whether the borrower can pay a just debt.'

Correspondence relating to land includes that of raising loans on entailed land. An entailed estate was one passing from father to son or other male heir. The father possessed only the life interest and could not dispose of the estate to defeat the right of succession. Thus, the enquiry:

'A nobleman in the south of Ireland having large estates there wishes to obtain a loan of £80,000. The property is entailed and, consequently, the security for the loan would be the life estate of the present proprietor with an insurance on his life.'

An interesting advice of 1850 to the merchant house of Brown Shipley related to a conveyance of land situate in Delaware USA by parents to their son Levi. The conveyance contained a condition that, if Levi should die without lawful issue, the property should pass to his brothers and sisters. After explaining that under English law, if the circumstances stated under the condition arose the property would go to the brothers and sisters, the advice continued:

'However, Levi by selling and converting the estate to you or any other person as his assigns avoids the condition even if he should have no issue surviving him. The question depends upon the law of Delaware where the land is situate. I can only advise as to the law of England. However, at the Declaration of Independence, they adopted the law of England as the law of the United States except where altered as an Act of the State.'

In 1850, the solicitors representing the American Chamber of Commerce submitted a request to the relevant Government Minister:

'Praying that they may take measures for the removal of the Wallasey gun powder magazine from its present situation so highly dangerous to the town of Liverpool with its shipping and vast population.'

It is surprising to learn that only one hundred and fifty years ago, this source of danger existed to Liverpool and to the homes of those living in Wallasey.

Other letters that reveal social conditions of the time include the answer to an enquiry relating to the substance of a proposed surety:

'We cannot recommend the gentleman as a surety for £4,000. He may be a civil engineer. However, they employ him here as a clerk to the works of one of the wells proposed for supplying this town with water. His salary does not exceed £150 per annum. He has been here about three years, but has not been receiving more than that sum. He is not supposed to have any property. We believe him to be a man of integrity.'

In relation to a road accident of the time, it was contended:

'You have been informed that your carter on Monday last by his gross negligence caused considerable damage to Mr. Hough's gig by drawing your cart against it. Mr. Hough had hoped that you would, ere this, have expressed your readiness to render compensation for this injury. Further, that it would not have been necessary for him to have required legal assistance to compel you to do your duty. We are instructed to commence an action against you on Saturday next to recover damages, unless you call upon us and pay the costs of repairing this injury.'

A notice summoning a general meeting of the Bread Bakers of Liverpool read:

'A meeting of several Bread Bakers held in Liverpool on the 18th July 1848 discussed a Bill now before the House of Commons. That Bill enacted under its first clause that they should stamp all

95

bread with its weight. The second clause subjected the Baker to a penalty of five shillings for every ounce that the bread should be found deficient in weight. We deem it desirable to hold a General Meeting of the trade to consider this important subject. Especially, as it is impossible for the Baker to calculate the loss that the bread will sustain in its baking.'

Following the meeting, the Bakers asked the Liverpool Member of Parliament to petition against the Bill on grounds that several provisions were impracticable of compliance by the Bakers.

Further, following construction of the Liverpool Corporation water works in the late 1840s, the Bakers sought legal advice. They asked whether the Corporation had power to charge for water supplied to the Bakers at a higher rate than for water supplied for domestic purposes. The advice read:

'The Act specifies certain rates for the supply of water for domestic use. It specifically declares that this shall not include water for any trade or business whatsoever. It is, therefore, clear that a Baker requiring water by for the purposes of his business cannot demand it under this provision.

'The Act empowers the Corporation to supply any person with water for baking or manufacturing purposes upon such terms as they shall agree. It follows, therefore, that any person who has not agreed terms with the Council cannot demand a supply of water for such purposes.'

An advice of 1850 concerning church pews read:

'The Consecration Deed of St. James Church, West Derby declares that the Churchwardens shall let the pews and receive the rents. Further that they and their successors shall be entitled to sue for the rents. The Deed authorises the Churchwardens to set aside a sum not exceeding ten pounds for necessary repairs to the Church. They are directed to pay the balance to the Minister for the time being. Notices relating to lettings have to be given to the Churchwardens and not to the Minister.'

As the nineteenth century progressed, joint stock companies became the recognised means of raising capital for the many developments then taking place. These developments included water, sewage, transport, fuel, insurance and building and civil engineering works and, especially, the railway.

The joint stock company was similar to the public limited company of today. The shares offered for subscription were invariably liable to additional calls upon shareholders as the project progressed. If the shareholder did not meet an additional call, his shares were subject to forfeiture with the loss of payments already made. Money subscribed was risk money in every sense. Shareholders could achieve substantial rewards but could suffer the loss of the investment if the project proved unsuccessful. Private investment was thus funding public works and very successfully as it happened.

3 The Arrival of the Railway

In 1826, Rowland Hill decided upon Bruce Castle. In that same year, a start was made on the building of the Liverpool & Manchester railroad. On the 15th September 1830, the Duke of Wellington and 'a splendid cortege of nobility and gentry' attended the opening of the railway. The train comprised thirty-two carriages carrying 752 persons drawn by seven engines. Tragedy marred the event. One engine ran down the Liverpool Member of Parliament who died of his injuries. From then on, the railway operated regular services between Liverpool and Manchester by means of the Planet steam engine. The journey took one hour. In 1830, horse drawn omnibuses made a first appearance in Liverpool.

On the 15th August 1836, the railway tunnel at Lime Street Liverpool was opened to provide rail services in and out Liverpool. In July 1837, the Grand Junction Railway Company (later named the North Western Railway Company) opened their service from Liverpool to Birmingham, which they extended to London in September 1838. Thus, only eight years after the first appearance of the railway, direct services between Liverpool and London replaced the rigours of the stage coach.

In 1847, Liverpool residents proposed a railway system connecting Liverpool to Crosby and Southport with intermediate stations on the route. The letter books contain much correspondence relating to this proposal. First, the Liverpool Crosby Southport Company was set up, and a prospectus was issued offering shares in the Company to the public at large. Many local people subscribed for the shares in what they locally termed 'our line.'

A first meeting of the shareholders took place on 25th January 1848. They resolved that, in the then state of the money market, to construct the whole of the railway was not expedient. Instead, they resolved to construct that portion of the line between Southport and Waterloo. For this they could raise a sufficient sum. Waterloo is only some five miles out of Liverpool, so that it does seem surprising that they could not raise a sufficient sum to construct the railway fully into Liverpool.

The area between Liverpool and Southport then comprised open country and scattered villages with increasing sand dunes on approaching Birkdale and Southport. There a thriving fishing industry prospered. Prices paid for the railway land varied downwards from £500 per statute acre for good agricultural land. The Company had power to compulsory acquire land on payment of compensation assessed by a jury or arbitrator under the then Land Clauses Consolidation Act.

The Earl of Sefton, Lord Derby, and the Blundell family of Great Crosby owned much of the land over which the railway was to pass. Mr.William Blundell was prepared to give a length of three and half miles in consideration of the Company meeting his wishes concerning stations serving the Crosby area. Those who were advising the Company reported:

'As to the station required in Great Crosby, we agree as to its desirability. As to the second station required in the area at Great Crosby, this is the nearest point to the village of Little Crosby and the Crosby Hall. It would be the station used by Mr. Blundell's family. He intends to make a road from Little Crosby to the line. As for the third station required, namely the Warren House, No.2 Little Crosby, the Company intends it for the accommodation for Ince. Those from the village of Altcar will also no doubt considerably use this station.'

A Reverend Rainshaw Rothwell opposed the Company and

its intended construction of a railway line on ethical grounds. He owned a field in Great Crosby through which the line was to pass. He refused to sell his land to the company unless compelled by law to do so. Ultimately he agreed to a sale.

The Company's consultant Engineer, George Robert Stephenson, prepared specifications. He was the inventor of railways and of Rocket fame. Work of construction commenced on 23rd March 1848.

It is humorous and poignant to refer to the problem of the rabbits and the letter of complaint to the Contractors:

'Mrs. Parker, the tenant of the Mission in Great and Little Crosby, has been with us complaining that two of the men here have been digging up her rabbits. We must really stop the men from taking the rabbits along the railway line. Mrs. Parker, who is a widow, pays a very large rent for the privilege of killing the rabbits and might suffer serious loss. We think, therefore, that it would not be too much to dismiss any person found stealing rabbits and not to employ him again during the progress of the works. The steward states that the damage to the rabbits may amount to £500.'

Rabbits were a valuable source of food when earnings were meagre and poaching a crime subjected to harsh punishment. Thus, Mrs. Parker was behaving with surprising tolerance.

By June 1848, arrangements were in hand for the opening of the line. On 24th June, George Robert Stephenson issued his Completion Certificate to the effect that the Contractors, Messrs. Holmes & McCormick, had executed all the work including materials at a cost of £12,000. The length of line completed was some sixteen miles, so the cost appears most reasonable even by reference to middle 19th Century monetary values.

A letter of 29th June 1848 to the Superintendent of Waterloo Station emphasises problems of the day. The truck mentioned would have been horse drawn :

'A person has been waiting at Edge Hill since two o'clock today with an engine. He says that you promised to have met him with a truck to take it to Waterloo.'

By letters addressed to the Liverpool Mail, the Liverpool

99

Chronicle, the Manchester Guardian and the Manchester Courier, the Company announced that the line would open on Monday 21st July 1848. The Company had only authorised its construction six months earlier. After that, it had obtained tenders and appointed Contractors. Actual construction occupied four months. A feat carried out at the midpoint of the 19th Century, which puts to shame the speed of much modern development. As to salaries, the Company paid the Chief Superintendent of the Railway two hundred pounds per annum and his assistant one hundred pounds. They paid station clerks eighteen shillings a week.

At the Waterloo terminal horse drawn omnibuses at a fare of 6d provided further conveyance into Liverpool. A passenger from Birkdale on the 7.19 a.m. train complained that insufficient omnibuses met the train. He and about fifteen other third class passengers had to wait at Waterloo for about half an hour. Another passenger suggested:

'Today I came from Southport by the first train. A number of third class passengers told me that they came almost every day, but that there were several others who still walked from Formby and Ainsdale. Do you not think that offering an annual contract for the second or third class might induce many more of this class of passengers to use the line?'

Distances thus walked were up to 12 miles or more.

Subsequently, the railway line was completed through to Liverpool, thus opening the coastal area lying between Liverpool and Southport to development. Much of this area now serves as a dormitory to Liverpool and even to Manchester.

The construction of the Liverpool to Southport railway line is but one example of the many railway lines constructed throughout Great Britain during the middle of the nineteenth century. Individually in private ownership, they together provided rail transport throughout Great Britain. For the next hundred years, the railway was to be the primary source of inland travel other than by horse. Steam was opening the door into modern civilisation.

100

4. The Coming of the Steamship

As the 19th century progressed, there were increasing indications of the revolution in sea transport that steam was to bring. Yet only a few of the time foresaw that steam would come to replace sail.

Until the second half of the 19th century, shipowners were building finer and larger vessels constructed of wood and powered by sail. Especially, the travelling public regarded the clipper ships as the grand mode of travel of the day. The Philadelphia line of sailing packets was a good example with their fully rigged ships and luxurious first class accommodation. These vessels, named *Wyoming*, *Tuscarora, Tonawarda* and *Saranah*, sailed from Liverpool to Philadelphia monthly throughout the 1860s as advertised by their Liverpool agents, Messrs Brown Shipley.

During the first half of the 19th century, steamships were making an appearance as river steamers. Thus, in 1807, the American engineer, Robert Fulton, built the steamship *Clermont* for passage in the Hudson River. In 1812, the Scots engineer, Henry Bell, operated the steamship *Comet* on the Clyde. Other river steamers followed to provide one day excursions. In 1819, the steamship *Savannah* became the first steamer to cross the Atlantic. She completed the voyage from Savannah to Liverpool in twenty-six days.

In 1838, the steamship *Royal William* of 617 tons burthen (gross) and 276 horsepower was the first steamship to cross the Atlantic direct. She sailed from Liverpool to New York carrying only passengers. She completed the outward passage in nineteen days and the homeward passage in fourteen days.

In those early days, casualties at sea both of sailing ship and steamer were frequent. Sometimes such casualties resulted from storm or other perils of the sea and at other times from collision. In 1831, the steamship *Rothesay Castle* plying between Liverpool and Beaumaris was lost with more than 100 Liverpool and Lancastrian passengers on board. In 1839, a severe hurricane off Liverpool caused the loss of two New York sailing packets outward bound and an emigrant sailing ship with the loss of 108 persons.

Such casualties not only caused much sorrow and suffering.

They entailed investigation and frequently action in the Admiralty Court to decide blame and assessment of loss. The Admiralty Court then formed part of the Ecclesiastical Courts served by proctors and advocates. The Court sat in Doctors Commons near St. Paul's Cathedral London. To bring an action in the Admiralty Court, it was first necessary to instruct a proctor. He in turn would brief the advocate to argue the case before the Admiralty Judge. The proctor or his instructing solicitor prepared the case including obtaining witnesses' statements.

The witness gave his evidence in affidavit form. If the other side sought cross examination of that witness, they examined him before a Commissioner agreed between the parties or appointed by the Court. Thus, the solicitors gave the following advice to the owners of the sailing vessel *Chas Carrol*, which had been in collision with a steamship:

'The Captain and Officers and crew of the ship who witnessed the collision must give depositions. They should state the circumstances of the collision, the state of the wind, the negligence of the steamer, and anything showing that the accident did not occur through their fault. They should also show that the crew of the ship were sober, as those in the steamship allege that some were intoxicated. Further, they should show that a proper lookout was being kept, that they properly navigated and steered the ship, and that they took all proper precautions to prevent the accident.

'Perhaps, it will be found that both vessels were to blame in which case, according to the rule in the Admiralty Court, each will bear one-half of the damage.'

Thus, unless a colliding vessel could establish a complete absence of fault on its part, the law required that each vessel should contribute equally to the total loss. In any collision it is always difficulty to prove a complete absence of fault by one of two or more moving vessels. Thus, in the case of the *Lusquehanna* in 1848:

'The Judge, Dr. Lushington, assisted by Trinity Masters decided that both vessels were in fault and consequently that they should divide the loss. They considered that as we, the steamer, did not see the sloop until she struck us, we had not a proper lookout. We urged that, even if we had seen the sloop, we could have done nothing more than we did. That was to hold on our course, which was according to the Rules of Trinity House. Further, that we had a good light and the sloop none. Yet they held negligence of our lookout fatal to us as far as respect a complete answer to the claim.'

A letter of the same year to the proctor relating to the colliding vessels *Sea Nymph* and *Port of Runcorn* shows difficulties in obtaining evidence:

'The *Sea Nymph*, a steamer, has today been lost. Her Owners have retained us. The Master of the other vessel *Port of Runcorn* is also lost. We took down the enclosed from the survivors of the *Port of Runcorn*. Though they repeatedly stated it was correct, they refused to swear it. They alleged conscientious objection as Roman Catholics. We could not remove the objection, though we got the presence of a Roman Catholic barrister and we offered a priest. We read the affidavit in his presence, and they again admitted its correctness. They wanted money. Can we in any way make use of the statement?'

By way of explanation, the witnesses interviewed were from the *Port of Runcorn* and to that extent must be considered hostile. To pay money to such witnesses would have been unlawful except in reimbursement of expenses and loss of working time. Without a signature a witness could deny his statement, although it could prove useful in cross examination if the other party called the witness.

In the nineteenth century, the life of the seaman was hard. Captains of vessels were master in every sense of the word. They enjoyed complete autonomy while at sea. Some seamen did enjoy some ship comforts. To most life was mean with poor food, cramped conditions and hard work. Ship masters had their problems in selecting their crews from those offering their services. They had to decide upon their competency and whether honest able-bodied seamen or rogues or vagabonds who would disappear at the first convenient port with ships' cargo or property.

Thus, in 1841, the Ship Masters' Association of Liverpool was seeking advice on a then novel proposition. Namely, the

103

Association setting up a Register of Seamen qualified by examination, and granting certificates of good behaviour. The advice read:

'I do not think that, according to the present Rules, the Committee has any powers to support the proposed establishment. The Rules state the objects of the Association as to establish a reading and coffee room, a museum and a library for the exclusive benefit of Ship's masters subscribing thereto.

'However, the prospectus printed along with the Rules declares three objects, namely first to disseminate amongst Ship masters useful information; second that the advantages derivable from the Association may be used for the advantage of seamen of every station; and third any surplus appropriated for the benefit of Ship master members may be employed for distressed seamen.

'The present proposal contemplates the examination of seamen and the granting of certificates of good character. He is to have an allowance upon each. Thus, the objects are to assist Ship-masters in the selection of crews amongst the best conducted seamen. This object, however desirable and valuable, does not appear to me to come within the meaning of any of the three descriptions stated without straining the obvious construction. I would therefore suggest that the Committee first obtain powers to make the proposed arrangements.'

A decade later, such registers were to become part of Government control over shipping exercised through the Board of Trade.

As the century progressed, Liverpool shipowners took the lead in adopting steam. That was to play a vital part in maintaining the greatest Empire of all times trading to all parts of the world. Yet among the greatest of all pioneers of steam was Samuel Cunard. He came from Halifax Nova Scotia to visit England in the early 1830's. The Liverpool / Manchester Railway and its speeds of up to 47 mph much impressed him. He realised that steam had come to stay and would revolutionise carriage by sea as well as by land.

In February 1839, Samuel Cunard came again to Britain with intent to establish a royal mail steam service between Liverpool and Halifax with regular sailings to a strict timetable. He teamed up with two shipowners, David MacIver of Liverpool and George Burns of Glasgow. They established what was later to become the most prestigious name in British shipping famed for the sheer luxury of its passenger ships. Namely, the Cunard Steam-Ship Company initially named the British & North American Royal Mail Steam Company.

The partners tendered for and obtained an Admiralty contract to carry mails by a fortnightly service between Liverpool and Halifax. They provided this service by wooden paddle steamers with feeder services to Boston and Quebec. The contract provided for imposition of heavy penalties in case of delay. In 1847 they extended the service to New York.

The first vessels built for the service were wooden paddle steamships barque sail rigged with a speed of between eight and nine knots named *Britannia, Caledonia, Arcadia* and *Columbia*. These four vessels were each 207 ft. in length, 34 ft. in beam and 24 ft. 4 ins. in depth and of 1155 gross tons and 619 net tons. Each vessel provided cabin (first class) accommodation for 115 passengers. As an indication of size, Cunard says that the *Britannia* could have been placed in the main restaurant of the later *Queen Mary*, stowed on the fore deck of the *Queen Elizabeth*, or enclosed within the forward funnel of either of these two luxury 1930 vessels.

The first of these four vessels to enter service was the *Britannia*. On the 1st July 1840, she sailed on her maiden voyage from Liverpool. She carried fifty-three passengers, ninety-three crew and mail for Halifax and Boston.

On the 4th February 1842, the *Caledonia* sailed from Liverpool bound on her normal voyage for Halifax and Boston. On the 9th February, she ran into heavy weather from the West North West.

Her Captain described it as' tremendous increasing to a perfect hurricane.' The vessel was making much water, especially in the fore cabin and in the engine room, and was sustaining substantial damage. The heavy seas stove in the bulwarks from the fore rigging to the forecastle. Later, 'a tremendous sea' stove in the starboard ice house that carried fresh meat and other provisions for the voyage. Those same seas also stove in the fore cabin and engine room domes

105

causing the vessel to ship large quantities of water. Later still, another tremendous sea stove in the starboard paddle box, quarter boards, stern cloth and stanchions and broke the windows of the wheelhouse and saloon. On the next day, in 'a terrific gale and hard squalls,' the rudder was found very much twisted and shaken.

The vessel and those aboard her were fortunate in that the vessel succeeded in limping back to Port Cove Ireland. After carrying out survey and temporary repairs there, she arrived back in Liverpool on the 17th February 1842. Those on board must have been overjoyed to be back safely in Liverpool after so appalling an experience.

In 1849, the Cunard paddle steamer Europa was in collision with the sailing vessel *Charles Bartlett* while voyaging in the Atlantic in thick fog. The collision resulted in a legal action. The judgement shows how the law was then evolving to meet the new situation of steam and speed in conditions of fog.

First, Admiralty law provides for the arrest and detention of a vessel for damage done by the vessel pending her owners giving bail commensurate with that damage. Accordingly, Cunard, as the owners of the *Europa*, took immediate steps to provide the necessary bail to obtain the release of their vessel without delaying the mail.

Part of the *Europa's* case was that her speed at collision was justifiable in consequence of her carrying mails. The owners of the other vessel challenged that contention. The issue came before the well-respected Admiralty Judge, Dr. Lushington, as a preliminary point of law. He held that the law laid down no particular rate of speed as unjustifiable under all circumstances. The only rule was that a rate of speed that would ordinarily entail danger was unjustifiable. It was for the Court to decide whether, under all the circumstances of the case including weather and locality, the speed was unjustifiable.

That decision allowed the *Europa* to argue her case. Namely that, as a carrier of Royal Mail, her speed was justifiable when voyaging well to the westward of the track ordinarily taken by sailing vessels. Her evidence showed that one hundred and thirty-five vessels sailed from England to America during June and July 1849.

Further, that the number of sailing vessels passing within the high degrees of latitude through which the *Europa* steamed was one in three hundred. That was as computed over a lengthy period by Lloyd's List newspaper.

The hearing before Dr. Lushington began on the 11th June 1850, and the Cunard case was presented the following day. The reader should have in mind that the Europa was carrying Royal Mail. That she was voyaging on a track where she would not expect to meet other vessels. That she was travelling at twelve and half knots in thick fog. Finally, unless the vessel was found entirely free from blame, the outcome must be an equal sharing of the loss.

The Cunard solicitor reported that Dr. Adams and Dr.Harding admirably argued the case for the *Europa*. Their address lasted from 11am to 4.30 pm. Mr Cunard was present and expressed himself well satisfied. He was sanguine enough to think that the *Europa* might succeed in full.

Nevertheless, the Judge, Dr. Lushington, held the Europa at fault for going at a speed twelve and half knots in a dense fog without taking additional precautions. Such precautions might have included an extra lookout, a second man at the wheel, and additional communication and arrangements with the engine room. The Judge also held the *Charles Bartlett* at fault for her lack of proper seamanship. Accordingly, judgment given was for an equal sharing of the loss between the two vessels. The Judgement was an important one given by a well-respected admiralty judge dealing with the vexed question of prompt delivery of overseas mail.

The Judgement was of particular significance to the mercantile community and, especially, to the Liverpool merchants. The latter had earlier approached the Post Office and Mr. Rowland Hill supporting a proposal for transmission of letters and, particularly, trans-Atlantic letters by private ship. In June 1843, they had petitioned the House of Commons seeking an enquiry into Post Office failure to give full effect to Mr. Hill's plan for improving the mail. Later, in June 1848, the American Chamber of Commerce in Liverpool had sought a postal convention with America fixing a uniform rate of postage despite the carrying vessel's nationality. Also, the merchants of Liverpool had sought a fixed hour for the Saturday weekly despatch of mail by the Halifax steamer. They pointed out that missing the steamer meant delay in delivery of a week.

Another interesting trial of collision was that of the steamship Orion with the Brig Revere. The latter was a square rigged sailing vessel with two masts. The Orion's solicitor reported the judgment to Liverpool by means of the new electric telegraph. This was first installed in the Exchange Building in 1847 and moved to the Royal Insurance Buildings two years later.

In considering the understated report back to Liverpool, the reader should have in mind two points. First, the obligation of every vessel always to go at such a speed and in such a manner as be appropriate in the particular circumstances to avoid collision. Second, that those in the steamer Orion were saying that, because of the dark, they failed to see the unlit brig in time to avoid collision.

'The decision is adverse as we had anticipated. Nevertheless, Dr. Lushington went as far as to lay down that, if as we aported we could not see a vessel under canvas without a light 300 yards distant, we ought not to have left the dock or at least ought not have put to sea. Accordingly, either it was too dark to justify us in going down the river or, if not, we ought to have seen the brig earlier. In the latter event, we should have conformed to the Rules laid down by the Trinity House and have put our helm to port instead of to starboard.'

Ironically a year later, the *Orion* was lost off Port Patrick. One hundred and fifteen cabin and forty-five steerage passengers and a crew of forty were on board of whom only about one hundred and fifty were saved.

By 1857, the future of the steamship was assured, especially for the regular lines that provided fixed sailing dates for the safe and expeditious carriage of mail, passengers and cargo. Nevertheless, the steamship still represented less than 10 per cent of British shipping. Many British shipowners and port authorities remained sceptical. Moreover, Parliament had repealed the Navigation laws that for two centuries had given preference to British shipping. It had thus thrown open the carrying trade of the United

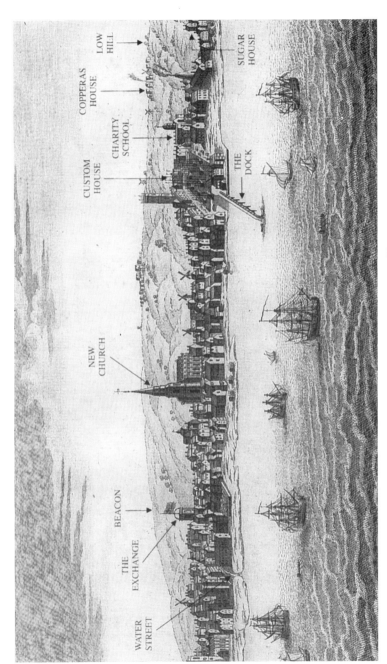

Perspective view of Liverpool c.1770

The Britannia at Boston - 1847

Kingdom and its Colonies to the ships of all nations. Shipowners, and especially the Liverpool shipowners with their large colonial trade, were feeling the effects of the repeal of these laws.

In these circumstances, towards the end of 1858, the steamship lines sailing from Liverpool convened a meeting under the chairmanship of James J. Bibby. His company had been among the first to establish a regular line of steamships trading between Liverpool and the Mediterranean. They established an association of steamship owners called The Liverpool Steam Ship Owners Association to protect and advance their common interests including opposing any new legislation prejudicial to those interests.

The Association appointed Andrew Squarey as its first secretary. He was a solicitor and a partner in the firm of Duncan Squarey and Duncan. A few years later, John Gray Hill became a partner in that firm, and the Association appointed him as their secretary. Thus began a unique association between the Hill family and the British Shipping Industry that was to continue for over a century.

CHAPTER 6

PRESTIGIOUS YEARS

The reader will recall James and Sarah Hill and their son Thomas Wright Hill (Tom) born in 1763. Sarah's disbelief that a lawyer and an honest man could be united in the same person thwarted Tom's ambition to become an attorney. Instead, he became the proprietor and headmaster of Top Hill School near Birmingham. Tom married Sarah Symonds. Of their sons, Matthew and Frederick each fulfilled the ambition denied to their father and qualified as barristers. Rowland introduced penny postage and helped by his brothers, Edwin and Frederic, modernised the Post Office. Arthur succeeded as headmaster of the family school at Bruce Castle Tottenham. His wife, Ellen, died while their four children were still infants.

The four children born between 1834 and 1839 and educated at Bruce Castle were in order of age Lewin, George Birkbeck, Laura and John Gray. Lewin, the eldest son, followed his uncles into the Post Office where he became an Assistant Secretary. George Birkbeck Hill (or Birkbeck as he preferred), the second son, was born in 1835 at Bruce Castle. He enjoyed reading and, with the aid of the school's well-equipped library, gained a good knowledge of English literature. From Bruce Castle, he went up to Oxford and entered Pembroke College.

While at Oxford, Birkbeck became a member of the Old Mortality Club, which had the reputation of including revolutionary young men who went as far as to read Browning. He met several young men, who were to make their mark on an exciting Victorian age. They included two young men studying law who were destined to become great lawyers of their day, Mr. Justice Wright and Professor Dicey. Also, he met a diminutive Balliol man with a mop of red hair called Algernon Swinburne. In a letter to his future wife, he wrote:

'Yesterday I was in Swinburne's room. I wish you knew the

little fellow. He is the most enthusiastic fellow that I ever met and one of the cleverest. He wanted to read me some poems he had written and have my opinion. They are really very good. Swinburne read them with such earnestness, so truly feeling everything he had written, that I for the first time in my life enjoyed hearing the poetry of an amateur. He was much pleased at the honest praise that I could bestow on them.'

Swinburne would not have been pleased to hear himself described as an amateur. He regarded himself as a talented poet and came to merit that self esteem. Birkbeck also met at Oxford the pre-raphaelite artist, Dante Gabriel Rossetti, who was to play a part in his later writings. At the time, Birkbeck described him as very quiet and saying little.

Illness thwarted Birkbeck in taking his final examination for his Bachelor of Arts degree. The University granted him an honorary fourth class in *literae humanories*. Subsequently, in 1886, he became a Bachelor of Civil Law and, five years later, a Doctor of Civil Law.

Meanwhile, Birkbeck became an assistant master at Bruce Castle. He married Annie Scott who was the daughter of a Wigan solicitor. Her brothers had been school fellows at Bruce Castle.

Later, Annie's father, a widower, married Birkbeck's sister Laura. To add to this family confusion Birkbeck's cousin, Leonora (Frederic's daughter) married Annie's brother, John Scott. It was he who later reorganised the Egyptian legal system and, as Sir John Scott, became Judge Advocate of the British army. Thus, reverting to Sara Hill and her views on the lawyers of her day, she became the matriarch of two legal families: the Hills and the Scotts.

Subsequently, Arthur Hill retired from the Headmastership of the school and Birkbeck succeeded him. A subscription by the Old Pupils of Hazelwood and Bruce Castle Schools raised £450 to establish a Memorial to Arthur's name. These monies provided an Exhibition or Scholarship at Bruce Castle to award those showing moral excellence. It was to continue while the Hill family maintained its system of education directed towards cultivating moral character in preferment to intellectual development. Afterwards, the trustees were to use the monies in the construction or purchase of a lifeboat

111

called the *Arthur Hill* lifeboat.

Meanwhile, Birkbeck was gaining the reputation of an academic and writer. He showed in his writings how far his views on religion differed from the stern Methodism of his great grandmother's household. Thus, he wrote:

'The thought of the wickedness of the teachers of the cruel God who condemns men to endless horrible and useless torment constantly moves me to indignation. The suffering they cause is terrible. They should teach such wicked doctrines, if today taught at all, only as shameful mysteries. Instead they teach them from the pulpit endowed by the State.'

He displayed his contempt for such religious teachings in rhymes he composed for his children. Such as his Hymn of the Pharisees on the Last Day:

> *Each saint took up a brand new broom,*
> *And swept along each trembling sinner,*
> *As crumbs are swept up after dinner,*
> *And threw them all upon the fire,*
> *So hot it made the saints perspire.*
> *While round about them all the good,*
> *With cheerful pious faces stood,*
> *And said Oh now we are so glad,*
> *That when on earth we were not bad;*
> *Far sweeter far 'tis sure to see*
> *Another burnt than burnt to be.*

In the early 1870s, Birkbeck Hill became a regular contributor to the *Saturday Review* and other Journals. However, a larger task awaited him. His Uncle Rowland asked Birkbeck to consider his draft history of penny postage and his early life with a view to publication. Thus began a labour of love that was to keep Birkbeck occupied for the next seven years. Yet Birkbeck was not of strong constitution. He began to find teaching and managing Bruce Castle increasingly fatiguing when combined with his writings

In 1873, a disastrous outbreak of scarlet fever took place among the pupils of Bruce Castle. It included the death of his sister Laura's son. This proved too much for Birkbeck. He suffered a prolonged attack of nervous asthma. He needed to find an easier life style. Nevertheless, he deferred any decision to give up this unique school to spare his aged father the sorrow of seeing it pass out of the Hill family after seventy-five years.

In 1875, the death of Birkbeck's father resolved his problems. He sold Bruce Castle as a going concern and gave up teaching. Bruce Castle is now a museum to the Post Office and to Rowland Hill and to the Hill family. A portrait of Birkbeck's children by the artist and his good friend, Arthur Hughes, still hangs there.

Birkbeck and Annie moved to Burghfield near Reading. There Birkbeck continued with his literary work. Yet, recurring attacks of nervous asthma made him a semi-invalid for the rest of his life. He generally wintered abroad in the more benign climates of Switzerland and Italy. In 1880, he published his *History of Penny Postage and Life of Sir Rowland Hill* in two volumes (publishers Thos. De la Rue) with the following opening dedication:

'To the Right Hon. WILLIAM EWART GLADSTONE M. P.
first Lord of the Treasury,
Chancellor of the Exchequer, etc., etc.,
Sir,
The following pages tell how much Sir Rowland Hill felt your kindness in a time of great trouble. In his Private Journal, I find even stronger expressions of his gratitude. I spoke he says in recording one of his interviews with you in strong terms and with emotion, which in vain I tried to suppress, of the feeling I entertained towards him for the uniform kindness, sympathy and support I have received at his hands. In asking you, therefore, to allow me to dedicate to you all in this work which is mine, I am sure that I have done what would have been pleasing to him.
I am, Sir,
With the highest respect,
Your obedient servant,
G.B. Hill.'

Birkbeck's next work was Colonel Gordon in Central Africa

1874-79. It was based on the letters of Colonel Gordon who later became General Gordon of Khartoum. The latter wrote of Birkbeck: 'I have given Dr. Birkbeck Hill all my private letters from the Sudan for publication. On terms that he never sees or writes to me and that he treats me exactly as if I were dead.'

Still, the completed work received Gordon's commendation. Thos. De la Rue were again the publishers.

Following his retirement as headmaster of Bruce Castle, Birkbeck devoted much of his time and research to Boswell's life of Dr. Johnson. In 1878, he published a small volume entitled *Johnson, his Friends and his Critics,* which contained some of his earlier articles dealing with the Johnsonian scene. The following year, he edited Boswell's *Tour of Corsica.*

In 1881, Birkbeck suggested to the Clarendon Press that they publish a new edition of Boswell's Life of Dr Johnson. He wrote:

'For many years, I have been collecting notes for an addition of Boswell's *Life of Johnson.* I believe I could produce an edition not unworthy of the Clarendon Press.'

It was to become Birkbeck's major preoccupation for some years. He moved his family to Oxford, so that he could more readily consult works of reference.

The new edition appeared in 1887. The literary world immediately hailed it as a masterpiece of spacious editing. They acknowledged it to give Birkbeck a prestigious place among the great editors of all times. Under the preface, Birkbeck tells that his interest in the doctor was first aroused in 1868 on discovering five little second hand volumes of Boswell.

More works on Dr.Johnson followed. These included two volumes of Johnson's letters and an entertaining account of a tour in Scotland entitled *Footsteps of Dr. Johnson.* He intended a similar work relating to a tour in Wales, but sadly his life span did not permit of this.

Other works included *Letters of Dante Gabriel Rossetti to William Allingham* (Unwin 1897), which he compiled with the assistance of his pre-Raphaelite artist friend Arthur Hughes. Artists today recognise it as a primary source for documentation on the pre-Raphaelites.

Birkbeck was elected an honorary fellow of his Oxford college Pembroke. He became a leading figure too in the Johnsonian Club in London in which he occupied the position of Prior. In 1892, he left Oxford to divide his time between the Hampstead home of his younger daughter, Lucy, and his wife's cottage at Apsley Guise. He also enjoyed his usual winter visits to the continent.

Birkbeck twice visited the United States of America where his writings were much admired. His first visit was to his eldest daughter, Margaret. She was married to the Professor of Economic History at Harvard University later knighted as Sir William Ashley. To please his American hosts, Birkbeck produced a short volume entitled Harvard College by an Oxonian.

His second visit was in October 1893 when he received an honorary doctorate in law awarded by the Williams College of Williamstown, Massachusetts. The college invited Birkbeck to come to Williamstown to receive the doctorate personally from the President of the College. The ceremony took place during a three-day centenary commemorating the founding of the College by Colonel Ephraim Williams in October 1793.

Birkbeck and Annie had a large family consisting of five boys and two girls. Margaret and Lucy are already mentioned. The youngest son Walter died at an early age. The second youngest Edmund took himself off to Australia under dubious circumstances. Birkbeck and Annie mapped out suitable professional careers for the three older boys. Their eldest boy Maurice was to go to the bar. The second Arthur Norman was to be a solicitor. The third Leonard was to practice medicine. Each achieved eminence in his chosen profession and was knighted for his services to that profession.

Birkbeck died in 1903 aged sixty-eight years. Little more than a youngster contrasted with his long-lived father, grandfather and uncles. He had earned a prestigious name in literature and continues well regarded. He outlived his wife, Annie, and was buried beside her at Apsley Guise.

John Gray Hill (or Gray Hill as he preferred) was the youngest son of Arthur and Ellen Hill. Born in 1839 and educated at Bruce Castle, his father articled him to London Solicitors. He attained a Certificate of Merit in the Solicitors' Final Examination and was admitted as a solicitor in 1863 aged twenty-four. He first practised in the City of London at Founder's Court, Lothbury. In 1865, aged twenty-six, he came to Liverpool to join mercantile solicitors, Duncan Squarey and Duncan, and specialise in marine law.

Three years later, in January 1868, the senior partner died while still in practice, aged seventy-two. His life had opened in the pastoral days of stage coach and sail and ended amid industrialisation, railways and steamship. Later that year, his successor, Andrew Squarey, suffered a serious illness that resulted in his leaving the practice. He had been handling shipping work including that of secretary of the Liverpool Steam Ship Owners Association. Thus within three years of joining the practice, Gray Hill found himself both senior partner and secretary of the Liverpool Steam Ship Owners Association.

Some comings and goings took place within the practice over the next six years, following which John Dickinson joined Gray Hill in 1874. The two of them continued in partnership under the name of Hill Dickinson and Co until the sudden death of John Dickinson ended the partnership in 1907.

Fortunately, Gray Hill preserved his private letter books comprising five volumes and other papers and a book written by him entitled *With the Beduins*. This has enabled reconstruction of his life and times to his death in 1914.

Gray Hill married Caroline Emily Hardy (Carrie for short) whose family were merchants and neighbours at Bruce Castle and lived at the adjoining Bruce Lodge. Gray Hill and Carrie first resided at Apsley House, Oxton, Birkenhead. This entailed Gray Hill in a daily journey to work by horse drawn carriage to the Woodside ferry stage, which was about three miles away. There he crossed the River Mersey by ferry to Liverpool. His carriage similarly met him on return in the evening.

As common at this time of low wages, Gray Hill employed a

John Gray Hill

Caroline Hill

Water Street, Liverpool 1864

Birkenhead Ferry c. 1830

coachman and other household domestic staff. The reader may find it of interest to compare his own modern day order for a new motor car with Gray Hill's order for a new coach:

'If you can reduce the price a little, I will have the carriage built following the enclosed sketch with the addition of a hood. I do not want to spend more than £50 beside the value of the old carriage. Perhaps you will make the new one of the best material and workmanship for £80 less the value of the old carriage £20 net £60. Also, do up the old carriage temporarily without charge to make it safe for us during the building of the new one. I will then accept that arrangement.'

Gray Hill was a remarkable man. He was hardworking and of great intellectual ability with much business sense. The shipping historian Sir Clement Jones later wrote of him:

'I knew Gray Hill personally because in 1910 I joined the committee of the Navy League Sea Training home for Poor Boys, of which he was chairman. It was there that I enjoyed watching his Draconian ruling. He was one of those men who carried about with him, concealed but always on his person, the mysterious weapon called prestige. He was a man who commanded our respect always, yet made us well aware that he would be fair and possibly formidable, both in appearance and manner, when it came to an argument.

A friend once asked Lord Rosebery, the Prime Minister, what was the relationship between Queen Victoria and her cabinet. After a moment's thought Rosebery replied: "We were all in an awful funk of her." I think we could say the same of Gray Hill and our Navy League Committee. He ruled us by a pleasant mixture of love and fear, but we were all in rather a funk of him.'

Gray Hill was much interested in the Middle East and its treasures. He was buying and selling art treasures from the Middle East and with his wife, Carrie, visiting Arabia and Europe by train and ship. He was a connoisseur of the arts and had a profound knowledge of the great portrait painters. Carrie herself was a portrait painter of considerable ability and, especially, of Middle East scenes.

Perhaps Gray Hill was fortunate in that he succeeded Andrew Squarey at an early age as secretary of the Liverpool Steam Ship

Owners Association. That of itself created many contacts, and he made the most of those contacts. As described, he had the gift of prestige. Moreover, he had the art of quietly analysing and forcibly expressing his opinions upon any problem, so that he left the recipient in no doubt that he must be right. Also, he had the good fortune to have come to Liverpool and its shipping at a time when both were growing rapidly as the gateway into an expanding British Empire.

In December 1873, Liverpool sailing ship owners invited Gray Hill to undertake the management of the Liverpool Sailing Ship Owners Mutual Indemnity Association, which provided mutual insurance of sailing ships to its members. He accepted and received an annual payment of one farthing per ton of the entered tonnage, so giving him a pecuniary interest in the future prosperity of the Association. Later, in 1889, steamship owners asked him to manage the newly formed Liverpool and London Steamship Protection and Indemnity Association on similar terms. Such mutual indemnity associations were becoming increasingly popular within the shipping industry. A century later, they were to extend their activities to include the professional risks of solicitors, architects and other professions.

Early in 1874, Gray Hill moved the practice to 10 Water Street where it was to remain during the next 100 years. The choice of these new offices was a good one. It put the practice in the centre of a thriving shipping and commercial city that was continuing to go from strength to strength. The bill book for the year contained many illustrious names of the day. They included Cunard, Burns & MacIver, Brocklebank, Brown Shipley, Thames & Mersey Marine Insurance and many steam packet companies from both sides of the Atlantic.

Gray Hill, especially, participated in the affairs of North Atlantic shipping at a time when that trade was expanding rapidly. Besides representing the Liverpool Steam Ship Owners Association and the American Chamber of Commerce, he represented the two pioneers of steam on the North Atlantic. They were the Cunard partnership and the Inman Steamship Company.

The reader will recall that the original Cunard partnership comprised Samuel Cunard, David MacIver and George Burns. In

1878, these family interests continued, but inherited by William Cunard, Charles MacIver, and John and J.O. Burns. Especially, Charles MacIver sought the setting up of a private limited company to take over the business of the partnership. He did so for the better protection and liquidity of the partner's interests and that of their heirs.

On 9th March 1878, Gray Hill reported to Charles MacIver on negotiations that had taken place between his two sons, Charles and Harry MacIver; William Cunard; and John Burns. As Gray Hill put it, 'ending in smoke.' He continued:

'Nevertheless, the discussion has cleared away some objections previously entertained to the scheme of a private limited company for the Cunard Line. You have now the full scheme of a company approved by Mr. Burns and Mr. Cunard. They satisfied me that they fully recognised the position of Mr. Charles and Mr. Harry and that you need not have much further anxiety on that score.'

In May 1878, following further discussion, Gray Hill wrote to William Cunard confirming receipt of the documents required for registration of the limited company and continued:

'Regarding the valuation, the Burns accept Mr. MacIver's proposal to place it at £1,200,000 with exclusion of the Gallia, which the new company is to take over at cost price.'

On 23rd May 1878, Gray Hill telegraphed the parties to confirm that all was completed, the new company registered and the Certificate of Incorporation issued. That was the beginning of the expansion of Cunard, which was to result in it occupying a unique position of British prestige.

In February 1880, Gray Hill reported to Charles MacIver who then resided in Malta:

'We have taken preliminary steps to turn the Cunard Company into a public one and to place it on the London Stock Exchange. We will offer half the issued share capital of Two Million Pounds to the public. This scheme will enable you to realise your property instead of having it tied up in the concern. It meets the necessity of providing money for new ships without the objections that exist to borrowing on debentures.'

Thus was the Cunard Steam-Ship Company Limit born with John Burns as its first Chairman. For the next century, Cunard was to sail the Atlantic between the old and new worlds with ships of ever increasing luxury and prestige. As the century progressed, so did Cunard prestige until Cunard became synonymous with all that was best of Britain and of Empire. Yet as the Empire later waned, so did Cunard.

Unhappily, disputes arose between the Cunard and the MacIver family to the embarrassment of Gray Hill who regarded himself as solicitor and friend to them all. Thus, on 5th May 1882, he wrote to a London colleague:

'A question has arisen between the Cunard Company and Messrs C.& D. MacIver. The latter are the Liverpool managing agents of the Company. The question relates to the rights of the latter to carry on, under their firm of Burns and MacIver, a separate business at Le Havre as agents for other lines. Messrs MacIver wish to take the opinion of Counsel as to their rights. As I act both for the Company and for them, I think it well that I should not act in the matter. Messrs MacIver have desired me to request your firm to act for them.'

On 12th January 1883, Gray Hill wrote to David MacIver, a third son of Charles MacIver and a Member of Parliament, explaining why he could not act for him in his dispute with Cunard.

In December 1885, Charles MacIver died in Malta. His will added to acrimony between his son, David, and his two other sons, Charles and Harry, concerning the family shipping and mercantile agency business of C & D MacIver. Gray Hill informed David MacIver that, if he disputed the will, he could enter a Caveat at the Probate Registry. This would then prevent a grant of probate without his prior knowledge. Gray Hill continued:

'But you will excuse my adding that there cannot be any doubt that the will is perfectly valid.'

Gray Hill wrote further to David MacIver:

'I am sorry to observe that you still contemplate legal proceedings against your brothers, especially that you think of

120

beginning them the day after the funeral. As a sincere friend, I must say (and you must bear with me for doing so) that such a course would be nothing less than shocking. It would put you in a most painful position in the judgement of all your friends. It would be so even if you had or thought you had substantial grounds for your threatened litigation. However, you tell me you intend to bring action after action. Not because you have a legal right to redress, but because you hope to coerce your brothers into a course that they are not under any obligation to adopt. This makes the proceedings that you contemplate still more indefensible. Moreover, I know enough of the family to be well aware that no MacIver will do anything under compulsion.'

Gray Hill went on to suggest that a solution might be found in giving up and extinguishing the use of the name of C & D MacIver. He then continued:

'This far, I have tried to act quite impartially as a friend to all and with a hope of composing all family difficulties. However, if you decide upon taking the proceedings, I consider myself bound to act on behalf of your brothers. I am sure that this is what your Father (who honoured me so fully with his confidences) would desire were he alive. To him I have always felt myself greatly indebted.'

Nevertheless, these quarrels within the MacIver family were to result in their severing links between themselves and, ultimately, with Cunard.

As concerns the other North Atlantic pioneer, in 1850 aged twenty-four, William Inman left his employment with a Liverpool shipping agency to set up his own business. He introduced steam ships on the North Atlantic named after various cities of the world, which provided the first emigrant service direct to the United States and Philadelphia. His first ship, the *City of Glasgow*, carried fifty-two cabin or first class passengers, eighty-five second class passengers, and four hundred steerage or emigrant passengers.

Inman much improved upon the former discomforts of passage in emigrant ships. A service that was previously known only for its evils of transit in the cargo holds of outward bound timber ships. To that end, he and his wife took passage on one of his first ships, so that they might see for themselves what the emigrants needed. In the result, his ships came to enjoy a good name for the speedy and comfortable carriage of emigrant passengers. He set up the Inman Steamship Company to carry on the business.

Yet Inman suffered his misfortunes. In 1854, the *City of Glasgow* sank at sea with the loss of four hundred and eighty lives. That same year, the *City of Philadelphia* became shipwrecked. Similar casualties occurred over later years. The American Civil War of the 1860's curtailed emigrant traffic. As the traffic revived, it required larger and faster ships.

Accordingly, in May 1875, Inman decided to raise additional loan capital. The Inman Steamship Company issued three, five and seven year bonds at 6% per annum that proved a highly regarded investment. Gray Hill was advising Inman on the loan and sought information from London about its completion. He wrote to Inman:

'Derby day is taking principals out of town again, and we cannot await much longer before closing.' In this respect, it seems that commercial life has altered little over the intervening years.

In December 1875, Gray Hill, as secretary of the Liverpool Steam Ship Owners Association, was writing to William Inman about the then contentious subject of load line. At the time, shipowners generally opposed the Conservative Government proposal for compulsory load line survey and classification of all ships. Charles MacIver of the Cunard partnership supported the Bill. By way of explanation, load line is the mark down to which a ship may be safely laden in the water. Classification is a measure of fitness of the ship.

The letter is interesting in two respects. First, it shows the general opposition of the time to a measure directed towards increasing safety at sea. Second, it expresses the political nature of Liverpool in those prosperous times. It read:

'One thing is quite clear. Whether Mr. MacIver is right or wrong, he will not alter his views and arguing with him is useless. Though why he should suppose that politics have anything to do with the actions of the Association, I do not know. It is strange, if politics influence the matter, that in a Conservative town like Liverpool

MacIver cannot get a single shipowner to agree with him. I do not know of any member of the Association who wants compulsory load line survey and classification for all ships.'

Such remarks read very strangely in today's more enlightened time. However, it appears from other correspondence that Liverpool shipowners of the day condemned these measures as a bureaucratic and unwarranted interference in ship owning. They were proud of their safety record, and they considered the measures would cause unnecessary loss of time and expense.

In July 1875, Gray Hill sought the Inman Line's assistance to arrange the passage home from New Jersey of a poor woman in the workhouse there. His letter is interesting in showing the cost to the steerage passenger of crossing the Atlantic:

'I have got the ticket but the Atlantic Lines have made peace. They have raised fares from £3.10s to £5.5s and by agreement between them they do not allow any passenger under that rate.'

An interesting domestic advice to Mr. Inman of the 13th January 1874 reflects social attitudes of the day as they contrast with modern day:

'The law is that you may dismiss a female servant at a moment's notice if she becomes pregnant after the service commences. Yet I do not know of any authority for saying that you may discharge a servant on discovering, after the service commences, that she was pregnant before it began. The rule ought to be the same in both cases.'

In 1882, William Inman fell ill and died at the comparatively early age of fifty-six. His son, Ernest, succeeded him. This was a very bad time for the Inman Steamship Company. Competition was cut throat in the North Atlantic trade. The company was awaiting delivery of a new vessel, the *City of Rome*, at a price of £200,000. The ship builders were guilty of late delivery, failure of speed trials, and failure to meet description.

Gray Hill advised:

'I think that you can as a matter of law insist upon the builders taking back the ship, for she does not possess the qualities that the contract requires. It is not that for which you contracted. I do not think you have kept her longer than necessary so to detect, and the builders cannot therefore say that you accepted her.

'Nevertheless, some doubt must always be whether you can legally return her, while the practical difficulties are very great. What is to be done with the ship if the builders decline to take her back? Her demurrage and lying up expenses would be a very heavy items for whom it might concern. Would it suit you if they sold the vessel with her speed put right to a rival company?'

All this was seriously affecting the Company's shares.

Gray Hill and Ernest Inman were the executors appointed under William Inman's will. In June 1883, Gray Hill advised that he was hoping to sell all the real estate at a sum that would cover the mortgages and leave a small surplus. Unsecured debts would then amount to £32,500 to be offset against assets of £8000 and 2,200 one pound shares in the Inman Company.

The real estate comprised the Upton Manor with its grounds and the Home Farm of about 120 acres in Wirral Cheshire. The executors sold this property for £35,950. Yet, after discharge of mortgages, this left less than £5000. Today, this former country estate has become a large suburban area serving as a dormitory to Liverpool and Birkenhead.

The executors were attempting to sell the Inman shares, but they could obtain no bid for most of the shares. The Inman Steamship Company was facing problems in the face of intense competition. The builders had settled the problems of the *City of Rome* by taking back the ship, but on terms of returning only part of the purchase price. The Company needed to raise funds to pay off debts and towards the purchase of a new ship costing £145,000. It was making calls on its shareholders for that purpose.

William Inman's estate had not the means to pay the calls. The Company forfeited the family shares. So the estate of this former vigorous and prosperous shipowner was insolvent. His death was bringing to its knees the Inman Steamship Company once the proud-challenger to Cunard on the North Atlantic.

Nevertheless, during the next two years, Gray Hill participated in attempts to save the Inman Line. The Company sold its New

York wharf and appointed a new agency there.

In May 1885, Gray Hill replied to a disgruntled shareholder fearing further calls:

'The Company is now working to a profit and will no doubt continue to do so up till November. The Government is taking up some of the largest and fastest of the Atlantic steamers as cruisers and transports, which is relieving the trade. A strong movement prevails to raise rates, when prospects will improve.'

Yet this was not to be. In 1888, the American owned company, The International Steamship Co., took over and merged the Inman Steamship Company to create the Inman & The International Steamship Co. Only a small minority of shares remained in the hands of former Inman shareholders. Subsequently, Gray Hill helped Ernest Inman in his application for a position offered by the Weaver River Trust. Also he helped his brother, Geoffrey, in supplying a reference to support his application for the position of Engineer Surveyor with Lloyd's Registry.

It is for conjecture to what extent the death of William Inman changed the course of British shipping. His death drastically changed the Inman Steamship Company and the future prosperity of the Inman family. Moreover, his death and that of Charles MacIver led to the shipping interests of each passing out of the hands of their respective families. That was contrary to the mode of the time when they regarded preservation of such assets within the family as sacrosanct.

Other well known Liverpool steamship companies advised by Gray Hill during the latter part of the nineteenth century included the White Star Line, Atlantic Transport, and Leyland. They similarly employed their ships in the North Atlantic trade and were destined to come under United States control. In that regard, although the Merchant Shipping Acts stipulated that no foreigner could own a British vessel, British company law treated a company incorporated in the United Kingdom as British. Thus, foreign companies were taking a controlling interest in British shipping companies or setting up subsidiary companies in Britain to sail their ships under the British flag. This could be valuable at a time when Britain ruled the waves.

Nevertheless, the Board of Trade maintained a right to cancel the registry of any ship that was not bona fide British owned. Thus, in 1902, the International Mercantile Company of New Jersey acquired a controlling interest in the British companies, White Star Line, Atlantic Transport, Leyland, and the Dominions Lines. The Board of Trade insisted that a majority of the directors of these companies should remain British as a term of continuing the British registration of the ships.

However, this was in the future. To revert to 1883, Frederick R. Leyland was having problems with his son Fred. The latter had been drinking heavily and was on the way to becoming an alcoholic. Gray Hill was attempting to persuade him in the ways of temperance.

Part of his letter to Fred of September 1883 read:

'I know what a hard task you have in front of you. Nevertheless, if you will put forth your whole strength, you will pull all straight again. For the sake of your wife and child as much as for your own sake you must do this. All their future happiness depends upon your success in this great effort. Upon the one hand, you have their welfare and your own and, on the other, the bottomless pit of misery and degradation. From my own experience, I know what trust and reliance a man may place upon a good wife. You have a kind and tender helpmate. Follow her advice and all will be well.'

Fred followed the advice, so that all did prove well for him and his family.

In autumn 1885, Frederick R. Leyland became seriously ill. Questions arose whether he should appoint Fred his partner in the Leyland shipping business. If not, valuable agencies could be lost on his death. Gray Hill proposed a short term partnership that father and son were to review on its termination, which was acceptable.

Father recovered to have an unfortunate relationship with a lady that resulted in the birth of a child. The lady was of fiery Irish nature. She gave Leyland a difficult time. She demanded large monetary payments. An offer of an annuity of £600 did not satisfy her, although no mean income in those days. The lady created violent scenes at the Leyland office. She began affiliation or bastardy proceedings against Leyland and threatened to notify his competitors of the bastard child. Gray Hill, at Leyland's request, personally handled the proceedings. He advised an acceptance of paternity to avoid a court hearing and resultant publicity and, at length, persuaded the lady to accept the proffered annuity.

During the later part of the 19th century, Gray Hill was becoming increasingly concerned with the attitude adopted by the Courts concerning the duties and liabilities of trustees. He replied to his brother Lewin who sought his advice on investing trust funds in a mortgage of property:

'You are at liberty to invest the trust funds in a mortgage. The difficulty is to find not merely a safe security, but one that the Court of Chancery will call safe. A recent decision makes it almost impossible to find a security that will be sure to pass muster. Perhaps, in an investigation conducted twenty years after the death of the trustee.'

He was expressing his disquiet at the manner in which the Chancery judges were treating trustees and their liabilities. He had no use for such judges and no hesitation in saying so.

Lewin Hill also sought his brother's advice on what he thought of the P&O as an investment. Gray Hill's reply reflects 19th century thinking on one of the few ship owning companies to survive and prosper to modern day:

'I do not think at all well of P&O. Competition is tremendous to the East and they have got for the most part an old and expensive fleet. They are old fogies, too far away from the scene of action and have become nursed too long on a mail subsidy. A board of Directors cannot compete with private individuals in the steam trade. Yet I cannot say that P & O's will not go up. The London brokers know best about that. I would sell when I thought that they were not likely to increase any more for the present.'

As earlier described, Gray Hill and his wife, Carrie, were inveterate travellers both in Europe and Syria. As he himself was later to write in his preface to his book *With the Beduins*:

'My wife and I had long felt attracted towards Syria. Many years ago, we had visited Beyrout and Damascus.Twice we had landed through the rolling waves at Jaffa, while the coast steamer lay off the port for the day. We had in our various autumn vacation trips coasted all around the Mediterranean Sea: from the Levant to the Pillars of Hercules and from the Gates of the Propontic and the Hellesport to the mouth of the Nile and the shores of Carthage.'

It is, perhaps, surprising that in the nineteenth century time and effort was found to visit so many then outlandish places. Gray Hill achieved this by taking autumn vacations of four to six weeks coupled with meticulous planning and his close connections with the shipping and the travel industry. Thus, long before the day of the holiday tourist, he was in regular communication with Thomas Cook & Son at Liverpool. He gave meticulous instructions for his journeys travelling by train to Rome and then by ferry to Naples and ship to Cairo.

Gray Hill was much interested in Middle East antiquities and ancient tiles and tapestries. He was always ready to buy both for his own retention and for investment. Thus, in October 1871, he and his wife, Carrie, were visiting Famagusta, Cyprus. There they got to know a Mr. Johann Hummel, a dealer in antiquities. Over following years, they were to purchase from Johann Hummel substantial quantities of ancient tiles with some tapestries. Also in September 1872, when visiting Corfu, they were buying antiquities that they shipped back to Liverpool on a Burns and MacIver steamer.

Gray Hill's interest in art and the prices at which he was buying and selling portraits is fascinating in today's circumstances of priceless treasures. On 4th March 1874, he was writing to offer some portraits for sale. These included a Botticelli for ninety pounds and several Dutch and German of the 15th and early 16th century for which he was seeking between twenty-five and forty pounds apiece. He stated that he had collected them in different places abroad. Also he was asking the dealer to look out for any really good old portraits of the 16th century whether by known artists or not:

'Anything like the Reichesberg portraits will suit me. I wish also to buy a really genuine Botticelli that has not been restored or repainted.'

In June 1875, Gray Hill was corresponding with M.A. de

128

Renders of the Marchand des Antiquities of Bruge about a purchase of pictures, saying:

'I shall be glad to hear from you when you have any good genuine old pictures of the Dutch or Flemish schools. I am anxious to buy a genuine good Rembrandt, so let me hear from you when you have bought the one of which you speak. I have a large collection of oil pictures, and I always pay at once for what I buy. You will have no difficulty with me.'

Subsequently he wrote to the same correspondent:

'I will buy the Pourbus Portraits for Fr. 800. I suppose they are by Franz Pourbus les fils who painted at Bruges. Am I right? . Let me know the prices of the other pictures that you mention. Is the artist Maas to whom you refer Nicolas Maas or which of the painters of that name?'

On 10th June1876, he was writing to the executors of the late Wynn Ellis:

'I purchased at the first Wynn Ellis sale a portrait of Betty Foster by Sir J. Reynolds. I should be much obliged if you could tell me from whom Mr.Wynn Ellis purchased it. Also, could you tell me whether any records or other means are available to show that the portrait really represented that lady. This interests me because of recent newspaper reports that the great portrait now missing represented Lady Betty and not the first Duchess of Devonshire.'

In 1884, Gray Hill lent to the Grosvenor Gallery New Bond Street London his Gainsborough portrait of Signor Fenducci, which he stated he had insured for £500.

The second half of the nineteenth century was a continuing period of development. Especially, the wealthy merchants and shipowners were building their large new houses in the pleasant outlying districts of Liverpool and Birkenhead. They favoured Bidston Hill with its fine views to the north across the River Mersey. There they had a good sighting of ships as they entered the river. Such a sighting put many a mind at ease, as the ship in which so much capital was invested hove into view.

The area provided equally fine views to the south across

129

the wooded Wirral to the River Dee and Welsh mountains beyond. The Earl of Shrewsbury owned much of the land there. He was granting building leases for constructing these fine homes in a beautiful place to live. Unfortunately, today suburban development has despoiled much of the area.

During the early 1880's, Gray Hill took such a building lease of land on the southern slopes of Bidston Hill at Oxton Birkenhead. There he built his new home Mere Hall. Initially he took four and three quarters acres and later he took a further similar acreage to extend his grounds. Gray Hill shipped in much of the building material for his new home, especially panelling, from Germany and elsewhere in Europe. Tiles and tapestries came from the Middle East. Some came from Mr. Hummell, the antique dealer, whom Gray Hill had met on holiday in Cyprus in October 1871. Carrie painted Middle East and other scenes on various internal glass panels.

The cost of building this new home as notified to the insurers was twelve thousand pounds. This was a considerable sum to pay in those days. However, Gray Hill had built a very fine home with delightful gardens and magnificent uninterrupted views across the River Dee to the Welsh Hills beyond. Then it was one of the most magnificent vistas of the area. Today, it is an oasis surrounded by suburban development, and the house converted into flats. Gray Hill employed a staff of seventeen at Mere Hall including domestic staff, coachmen and gardeners. This was not a large staff by late 19th century standards for such a large house with its extensive grounds when employment was scarce and wages low.

Perhaps, a most surprising aspect of Gray Hill and his wife, Carrie, was their love of travel and the abandonment of their luxurious home for remote and perilous places. As Gray Hill wrote under the preface to his book *With the Beduins*:

'A time at last came when I obtained a longer respite from the toils of a labourious profession. I became free to choose our own season for an annual flight from the east winds and leaden skies of England.' An annual flight that was to Syria. A Syria that then included what is now Israel, Palestine and the Lebanon but was under Turkish domination.

Gray Hill described the first flight as taken in 1887 to the beaten track of Jerusalem, Palestine, Nazareth, Damascus and Beyrout, and continued:

'In a month of riding and camping, we had found new health and life, opened a fresh source of happiness, and imbibed the spirit of the country. That which had charmed us most was the glimpse that we had gained into the life of the Arab Nomads' tribes. Especially, we delighted in the simple pastoral existence of the Beduins and the silent impressiveness of the great solitudes. We breathed the air of the wilderness and sat with Father Abraham under the great tent. We beheld Isaac and Jacob in their habits as they lived and watched the flocks and herds go forth to feed at dawn. We came home to our tents by the light of the setting sun and camped alone in solitary fastnesses or upon boundless plains. We gazed into the starry depths of a Syrian night and saw the great disc of the full moon rise across the eastern desert lone. Until the splendour of its light irradiated the barren gorges and changed the dark and silent surface of the Dead Sea into a luminous floor of water.'

In the first chapter of *With the Beduins* Gray Hill introduces George Mabbedy, our faithful friend and our guide and companion in all our travels, and continues:

'In his way George Mabbedy, our dragoman, is one of the most interesting men I know. He is by race and religion an Egyptian Copt, which is the smallest of the Christian sects. He was born in Jerusalem and educated at the English Bishop's school there. Having learnt our language through instruction in the Bible, he speaks a kind of sixteenth-century English. This is often quaint and expressive and tends to that brevity that the present age prizes. He is very proud to have descended from the ancient inhabitants of the land of the Pharaohs. He believes the Copts to be the chief depositories of the Christian virtues and, in succession to the Jews deposed, the chosen people of the Almighty.

'Mabbedy is short and strongly built with a broad forehead and a very dark rather fierce-looking and handsome face. He is a splendid horseman of great muscular strength, very brave, absolutely honest, faithful, and devoted to us. He expresses the wish to come to England with us and to help me at my office. His main idea is that I must be constantly engaged in divorce and murder cases and that those whom I am opposing must always be seeking my life. He wants to be my guard against avenging knives.'

Thus, Gray Hill and his wife, Carrie, came to live a double life. In the one, he was a prestigious mercantile lawyer in prosperous Liverpool, and they were living luxuriously at Mere Hall surrounded by beautiful furniture and works of art. In the other, he and Carrie were exploring by horse and tent unfrequented and perilous parts of Syria little seen by European eyes of the day. Often, they endured considerable discomfort and risked serious illness and danger of violent attack, robbery and murder. Any tale of their lives would be incomplete without some description of these travels.

Gray Hill's book *With the Beduins* described three journeys. The first taken in 1888 was to *East of the Jordan*; the second taken in 1889 was to *Palmyra*; and the third taken in 1890 was to *South and East of the Dead Sea*. Gray Hill shows the route of each journey on the annexed map. The Author invites the reader to journey back in time into the mind and thoughts of Gray Hill as he undertook these travels.

George Mabbedy

Some of our faithful servants

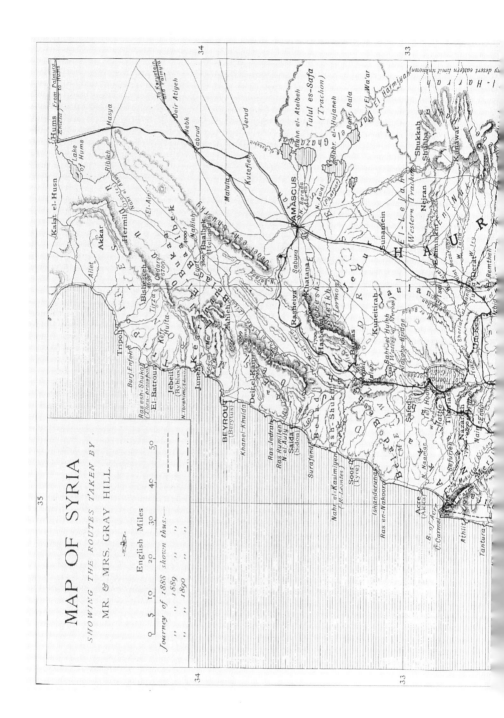

MAP OF SYRIA

SHOWING THE ROUTES TAKEN BY
MR. & MRS. GRAY HILL.

English Miles

0   5   10   20   30   40   50

Journey of 1888 shown thus:—
"   "   1889   "   "
"   "   1890   "   "

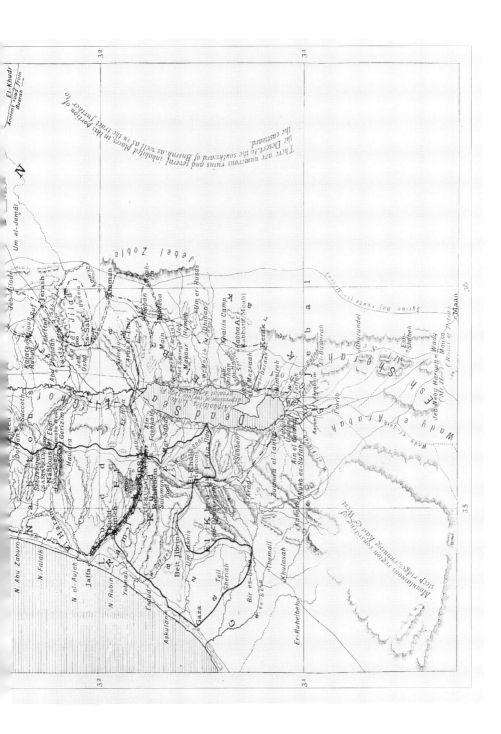

Caroline Hill

John Gray Hill

Riding in the desert

CHAPTER 7

WITH THE BEDUINS

PART 1 - 1888   EAST OF THE JORDAN

This was a journey that we took from Jerusalem crossing the River Jordan to Hesban. We then went on via Mashita to Amman, Es Salt, Jerash, Alijoun, El Husn, Gadara to the Sea of Galilee. We returned along the western side of the Sea of Galilee and via the Wady Hammon, Hattin and Mount Tabor to Nazareth, Haifa and our port of embarkation Jaffa.

Upon arrival in Jerusalem, we arranged with Sheikhs Fallach and Ali Abdul Aziz of the Adwan tribe encamped at Hesban for us to spend nineteen days under their protection. Of course, the sheikhs began by demanding an extravagant sum. Of course, George Mabbedy jumped up several times with horror struck and indignant looks as though the proposal to visit the lands of Moab and of Gilead was at once and forever withdrawn. Of course, after an hour's gesticulation, we settled all. For the sum of sixteen French napoleons and a backsheesh (backhander) that we would pay if all went to our satisfaction, we were to spend nineteen days in their camp.

After staying two nights at Jericho, we crossed the wooden bridge built over the Jordan a few years ago. Then we began to ascend the foothills of the mountains of Gilead. We had splendid views backwards. These were of the Dead Sea, the Plain of Jericho, the valley of the Jordan and the Judaean mountains beyond in a Constable-like effect of cloud and sunshine. We found our camp fixed at Tell Nimrin. The next day, we journeyed to Arah el Emir. To reach our camp there, we followed the windings of a very rough mountain track through grassy country ascending high above the Dead Sea.

The following morning, scrambling on our surefooted little horses down the steep slope of the hill, we reached the stream below. This flows through thickets of oleanders covered in red blossoms. We cover the headgear of our horses and the tent pole with them, for the many snakes will not come near the oleander. Then again along a winding track, we climbed a steep hill, down into a deep valley, and up again a steep ascent. From there we once more obtained those splendid views. Thus, following our Beduin guides, with well-deserved confidence in the surefootedness of our horses, we came to the Adwan camp. We found our tents pitched about half a mile from the great tent of the Sheikh Ali Diab who is chief among the Beduins of this district.

We found him polite in manner although taciturn, but as George says 'a high man does not speak much.' He is liberal concerning wives marrying a new one every three or four months and divorcing old ones. These he generously bestows upon the less important members of the tribe. He complained to my wife that his wives were always quarrelling and that it made his head ache. She had little sympathy.

They entertained us with much feasting in our honour. Sheikh Ali Abdul Aziz invited us to visit his latest bride. After the usual coffee and cigarettes, a remarkably fine camel appeared. They had caparisoned the creature with many carpets arranged like a howdah among which the bride sat. It was the same animal and trappings that they had used in her marriage procession. She made the camel kneel down, descended from the seat, and placed my wife on his back in her stead. The camel rose again and bore my wife to our tents amid the applause of the beduins. They sang a bridal song as the beautiful creature moved off.

We journeyed from the Adwan camp at Hesban to Madeba. We were anxious to visit the extensive ruins at Mashita, first discovered in 1871, which are supposedly the remains of a Persian palace of the seventh century AD. Mashita was four hours' ride from Madeba, but was in the territory of the Beni Soki Beduins. So, although our Adwan had agreed to take us there, they made objections when it came to the point because of the risk of attack from the Beni Soki. Nevertheless, we insisted upon their carrying out their agreement and got them to make an early start on the morning of the 20th April 1888. Though, only four Adwan now accompanied us including Sheikh Ali Abdul Aziz.

The country through which we had to pass was undulating. We found it curious to see how these men reconnoitred that country. On approaching each eminence, they separated and mounted it from different points rushing up at a gallop. When they reached the top, they dismounted and examined the country around. Satisfying themselves that no one was in sight, they descended and went on to the next eminence up which they rushed in the like manner.

On reaching and walking over the ruins, our guides only allowed us sufficient time for my wife to make a sketch and for us both to take a little lunch. They then hurried us off towards Amman and went on with extreme caution. On approaching the first hill, they caught an Arab bearing a heavy club such as a Beduin on foot generally carries. Our guides thought he was acting as a spy for some Beni Soki lying in ambush. They were proposing to kill him at once. Fortunately, George knew the man who sought his protection. They allowed him to go free on my request. We continued our journey to Amman and then on to Es Salt.

At Es Salt, we met again with Sheikh Ali Diab. It appeared that one of his tribe residing there had the misfortune, as he put, it to kill his servant for stealing. It struck as an unreasonable thing for a Beduin to kill anyone for that. The man had already been in prison for twenty-one days. Ali Diab had come to pay something to the parents of the murdered man and to arrange matters with the Governor. He hoped to have his man out of prison shortly.

The journey to Jerash was delightful over charming country abounding in wild flowers. We were again riding in air like an elixir of life. At Jerash, the effect of the moonlight pouring down upon the street of columns, the pillars of the Forum and the temples and theatres is magnificent. It is a sight we shall never forget. It would be a pleasant task to take up residence at Jerash and to rebuild the splendid street of columns. Earthquakes have shaken these down and separated them into the sections or drums of which originally composed. We could easily rebuild them. The local Circassians would readily accept the offer of employment. However, one would have to look out for the snakes that are numerous there.

135

At Jerash, we parted with our Adwan friends. The night before they left us, we had a fantasia in the dining tent consisting of singing, dancing, smoking and pistol firing. There was singing with a chorus in Arab style accompanied by much clapping of hands.

We contracted with the Sheikh of Suf to accompany us as far as Tiberias (on the west side of the Sea of Galilee) for the price of five pounds sterling. They allowed nine days for the journey. Thus, passing on to Abijan, we pitched our tents in a grove of fine old olive trees just above a beautiful clear stream. All the population came out to sit in rows in front of our tent. The Turkish Kaimakam (Governor) told us that when first he came the people of the district had been very troublesome. He had sent 150 of them to prison at Damascus where 120 had the misfortune to die. Since then, the people had behaved better.

At a great height above this place stand the ruins of an enormous Crusaders Castle (the Castle of Rubud). I rode up to inspect it. Getting into it is difficult owing to the dangerous state of the bridge and the dry moat, but the view from the summit is magnificent. The valley of the Jordan, the plain of Eschraelon, the Sea of Galilee, and Mount Hermon are clearly visible from it.

Just as we were about to start the next morning, the 27th April 1888, we saw a very pretty sight. Along the path through the olive trees just above our camp came a procession of about twenty men on horseback. They were accompanying four camels that had erections like howdahs on their backs in which sat women and girls. This was a wedding party going on to a neighbouring village. In the dappled morning light, the picture was a charming one. Especially, the guns and spears of the horsemen glancing in the sun, the light colour of the dresses, and the trappings of the camels gave a joyous look to everything.

That day, after descending a long valley in which the afternoon sun was extremely oppressive, we found ourselves at the large village of El Husn. We pitched our tents in a grassy hollow nearby. That night was one of the most anxious I ever passed. The heat had brought a very severe feverish attack upon my wife. An extremely high pulse accompanied shivering. By midnight, she was in a delirium.

I never felt so helpless. We were several days journey from the nearest doctor. The mosquitoes that had not troubled us in any other place were here almost maddening. There seemed no possibility of restful sleep.

Very happily, I had brought a very strong dose of sleeping medicine with me for emergencies. This and holding her hands enclosed in mine while I covered her face with handkerchiefs to protect her from the wretched insects at last got her some sleep. Thus, after many hours, the restless tossing to and fro yielded to something like rest. All night, I sat in the chair by her side looking out into the splendid moonlight and wondering whether I was going to bury her in this distant land.

In the morning, I got her safely to higher ground where the air was fresh and cool. She began to mend at once. All anxiety was over. We stayed there a further two days, so that my wife might gather her strength. This she did very rapidly, and on the third day, 30th April 1888, we continued our travels to Umhers, which is the ancient Gadara.

It was a beautiful morning. The larks were singing and the storks were floating lazily in the air. After a ride of about seven hours, we reached the village of Umhers. We encamped on a hill west of the village from which we could see the Sea of Galilee. The people of Umhers bear a bad character, and the village is a refuge to the outlaws of Tiberias and other places west of the Jordan. Nevertheless, no one had molested us in our journeys thus far, and we did not think of any danger. We went to bed early intending to rise with the dawn.

About half-past eleven, when we had been asleep for two hours, the firing of guns and pistols, the running of feet close to our tent and general hubbub awakened us. Jumping up and getting outside the tent, I found all our men firing away as fast as they could. I had no weapon with me not having carried a revolver thus far. Never before had I felt so much like a rat in a trap. I decided that I would not go to Syria again without carrying a weapon for our defence.

It transpired that one of our Beduin guides had seen a man creeping up to our sleeping tent. The marauder had lifted up the canvas at the bottom at the side next to my bed. Our Beduin had also noticed other men about. He had aimed his gun at the man and threatened to shoot the first that moved onwards. Also, George saw other men creeping towards our tent and similarly threatened them. The assailants, eight in all, replied by firing at George and the Beduin. The latter returned the shots. Then all our men came running out with their weapons. The robbers fired about a dozen shots in all and then made off. A good deal of blood was found in the morning in the direction in which we saw the men, so that we must have wounded one or more of them. Not one of our men was hurt.

It occurred to me that, if we remained another night at Umhers, we ran a great risk of being attacked again. Further that no assistance was obtainable in this wild place. George agreed, so we had the tents taken down and loaded on the mules. We descended on foot the very steep hillside that led to the gorge of the Yarmuk. We forded the beautiful stream at the bottom fringed deep with red flowered oleanders that rose above our heads as we sat on horseback.

Later that day, we descended to the plain of Jordan and passed to the south end of the Sea of Galilee. We came to the spot where the river flows out of the south west corner of it. Here we found a sweet pastoral scene. The lake was perfectly calm and of a light blue colour. The sparkling waters swept out of it down into the river bed. Some pretty little black and white cows were grazing nearby. Swallows, water birds and the lovely yellow blue and red warawaras with their most brilliant plumage were flying backwards and forwards.

Here I bathed, swimming from the lake into the Jordan. On attempting to return, I found it quite impossible to make headway against the stream. I had some difficulty in regaining a footing and scrambling out again. It was well that I did not venture farther down the river since, as I subsequently learned, just below is a dangerous part overgrown with weeds. If one gets swept into it, no escape is attainable. Three people from Tiberias had drowned there the previous month.

We then forded the river. The sheikh of the ford led the way. The water rose above the bellies of our horses as we passed over. From this point, we had a very pleasant ride for about an hour and a half along the west side of the lake. We passed great quantities of oleanders and large flocks of sheep and goats and herds of cattle brought down by the shepherds for watering.

On approaching Tiberias, we felt at home as we had visited the place in 1887. Here the weather was extremely hot, and the flies and mosquitoes were most troublesome. A local boatman advised us to make a fire of cow dung in front of our tent and to let the smoke blow through it. We got rid of both mosquitoes and flies, but were doubtful whether the remedy was not worse than the disease.

After staying two nights at Tiberias, we journeyed first to a place called Khan Yubb Yusef. This is over twelve hundred feet above the north end of the Sea of Galilee and provides a very fine view of the Sea. The next day, 4th May, we went on to Safed supposed to be the City on the Hill referred to in the Sermon on the Mount. Reaching Safed, we climbed to the highest point. From there the view is extensive and includes the Sea of Galilee, Mount Tabor and the peaks known as the Horns of Hatten, the supposed Mount of the Beatitudes. The Jews of Safed are reputed to be very fanatical. Many people scowled at us as we passed through the streets, but they did not molest us in any way.

The following day, we started at a very early hour. We passed along the edge of a ravine. The rocky perpendicular side contained many large caves. Some had storeys one above another that apparently communicated internally. This was a most remarkable place. I do not think that we should have seen it if we had not lost our way a little. I have not come across any account of this ravine that would be very interesting to explore.

The track now brought us down to the Sea of Galilee at the north west end believed to be the land of Gennesaret. Instead of continuing along the margin of the lake, we turned to the west and soon entered the Waddy Hammon. After a ride of five hours, we stopped in the valley to lunch. Above us on each side towered very high cliffs in which were many caves.

Among these were the ruins of the Castle of Kal'at ibn Ma'an. This consisted of caverns in the rock that were several storeys high and connected by passages and protected by walls. In the time of Herod, this was the stronghold of a great robber chief who with his crew spread terror all over the neighbourhood. Soldiers captured them only when let down by ropes from the top of the cliff.

Our chief mulet and I with some difficulty got our horses up to the bottom of the almost precipitous ascent to the castle. We scrambled up the rest of the way on foot. Riding down again was impossible. I had to walk in the heat of the sun, which upset me. However, George soon put me to rights by pouring water over my head from the brook while I sat under the shade of a wild fig tree.

We set off again winding up the Hady Hammon and ascended a steep hill to Hattin. This is the filthiest mud village that I ever saw, but surrounded by lovely orchards in which pomegranates were in full flower. Passing through the village, we encamped above and on the slope of the hills behind it. The local Druse inhabitants told us that travellers seldom came to Hattin. They asked us many questions about England.

That evening George was very ill with shivering fits followed by fever. My wife applied remedies and nursed him with the greatest care. He threw off the attack after a night of delirium. That same night, at two o'clock, the firing of guns awakened us. We found this to be the Druse guard firing at a prowling hyena. We went comfortably to bed again.

The next day, our journey lay across the plain of Hattin. It was the scene of that great defeat of the Crusaders, which practically ended their dominion in Palestine. We reached the top of Mount Tabor There we found our tents pitched in the Latin Monastery. The next morning, we walked down Mount Tabor leading our horses as we descended by a rough track. We got to Nazareth by ten o'clock. The heat was very great.

The following day, we came to Haifa and entered its streets. It is a small place and much cleaner and more modern in appearance than any other town we have visited in Syria except Beyrout. A distinction that is no doubt influenced by the adjoining German colony. Here we found a telegraph office and sent a message home reporting our safe arrival.

We stayed for three days on Mount Carmel. On the third day, we departed along the forest clothed mountain to the south east. As we rode, we found a poor native of the country stretched on the ground crying out in great pain. He was apparently suffering from the colic. He appeared almost at his last gasp. Fortunately, my wife had bought from the monks at the Monastery some bottles of medicine that they prepare from herbs. This has a great reputation in Palestine. Poured down the throat of the victim, it had a marvellous effect. In about half-an-hour he got up and walked away.

That night a heavy storm of wind and rain swept up from the sea over our tents, which were in danger. Fortunately, all went well. The storm had cleared by the following morning when we started our ride along the coast to Jaffa. Marauding Beduins frequently infest the plain of Sharon. Thus, the Turkish authorities recommend taking a guard of soldiers on this route to Jaffa. We had not thought it necessary to follow that advice. George said we must all carry arms and furnished me with a pair of flint lock pistols.

We reached a place where the cliffs come near to the sea to leave only a narrow road. Our muleteers with the baggage mules were a long way behind and out of sight. Three Beduins approached us with their hands on their guns and their eyes fixed on ours. We watched them in like a manner with our weapons in our hands. They went by in peace. George fell in with one of these men in 1889. He learned from him that he and his companions were then looking for travellers. They would have attacked us, but that we were equal in number to them and were as well armed.

We learned at Jaffa that there had been a report that bandits had murdered all of my wife, George and me at Kerak, which we had not visited. George's wife and mother were in great grief. They had been throwing ashes over their heads for some days. As a result, the mother had become blind.

The time had come to leave. How hard it was to leave this happy life, even with the hope of returning to it again at no distant period. In prospect, how forbidding appeared the gloomy days, the monotonous daily toil, the party (parliamentary) cries and striving contentious life of our native country. How attractive was that restful acquiescent spirit of the East.

As the steamer bore us away, our faithful followers stood watching from the little landing place until they themselves had melted into thin air. Even the white houses of Jaffa, ceasing to sparkle in the light of the sunset, had faded like the baseless fabric of a vision and left not a wrack behind.

PART II 1889 - A JOURNEY TO PALMYRA

Early the 9th March 1889, we returned and landed at Jaffa. There George and some of our old servants received us. The kind welcome, the warm sunshine, the blue skies, the cooing of doves and chirping of birds soon made us forget the little disagreeables of a rough voyage. Our itinerary was across the plain of Sharon to Gaza and Beersheba and then via Hebron to Bethlehem and Jerusalem. From Jerusalem we were to go to Damascus. From there, we planned to visit Palmyra.

The beginning of our journey was over a gently undulating plain that the local inhabitants partly cultivated. Then we passed through a few plantations of olive trees and by orchards of pomegranates and figs. Here, for the first time, we saw camels ploughing. Some alone and others joined with an ox or donkey. We came to Gaza on the 14th March 1889.

There George sought two soldiers to accompany us to Beersheba and on to Hebron. However, we received reply that we could not have the soldiers for two days, because they were all dispersed collecting taxes. As we had two Beduins with us, we decided not to wait for the soldiers but started at an early hour the next morning. A trooper joined us and said that another trooper was to follow, but he did not come.

We remained the night at Wady es Sheriah. A stream flows at that place, but no other water is to be found between there and Beersheba. We pitched our tents above the stream. It was very warm. The horses much enjoyed a swim in the water, and the men enjoyed a good wash.

The next day, the 16th March, we left for Beersheba taking

142

a circuitous route. We followed the soldier, as he led us to avoid the Beduin camps. Many vultures hovered about. We saw the beautiful storks. They appeared first as single spies and then in battalions. A flight of several hundreds of storks is one of the greatest sights of Syria.

We arrived at Abraham's Wells very tired and hot and camped there overnight. The water out of the well was cool and welcome to the taste. The letting down and drawing up of the bucket ropes over many generations had cut deep into the hard stone sides of the main well, which appeared of great antiquity. We had come through a true wilderness that was void and empty of man and beast. What a refuge for the thirsty and exhausted was this place of cool springs of water that never fail.

On 22nd March, we reached Bethelem. We found a place of rest and food a little distance from the town, which commanded a fine view of the Church of Nativity. We reached Jerusalem the following day and Damascus on the 6th April.

For years, we had talked about Palmyra longing yet fearing to make that difficult journey. Heat, cold, fatigue, thirst, sand storms, and Beduins seemed to threaten our path and warn us from the attempt. We engaged Sheik Nasr of the Aenezeh tribe, whose area included Palmyra, as our guide and protector. We supposed his authority would be sufficient to prevent any robbery by Beduins.

On the morning of the 9th April, we took our departure from Damascus. Our company consisted of my wife, myself, the faithful George, Haled our cook, Tanus our waiter, Selim our chief muleteer, three under-muleteers, and Nakhli our man of all work.

Whilst we stopped for lunch, our muleteers and baggage animals passed us. They were making for the place where George had arranged to camp overnight. However, the country was strange to them. They wandered from the track, or rather from the direction, for no particular track was there.

We did not find them that night. We had to make for the nearest village. There, after much palaver, they ushered us through a courtyard into the family living room of which the house proper alone consisted. The woman of the house lighted a fire of sticks and cow dung under a rude chimney. She threw us some mats and coverlets. We slept as well as possible. This, in truth, was little, for the place was damp and got very cold as the night dragged its slow length along. The next day Sheikh Nasr found us, and we all continued together.

On the fifth day from Damascus, we reached Karyaten where the waterless desert begins and extends to Palmyra some fifty miles away. My wife was unwell, which detained us here two days. The Governor of the place called. He told us that the Governor of Damascus with fifty soldiers had just returned from the desert with eighteen captive Beduins. He had charged them with robbing caravans going from Baghdad to Damascus and with stealing cattle from Karyaten. He had marched them off chained together to Damascus. The Governor of Karyaten said that we must take four soldiers with us, for the desert was not safe from predatory Beduins.

We had decided to start from Karyaten in the evening. George and the Sheikh wished to travel as far as possible at night to avoid the Beduins. We were also anxious to escape the heat of the sun that was very oppressive in the daytime. The soldiers did not arrive. We decided not to wait and set off an hour before sunset having engaged three camels to carry water. Having read much about the cold at night in the desert, we dressed warmly. Yet a Sirocco or Khampseen wind blew, so that it was very hot and oppressive.

We left the gardens and the cypress trees behind us. Then, through the haze of the Sirocco, we went out, as it seemed, into space. We lost sight of everything but our own men and the ground beneath our feet. The moon was at the full. The dull hot wind blew across our faces, and we breathed with difficulty. We went at a quiet walking pace or amble. The sheik led with the foot stepping horse. We followed him one by one breaking into a trot now and then to keep up. No one said a word.

Before us lay the desert. On and on we rode throughout that long night. Occasionally, a burning breath swept across us leaving behind it a feeling of sickness and exhaustion and making our hearts beat quickly. It seemed that we were going on in a dream. We called a halt for a brief period of rest, lay down on the warm sand,

and fell into dreamless sleep from which we had difficultly in awakening.

That night of riding was the strangest which I ever passed. The thin dusty haze seemed to make every object unnatural, mysterious and ghostly. While, as I knew, we were plunging deeper and deeper into the wilderness. As the day broke with the morning sunlight pouring in upon our tired eyes, we pitched the tents and were soon in oblivion. Even to the high range of hills each side of the desert plain that is about ten miles broad. From these hills the Beduins descend to plunder caravans.

On awakening, a ride of six or seven hours through great heat brought us to El Beda. The same sirocco haze lasted nearly all day. The illusions of the desert continued. We had a mirage always ahead of a lake of clear water, the shores of which we could never reach. Once we saw three islands on it and the imposing buildings of a phantom city on the middle one. Then, islands, buildings and city all disappeared, so that nothing was left but the strange atmosphere of the sea of air which surrounded us.

About noon, we saw some distant objects like giants walking towards us. We all halted. Sheik Nasr said he thought it was a trading caravan. However, this did not satisfy the soldiers. They unslung their rifles from their backs and galloped forward. George soon followed them. As we drew nearer, the giants seemed to vanish entirely. Then the figures appeared again looking like cows. Finally, as we closed with them, we found a flock of sheep and goats. Sheik Nasr jumped off his horse and nimbly caught a she-goat by the leg. He borrowed a metal cup from one of the men and gave us each two cups of delicious fresh milk. We never tasted anything so pleasant in our lives.

We camped overnight at El Beda by a well of water. We found it very brackish and nasty. The next morning, just as we were going to start, the sheik's horse gave me a nasty bite on the leg. This caused me a great deal of pain. I was lamed more or less for about ten days, so that I required lifting on and off my horse.

After six hours ride, we reached Palmyra and the tall round tower-tombs that stand before the entrance to the ruined city. The wide stretched solemn ruins stood before us. We rode up the celebrated street of columns that lead towards the great Temple of the Sun. We found our tents pitched close to a stream of clear water.

We intended to remain in Palmyra for a week. However, after three days' stay, the heat drove us away. It was most exhausting and overpowering with the Khampseen wind still prevailing. Nevertheless, it was with a sad heart that we paused at the gorge in the hills to take one last look back upon Palmyra.

The first day out of Palmyra, we only rode as far as El Beda. The journey was most trying. A strong west wind arose bearing great quantities of sand burning like the blast of a furnace. Eyes, nose and lips became intensely irritated. For hour after hour, we had to struggle on with faces muffled up and eyes almost closed against the wind. The wind increasing, we had to hurry forward as hard as we could for the last half hour through the sheets of flying sand. We had to leave it to our horses to find their own way, for we dared not uncover our eyes. We feared lest the animals should be overwhelmed. After six and half hours of struggle, we reached El Beda. Our men put up our tents there with many efforts and made fast.

The next day we had a very fatiguing ride of nine hours. As we ascended the northern hills, the wind became very cold. It seemed to cut through the few extra wraps that we put on. I felt very ill. By the evening of this day, the temperature had fallen some thirty-five to forty degrees from what it had been at Palmyra. We encamped at the final spring of a waterless desert.

The following day, after we had been riding for some two hours, George pointed out three horsemen on top of a hill. We knew this to be an outpost and that there would be more men behind the hill, so we assembled our men. Then we observed a sheik on a white horse. He carried a long lance in his hand and was riding towards us. We prepared our revolvers. Sheik Nasr fired a warning shot. George advised me that, if attacked, we should fire at the horses and not at the riders. For while the Ishmaelites value their horses so highly that they might retire rather than risk their loss, by

146

their code of honour the blood of the slayer must avenge the death of one of their tribe.

Sheik Nasr and George rode out to meet this warrior on the white horse. It happened that Sheik Nasr was related by marriage to the warrior, so all was well. He explained that the previous day Beduins from the desert had attempted to seize their camels. They had only prevented this by bringing out all their force at once. Seeing us coming from the same direction from where none but marauders come, he thought that we were the same Beduins back again. He explained that he had his men ready in case of an attack or attempt to steal the camels. In that event, his men would sweep round from behind the hill upon the marauders.

Following this incident, we continued upon our journey. After a ride of eight and half hours against a cutting wind that got colder and colder as we advanced over the hills, we reached a miserable little village. The people there received us kindly enough into one of their hovels. They made a fire of cow dung to warm us. We were glad of even this wretched protection from the furious and bitter blast, while our men struggled to put up the tents under the shelter of a wall. However, the hovel had no chimney, so the smoke soon drove us out again. By this time I was in a miserable state through illness.

However, the next day we reached Homs where I could obtain some medical assistance. Still, I was a long time in recovering from the horse bite and the chill that I caught in those cold winds after the intense heat of Palmyra. At Homs we encamped near the town by the wall of a lovely garden containing flowing waters and beautiful trees and shrubs.

Four days' journey from Homs via Nebk and El Kutifyeh brought us back to Damascus on the 27th April. That was the 19th day after we had left it for Palmyra. We purchased at El Kutifyeh some beautiful old embroideries and silver ornaments from the villagers.

We returned from Damascus to Jerusalem. From there, on the 13th May, we took our last ride passing in full moonlight through the corn lands of Philistia. We arrived at Jaffa at four o'clock in the morning after nearly eleven hours in the saddle. So ended a journey during which we had spent sixty-two days under canvas and ridden about twelve hundred miles.

PART III 1890 ADVENTURES SOUTH & EAST
of the DEAD SEA

We had visited Palmyra and were now bent on getting to Petra. Both the British Consul at Jerusalem, Mr. Moore, and our good and trusty friend and dragoman, George Mabbedy, strongly advised us against the journey as much too dangerous. Yet we had come from England to make the attempt, and they were not going to dissuade us from it.

Sheik Selim About Dahook of the Jehalin tribe was to accompany us. He made a formal contract with us before the Consul for twenty-five napoleons to conduct us safely to Petra with a sufficient escort. We were to pay one half before starting. He had at first demanded one hundred pounds sterling. We took two days of wrangling to reduce his demand to a reasonable sum. He was a restless, grasping, wild-looking man and we felt some hesitation in trusting ourselves to his care.

We had the usual provisions of tents, men and baggage mules. We preferred to ride horses to camels but hired two camels for carriage of water. Our servants comprised a dragoman, George Mabbedy, a cook, an old soldier from the Crimea War, a waiter, five muleteers and a young man of all work called Nakhli. We also had with us a Holy man or kind of Dervish whom we knew and met again on our arrival at Jerusalem.

We took with us gold and silver coin to the value of about seventy French napoleons. The rest of our money and valuables we left at Jerusalem, lest we should encounter robbers. We thought that the cash would be enough to pay our way to Petra and back again to Jerusalem through Ma'an and Kerak. The latter places lie to the east of the Dead Sea by which route we intended to return.

Before we left Jerusalem, the Consul warned Sheik Selim of the dire consequences to him if he failed to provide for our safety.

148

Also, upon our arrival at Hebron, the Kaimakam or Governor there summoned Sheik Selim before him. He calmly informed the Sheik that, if he failed to bring back a letter from us reporting our satisfaction with his conduct, he would put him in prison. This was somewhat arbitrary but made us feel more comfortable.

We journeyed past the pools of Solomon through Hebron and down the bare wild and rugged passes. Then we passed along the desolate west shore of the blue waters of the Dead Sea to leave the south end of the lake behind us. At the end of the sixth day after leaving Jerusalem, we reached a place called El Eskrib. This is within two long days' journey of Petra. We had kept Jebel Haroun (Mount Hor) constantly in sight all that day, knowing that hidden in a deep valley there lay the dearest object of our hopes Petra.

We had not travelled far on the seventh day, when a man came from behind a rock and hurried towards us. He told us that the Beduins were fighting in Petra and in the country between us and that place. He strongly advised us to go back, as we could not go forward without the greatest danger, and even in that place were in risk of attack. No alterative was available but to accept the advice. Three thousand Beduins were on the war-path.

George advised return to Jerusalem. However, we could not make up our minds to retreat ingloriously without accomplishing anything. We decided, against his advice, to go to Kerak (Kir of Moab) in the mountainous country bordering the east side and the south end of the Dead Sea. We retraced our steps. To the east rose the bare mountains and all around us spread the desolate sands with not a trace of a living thing. Yet, journeying northwards, we passed along a depression full of immense reeds with plume-like tops. An opening appeared. We found the spring, Ain el Beda, bubbling up in the midst of dense vegetation.

Here we set up the tents. The camp was composing itself to coffee and narghiles. We were gazing dreamily out of the tent-door watching the red glow of sunset fall upon the eastern mountains. Three horsemen, coming from the eastwards across the valley, pushed through the reeds, tethered their mares to the tall stems, and walked up to our tents. They were the head sheik of the warring

Howeytat and two of his brother sheiks. They pointed out the direction of their camp. They carried Remington rifles, flintlock pistols and swords and daggers. They were very surly in manner, and their behaviour was such as to make us extremely suspicious of their intentions.

Nor did following events lessen our fears. For soon afterwards, another Howeytat came out of the reeds. Then followed another and another and so on until overnight their number increased to twenty-two. From the time when darkness set in, we could see the huge red flames of the campfires of the Howeytat shooting high up into the air. They were six or eight miles eastwards of us on the other side of the valley. We knew that plenty of the Howeytat were there. Would more follow? .

The situation was a most anxious one. We could not tell how many might then be crouching in the reeds or were still to come. We felt from the way in which they looked at us and held whispered conversations together that they were discussing among themselves whether to attack and rob us. Robbery by Beduin custom involves stripping. Unsuccessful resistance would no doubt result in murder.

George and I distributed our weapons to the best advantage. We let them see clearly that we would defend ourselves. Our servants and the Jehalin formed a circle round our sleeping tent. We were very tired and lay down in our clothes with a revolver by my side. I got some troubled sleep expecting that the first shot would awaken me. I do not think my wife slept at all. She was very quiet, kept an anxious watch, and waited for the first flush of dawn. Until it came, our men and the Howeytat sat watching each other gun in hand.

When the blessed dawn appeared and while the baggage was being placed upon the mules, the Howeytat began to ask for our backsheesh. We would give no answer until we were starting. We then gave the sheiks of the Howeytat a Turkish pound and left them grumbling and threatening. However, they did not follow us.

That day we steered a most circuitous course to avoid wandering Beduins until we got within about a mile of the south end of the Dead Sea. There we picked our way across the wet salt

150

sand that contains dangerous places in which both man and beast might be lost. We crossed a small stream, and, although the water was only a few inches deep, several animals sank up to their bellies. That night we had a splendid sunset as the eastern mountains turned a deep crimson in the evening light.

Our camp was in motion the following day before the first rays of the sun had touched the summits of the western mountains. The Sheik of the Ghawarineh had found us and was demanding one hundred and fifty medjidies for our safe passage to Nimeirah. When we refused, he threatened to make me a prisoner. However, we were firm and only offered to pay him what we thought right for guiding us to Nimeirah. When it came to the point, he was afraid to attempt to detain us by force despite his loud talk. He came as our guide attended by three of his followers.

Part of our journey lay along the southeast side of the Dead Sea. The clear deep blue water was most inviting for a swim, but I could not be sure whether the Howeytat or Ghawarineh Beduins had followed us. Thus, I did not stay behind for a dip. At Nimeirah we gave the Sheik of the Ghawarineh a Turkish pound and sent them away cursing and threatening to return. That old sheik had the most evil countenance that I ever saw. Had he not been a coward, he would no doubt have robbed us. We camped overnight at Nimeireah alongside a clear stream of pure water that flows from a deep gorge there.

The next morning, being anxious to get to Kerak that day, we arose at three and had the camp in motion by half-past four. Thus, we had two hours' riding before the sun became hot. As we ascended, the views of the Dead Sea became ever more beautiful. As the northern part opened out to view, a haze caused by the warmth of the morning sun arose from its surface. It appeared as a lake of silver receding away into the distance.

Nine horsemen of the Keraki tribe joined us to provide a safe passage through their territory. They were tall, dark, dignified men mounted on fine horses. We reached a place called El Drab (the stream) where a rushing little brook pours down a hollow. Although still very early, the Keraki said that they were too tired to go on to Kerak that day as it still entailed a six-hour ride. They represented that they had come to us at great speed the previous day. They also represented that no water was available between El Drab and Kerak, and that we should pitch our tents there for the night. We could only acquiesce being unaware of ample water farther on. About an hour later, a son of Sheik Saleh arrived, followed by Sheik Saleh accompanied by two more horsemen.

Sheik Saleh is a fine looking man of about forty-five years of age. He is of distinct Jewish features of the handsomest type with a black beard and moustache. He has the air of being a very great man. We invited all into our dining tent and handed round coffee and cigarettes. We made a raised seat for the sheik with carpets. Fifteen more Keraki arrived later in the day.

The sheik asked what we intended to present to him. He suggested that, whatever we wished to bestow upon him, we might conveniently give at once. Because, when we got to Kerak, he might be a little busy. The idea of his being busy was amusing, but just then we felt too anxious to see the humorous side of it. We began at a low figure and suggested one hundred francs. The sheik asked for one hundred pounds. After some wrangling, the sheik reduced his demand to forty napoleons.

However, in the morning, Sheik Saleh said that sixty napoleons was the smallest sum that he would accept. We tried refusal, indignation and remonstrance in vain. Clearly, they would not allow us to go to Kerak unless we paid sixty napoleons. They handed us a letter from Sheik Khalil of Kerak. This stated that he would not permit us to enter Kerak unless we paid what Saleh demanded, but that whatever we settled with Saleh would be binding upon him Khalil.

We decided that, rather than pay this amount, we would go back and try our luck again with the Ghawarineh and Howeytat. We so informed Sheik Saleh. It was of no use. He assumed a very threatening attitude and said that we should not stir north, south, east or west unless we paid him sixty napoleons. He despatched some of his men down the hill to prevent our retreat.

We tried appeals to his honour. We had come to him as a

152

guest with a letter from the British Consul. He had met as a friend. Bidden us welcome. Eaten with us. Did he intend now to rob us? He made a deprecatory motion and said he must have the sixty napoleons. What could we do? He and his men carried Remington rifles and other arms. To think of resisting such a force was useless. After a very long attempt to better the terms, we decided that we could no other than to yield.

Yet we arranged for this sum that they should safely conduct us not only to Kerak but through the Keraki territory down the great Mojeb pass. The river Arnon flows at the bottom of this pass, and it is within one day's journey of Madeba. We knew that we should be safe there. At last we started for Kerak. On the way, the Keraki were quarrelling among themselves about the division of the spoil. I am afraid that we hoped several times that they would come to blows, but they quietened down as we approached Kerak.

Kerak is protected to the north and south by the mountains, to the west by the Dead Sea, and to the east by the desert. The Keraki can muster from sixteen hundred to two thousand well-armed horsemen. Thus, protected by nature and having long enjoyed independence, they have come to believe themselves invincible. They express contempt for the Turkish Government who have previously left them alone.

We knew the Keraki to have an evil repute. That here they had plundered Burckhardt, held to ransom De Sauley and his companions, and much harassed Canon Tristram. The British Consul at Jerusalem had also warned us that it was a most dangerous place. However, we knew an English missionary to have lived there for the last three years. We had supposed, therefore, that we would not be likely to meet any serious misfortune in entering the territory of the Keraki.

We pitched our tent in an open space at the edge of the town and on the summit of the hill. Sheik Saleh wanted us to pay him the rest of the sixty napoleons in the absence of his followers. We were not paying without witnesses and in the presence of some of the escort. Nothing was finished that evening. Wearied and dispirited we went to bed.

153

In the middle of the night, a messenger came from Sheik Khalil. He told us that we must not leave Kerak until we had seen that personage. In the morning, Khalil's two fierce looking sons, Ibrahim and Derweesh, came with a repetition of the same message.

At last Sheik Saleh was ready to take us from Kerak towards the gorge of Mojeb. Khalil's two sons had joined the party, but where was Khalil? We felt sure that they were leading us into another trap. It was a very hot morning. By the time we had reached the bottom of the valley, the heat, anxiety and exertion of scrambling down on foot caused my wife nearly to faint.

When we got to the top of the hill, we saw some horsemen armed with spears and rifles. We found Sheik Khalil seated amongst them awaiting our arrival. We saluted him and then continued surrounded by the whole array. Sheik Khalil is an older man than Saleh with a grey beard. He is tall, strong and determined looking. He has the reputation of being less treacherous and grasping than his relative.

Two hours' riding over grassy uplands bare of trees brought us to the ruins of Ar of Moab through which we passed. We regretted that we had not the opportunity of inspecting them properly. We then still hoped that we should get across the Arnon and within easy reach of Madeba that day.

Early in the afternoon, we arrived at the encampment of Sheik Khalil. Here they invited us to descend. We declined saying that we wished to go on towards Madeba. They insisted and we continuing to object. Khalil's sons put their pistols to George's head. They forced us to stop and pitch our tents.

We thought it best to accept an invitation from Sheik Khalil to eat with him. With the best grace, therefore, which we could summon out of very indignant hearts, we sat down in his tent. They confronted us with various unpalatable messes. We drank coffee and administered pills to various applicants. Then we retired to our tents. A crowd speedily followed us. They sat in front of our tents and gazed at their contents with covetous looks.

Later in the day, Khalil put aside formalities and courteous shows. He and thirty of his men crowded into our dining-tent. He must have sixty napoleons the same as Saleh. George and we made remonstrances. We asked to see Saleh. Khalil replied that Saleh would not give them their share and that, if he would give them half of what he had received, they would ask for nothing more. We became satisfied by all that we saw and heard during our detention by Khalil that political motives rather than greed induced their demand.

Saleh made excuses. He had given all but eight napoleons to his followers, and he had spent all his share. We pressed him as hard as we could. A most wearisome discussion followed in which we introduced the Consul, the Queen, the Sultan, and the reputation of the Arabs for hospitality without the slightest effect. Khalil rose angrily and withdrew.

Clearly, Khalil was intent on satisfaction and to be placed on equal position with Saleh, who did not intend to satisfy him out of his own pocket. Therefore, the satisfaction in the end must come from us. Discussions continued the next day and on the following day. At last, they agreed or pretended to agree that they should share equally. They say that, if we will pay the residue of the sixty napoleons to Saleh, we shall go free.

We pay the residue of the sixty napoleons. Saleh's mare stands close by. No sooner does he get the money into his hands than he slips it into his saddle bag and leaps on to her back. He is off at full gallop on the road to Kerak followed by his sons and other adherents. He has got our money. Yet, instead of conducting us safely through his country, he has left us to the tender mercies of Khalil with only about fifteen napoleons remaining in our purses.

Great uproar arises in Khalil's camp. They crowd round our tents and threaten us. They repeatedly demand The money! The money! We tell them that we can only get it by sending to Jerusalem. They reply that we shall not send there. They fear, no doubt, government interference.

The next morning, Ibrahim forces himself into our sleeping tent while we are yet in bed. It is with great difficulty that we turn him out. He wants some other articles and always The money! The money! We send to Khalil to complain of Ibrahim's intrusion. Much

155

to our satisfaction, the old sheik administers a paternal blow of a substantial kind to his son of the greedy eyes.

My wife is very poorly. We think of painting red spots on her cheeks and giving out that she has the plague to be free from this continual harassing. We cannot go on like this much longer and must try something. During the previous night, the cook was beaten, the food at the fire snatched away in spite of him, and half our bag of bread stolen. The Keraki threaten to starve us into payment. They will sell us nothing. Our charcoal is failing.

Ibrahim comes again. He threatens to take our clothing and tents and all. George tells us to be ready to make a rush for it in case of necessity. The weather is cold and threatening. We are forced to wear double underclothing, lest we should perish of exposure on the road if we have to fly. Our Chief Muleteer tells us that they are threatening to kill his two sons if they do not receive the money.

We ask our Holy Man to go with a letter to raise the money at Madebo. We tell him, if he cannot raise it there, to place our missive in the Consul's hands at Jerusalem. He mounts George's horse as the best we have and hurries away.

My arguments, appeals and indignation being of no avail, my wife sends for Sheik Khalil. He comes attended by his sons. She makes George translate to them word for word the following little speech:

'We have travelled among Beduins before. They have taught us to believe that, from the time of our father Abraham until now, if anyone came as a guest into their tents, their hospitality would be full and true. Nevertheless, we have lived to find ourselves mistaken. We have entered the tent of Sheik Khalil, broken bread and drunk coffee with him and he has treated us outwardly like welcome guests. Yet, we find ourselves robbed and kept as prisoners. Is this well done?'

They listen with the utmost attention and look, even if they do not feel, ashamed. They cry out, " Clever! Clever!" and say:

"Tell the Sitt (lady) she speaks well and we swear by our heads (placing their hands on them) that we shall not harm her. She and

156

the gentleman shall go in peace, but we must have the money."

After this, things went more smoothly and we felt tolerably free from danger or personal violence. The little speech had produced an excellent effect. The sheiks said to George whoever speaks with the Sitt will break his head meaning must submit to her.

They now seem at last to understand that they must await the return of our messenger before we can pay them. Nevertheless, they take precautions lest we should escape. They do not allow us to ride or even to walk out alone. They keep an especially strict watch upon George.

The rain comes. How it pours! The ground in front of us is like a marsh. How shall we get the baggage mules along when the money comes and they allow us to move? It is wearisome waiting! George seems sickening for fever lacking the season of all natures sleep. I guard the door of his tent and dose him with bromide. He starts and tosses and shouts in his slumbery agitation without a moment's repose. The men of the Hameydeh tribe have been waiting at Khalil's camp for some days to take us on to Madebo. We learn that they are preparing to ask us for a large amount.

On the seventh day of our captivity and the fifth since our messenger left for Jerusalem, we make out a horseman through our glasses. He is coming down the shoulder of Jebel Shehan, a high hill near to us on the west side. Presently, we recognise our little Holy Man. We go out rejoicing to meet him, and he comes on radiant with smiles. He enters with us into our sleeping-tent. He opens his breast and cuts a string that fastens a sealed packet beneath his shirt. It contains a letter from the Consul and the hundred napoleons. We summon Sheik Khalil and tell him that we have got the money. We offer to pay half down and the rest when he has taken us across Mojeb. To this he agrees.

The next day, Good Friday the 4th of April, we rise very early. After sitting down to breakfast, the sheiks and their followers crowd into the tent. They now say that we must pay the whole amount before starting. We remonstrate suspecting some trick. Khalil assures us that he would not like Saleh 'leave a stone in the well' but would carry out his agreement. A long journey is before us, and

157

we have no time to lose in fruitless discussion. We pay the money that seems to take a vast time to count and recount.

At last - how long it had seemed - we were off. We have to make a long detour to avoid the swampy ground. After some hours of riding over undulating uplands, we come to the brink of the mighty pass of Mojeb. This is a deep chasm down which it makes one almost dizzy to look. On the south face of the cliff was a goat path as difficult of descent as rocks and the precipice could make it. All here dismounted from their horses and one after another descended the deep ravine.

Shortly afterwards, the Keraki left us. With the feeling that a chapter in our lives was closed, we watched them ride slowly down to the stream. We turned to scan the Hameydeh. They had joined us as we went on. I perceived fifteen of them and with great satisfaction that there was not a rifle among them. Every man had a sword, dagger and flintlock pistol and six or eight carried spears. The sheik carried a good six-chambered revolver. Still, these fellows did not look to me so redoubtable as the Keraki. We followed them up the toilsome ascent to the northward, which was even more labourious than that on the south side. It was a hard portion of a very hard day's work.

Two or three hours farther on, we entered a narrow grassy valley where the Hameydeh invited us to stay for the night. No, we wanted to get on to Madeba. They pressed us urging various reasons, but we were firm. They insisted and began to threaten. We had paid each sheik of the Meyelli sixty napoleons, and we should pay them as much. We answered them that we would pay them what we thought proper and no more.

While we discussed, our baggage mules were going on in front. The sheik's brother and his spear men stopped them. Agreeing with George that we would fight if necessary, I galloped forward with him. He beat on the mules and pointed his gun at the sheik's brother. I covered the same man with my revolver across the mule that separated me from him. We told him that we would shoot him if he did not let us pass.

After a tumult of about half an hour, the spear men dropped

158

behind and allowed us to go on unmolested. They again urged us to stop but did not renew their threats. We pushed on as fast as we could for several hours and then encamped for the night. We only set up two of our tents to be free to move the more rapidly in case of any further trouble. The Hameydeh bivouacked on the south side of the watercourse opposite to us.

We were afraid that the Hameydeh would send for more men in the night and renew their attempt in the morning. However, only one other man arrived. Although they again asked for payment on the same scale as the Keraki, we told them that we would pay nothing till we saw Madeba. So we started as soon as it was light, and grumbling they followed. At length, they stopped in a deep valley and insisted upon payment right then. They said that on the hill beyond was an encampment of Christians with whom they had a blood feud. Therefore, they would not take us farther. We gave them thirty medjidies.

On reaching the top of the hill, we saw the Christian encampment lying in a hollow to the south east of us. In three hours' time, we came in sight of Madeba. The Sheik Khalil Sena received us. He is a very fine and benevolent looking man of about fifty-five years of age. He and all the principal inhabitants welcomed us as Christians who had escaped from the Moslem tyranny of the Meyelli.

How delightful it was to have a mighty wash and a quiet sleep; to put on clean clothes; and to feel that all anxiety was over after thirteen days of anxiety, danger and ceaseless harassing. We much enjoyed the peaceful tinkle of the church bell that awakened us on that Easter Sunday, 6th April.

After further journeying and visiting Hesban, Amman, El-Salt and Basrah, we made our way to the Mount of Olives. We pitched our camp at the northern end and highest point of the ridge upon the hills that stand above Jerusalem. We had bought there a little piece of land with a cave to call our own in the land that we love. There we remained for three weeks riding about Jerusalem. When the time came for us to part from our faithful servants, they were all of one word: "Why should you leave us? Why not always live in this our country?"

Why should we leave them? Why not always live in their country? Why not dwell upon this quiet solitary spot far enough from Jerusalem to be free from its religious animosities and yet near enough to drink in its great past? Why not rest here to watch morning after morning the dawn break in unclouded beauty over the mountains of Moab and the Dead Sea. To see the first rays of the rising sun strike across the deep valley of the Kedron. To watch the sun light up the domes and minarets of the Holy City and creep slowly down the mighty walls of the Haram?

Ain el Bêda. The Howeytat come out of the reeds

Walking for a change

Sheik Khalîl of Kerâki and another of his tribe

Kerâki discussing division of spoils

CHAPTER 8

BIRKBECK'S SONS

So Gray Hill thought about remaining permanently with the Beduins and upon the Mount of Olives. Yet, such was the stuff of dreams. He had too many other interests. He was too much involved at the centre of affairs in Liverpool and all that was happening there. Still, he did build a second home upon the Mount of Olives overlooking Jerusalem.

The reader will recall Birkbeck Hill and his wife Annie Scott and their three boys brought up to enter upon professional careers. Maurice was to go to the bar, Arthur Norman was to become a solicitor and Leonard was to practice medicine.

Maurice qualified as a barrister in 1888. In June of that year, Gray Hill was writing to him:

'I do not see how you can manage on less than £100 a year and managing on that will not be easy. From what you tell me, I presume that you can count upon earning about £50 a year in barristers' fees. Aunt Carrie and I will be answerable for the other £50 until you earn enough to support yourself. I fear that I cannot help you professionally at the present. We are bound in our clients' interests to go to more experienced counsel. I do not personally conduct litigation now. We can likely do something later. Meanwhile, I hope you will distinguish yourself at the criminal bar. Yet it is a slow wearisome business that of advocacy in its beginnings, and legal times are bad just now.'

As Gray Hill had warned Maurice, legal times were bad. Briefs were slow in coming until Maurice had established himself as a busy junior at the admiralty bar. Later he became Queens Counsel and later still the Admiralty Judge. The reader will meet him again in later chapters. Gray Hill referred further to these bad times in his reply to a father seeking articles for his son:

'I may say that, unless your son is very industrious and has really good abilities bringing him up as a solicitor would be useless.

I say this because of the numbers now entering the profession. Of this you must judge. Do not let him come too soon. Age seventeen and a half is quite young enough I think. The premium is 300 guineas and a Government stamp of £80 is payable on the Articles as a Solicitor.'

Arthur Norman Hill (or Norman as he preferred) was born in 1863. Like his uncle Gray before him, he was born at Tottenham and educated at Bruce Castle. He served articles in London with solicitors, Gregories, and qualified Michaelmas 1885. The following year, he joined Gray Hill at a salary of £200 per annum rising £50 a year to £300. In September 1888, the junior partner left after suffering a breakdown in health due to excessive alcohol. The firm appointed Norman Hill a junior partner in his stead with a profit share of 5% providing about £500 per annum.

Norman was then seeking the hand of Mary Danson in marriage. Mary was the daughter of a well known marine average adjuster. Thus, the marriage would appear an ideal one. Unfortunately, Mary's father was exceedingly possessive of his two daughters, Mary and Polly, to the point of downright cruelty. Much in the courtship resembles that of the poet Browning and Miss Barratt of Wimpole Street.

Norman at one stage despaired of ever achieving the marriage. During 1888, he wrote in most gloomy terms to Gray Hill to receive the reply:

'Your letter of yesterday much touched me both as concerning yourself and one so like my own as dear Mary. I had not felt the certainty of your affection for her, and was so glad to know it. I think it better to wait a little, but to await with hope, as I feel it will come in the end. You are down hearted and oppressed by work. Yet I see a brighter future in store and a year or two is not much at your time of life. I have felt that she had more than a liking for you. Waiting is nothing for true folks. I have felt all along this was not the time to do anything else. So we are only where we were, except that you have been so trustworthy as to open your heart to me. In spite of the gloomy outlook expressed in your letter, it has made me feel quite happy. I know your happiness would be so safe with her

162

and hers with you and we should be so happy in your united love for us.'

In December 1888, Norman determined to seek the consent of Danson to his engagement to Mary. He sought a meeting with Danson to that end. He advised his parents of his intentions. His mother, Anne, wrote in reply on 23rd December 1888:

'Father and I think you have done quite right. We believe that you will find the terms on which you and Mr. Danson are to meet will be all the better for the explanations of this week. Even if you think it wise to marry almost at once and without his sanction, I feel convinced that the consequential estrangement would not last long. Father and I are quite ready to settle your share of my money on Mary on your wedding. We are also ready to do anything else that we can to enable you to marry.

'Far better marry Mary quietly from here in case of any difficulty. Let her come to me. Your sister Lucy and I will get her anything she needs and help to make the wedding dress. We are delighted that you will bring her to us on the 5th January. I quite agree with you that she is best away from home for a time and could not be anywhere so well as with your father and me. We are ready to love her and give her a peaceful rest after all her troubles. I cannot bear to think of your being all alone on Christmas day, and we were wanting you so here.'

The meeting with Danson took place. Norman received the following confirmatory note from Danson dated 26th December 1888:

'I might have made my consent to your engagement conditional. I do not and exact no promises in return. I have told you that I cannot give agreement to Mary's marriage before she will be twenty-six years of age. I have told you the facts that have brought me to this conclusion, which I have not hastily adopted and will not easily change. I rely on broad facts easily ascertained as to the general rule of prudence in such matters. I have given the special reasons that convince me that here we should observe it with unusual ease. I appeal only to your own good sense. Yet I do not forget that you are a lover and I am a father. It is not a question that needs be

163

decided today or tomorrow. Let me advise you to take time to consider it and to consider it well. Then contest your feelings and do not mistake them for well-founded opinions. Then to do your duty, and I will do the same.'

Carrie returning to Damascus from Palmyra in April 1889, wrote to Norman:

'It is lovely here and the sunshine makes me so happy. The time is going when you will soon be in possession of a sweet little wife and her the best of husbands. I think it will aid Mary to know she has two other homes ready to receive her. Mr. Danson will feel this and realise it, though nothing can ever prevent these disgraceful outbursts of passion. For many years, I have felt either of the girls might arrive at our house at any hour and claim and get protection. I think the knowledge that our arms were open for them has stayed them in many a dying hour. It reposes me that dear little Polly's hour of deliverance is at hand. I suppose they have settled nothing about the wedding, but we are ready to manage it if need be.'

To complete this happy tale was the following letter of 8th July 1889 addressed to Norman by the pre-Raphaelite painter and friend of the family, Arthur Hughes:

'I understand that a certain glorious event comes off on the Twelfth. Others might have expected that I would be ready with something more than good wishes for your own and your beloved one's happiness by that date. Yet that is all the ignorant know about it. I feel quite sure you know my real value much better. How the keeping of appointments or the coming round of quarter days and so on can never trammel genius of a very tremendously superlative description. They must allow it to have its way to keep dark or blaze out upon a benighted universe just when it pleases. Perhaps, therefore, as the little sketch I am going to ask you to honour me by accepting will not be quite ready by the 12th, you may consider it better to put off the wedding. That is until I can inform you that it is ready. Still, if you are headstrong and determined to proceed, why then I shall hope that it is ready for you on your return from honeymooning. In sober seriousness, dear Norman, meanwhile accept all our heartiest good wishes and love.'

For Norman, then a partner in a prestigious legal firm and married to his beloved Mary, all was set fair for his future. Especially, as passing out of the 19th century into the 20th century was a time of continuing expansion and prosperity for the United Kingdom and specially for Liverpool.

Thus, in 1888, a tunnel was opened under the River Mersey to provide direct rail services between Liverpool and Wallasey, Hoylake and West Kirby. In 1890, the Manchester Ship Canal Company opened its canal from the River Mersey through Eastham Locks to Ellesmere Port. Shortly afterwards, the Company extended the canal from Ellesmere Port to the River Weaver with a twenty-six foot depth that enabled vessels to trade directly into Manchester. In 1893, an electrical overhead railway was opened to provide easy access throughout the Liverpool dock system.

The mercantile community were creating new businesses and forming new companies to carry on trade of every kind. Changes over the century had been phenomenal. Mankind was transforming the future. Great Britain was great in every sense of the word. She headed the greatest Empire of all times occupying one quarter of the world's surface. An Empire on which its peoples proudly proclaimed the sun never set.

The steamship was the arterial system serving that Empire. Steel was replacing iron in its construction. Propelling machinery was reliable and auxiliary sail discarded. Passenger ships were becoming larger and more luxurious. As early as 1870, the White Star Line had introduced the steamship Oceanic of 17,000 tons on to the Atlantic. They described her as fulfilling the vision of the steamship as a travelling palace. A vessel fitted with electric bells to summon stewards, water taps instead of jugs, oil lamps instead of candles, and adjoining lavatories instead of chamber pots. Also, the ultimate luxury, fitted with bath tubs and central heating.

From then on, progress in shipping was rapid dictated by competition to satisfy the demands of a new travelling public that believed how you travelled reflected your worth. The age of the great passenger liners was dawning with all their comfort, elegance and opulence for those travelling first class.

Liverpool with its trading connections occupied a unique and prosperous position. Its merchants were fortunate in their way of life, which compared dramatically with those less fortunate. A great divide separated those with and those without wealth that could be overcome by success in business. Equally, in the reciprocal direction, wealth could be swept away by failure in business or investment. This was all part of an evolutionary process that would ultimately offer mankind the choice between riches beyond imagination and its own self destruction.

Gray Hill was becoming ever more involved in the commercial and political activities of the day. He was engaged in the flotation of companies and taking founders' shares highly prized by the business community. Companies were offering him numerous directorships. Many of these he had to refuse because of his already heavy commitments. One he accepted was that of the Law Guarantee & Trust Society Limited established by Lincoln's Inn solicitors for providing guarantees of various kinds. Gray Hill suggested that the company undertake the guarantee of bail bonds in Admiralty, which he recommended as a safe and lucrative business:

'This business is a safe one according to my experience. Cost of providing bail in collision and salvage cases falls on the underwriters. The liability on the bail bond is to pay the collision damages or salvage award if the shipowner does not. Yet underwriters are also responsible for paying that amount. I have a special hold in these cases as I am manager of two Protection Clubs: one for steam and the other for sail. In case of collision, the Club covers one quarter of the risk of the liability of the ship entered in the Club to the other colliding ship. Owners have entered about one-third of the whole tonnage of the UK in my Clubs. I may say that after twenty-four years of Admiralty practice, I have never known a case of loss on a bail bond. The premium generally charged is now 1 per cent, but there is grumbling among the underwriters at the cost. If we could quote ten shillings, I think we might get the business.'

Gray Hill was looking to spend more time in Syria and at his second home on the Mount of Olives. Thus, he sought a lessening of his work load. In 1893, he proposed Norman as his successor as secretary of The Liverpool Steam Ship Owners' Association. The Association appointed Norman and sixty-five years later said of him under its Centenary History:

'There then began his long and remarkable connection with the Association, which was to enhance its prestige, add to the weightiness of its pronouncements, enrich its annual reports with literary touches, and voice opinions in forthright language.'

Thus, Birkbeck and Anne Hill saw their two eldest boys, Maurice and Norman, established in the legal careers that they had chosen for them. Careers in which they were later to become much distinguished.

Leonard, their third son and the author's grandfather, was born in 1866 and educated at Haileybury College. He received there the customary classical education but no scientific training at all and very poor mathematical teaching. In a letter home on his seventeenth birthday, he wrote:

'Sunday is the best day for letter writing without the inconvenience of work. Yet Sunday is not that free with three and half hours' Greek testament work and three hours' chapel.'

At Haileybury, Leonard acquired a life long devotion to swimming and other exercise as a relief from brain work. Again he wrote home:

'I have learnt by experience that knocking off exercise means waste and not a gain of time.'

On completion of his Haileybury schooling, Leonard entered University College London to study biology. He did well despite his absence of scientific schooling and his initial difficulties in endeavouring to dissect a frog. He achieved the award of the Bruce gold medal for surgery and medals for anatomy and physiology.

He underwent the usual training of a medical student at University College Hospital that concluded with him acting as house surgeon. This was at the time of the Jack the Ripper murders. Thus, although his hospital was some miles from the East End of London where this mysterious individual met his victims, he found himself

167

challenged more than once. Perhaps, not surprisingly, as he hurried, doctors' bag in hand, through the mean streets of St. Pancras to some urgent midwifery case.

In 1889, Leonard visited Norman in Liverpool. Writing to his future wife, Janet Alexander, he described the port thus:

'It is a wonderful place this Liverpool with its Turner sky and the frosty sun streaming through the mist and the long line of gold on the waters. We see the shadowy forest of masts in line upon line till the mist hides the rest. Then a mighty Atlantic liner in the foreground with its dozen cranes and scores of men rolling out carcasses of frozen meat and tubs of cheese, till one thinks man is nothing but one great belly. The corn ships with their endless buckets worked by steam ever dipping into the hold and pouring the grain into the huge warehouse. The sugar in rough bags piled ceiling high and streaming out over the floor from rents and tears. The great timber ships with six horses which haul out great logs of mahogany and the cattle ships which turn out troops of live oxen. Then the men from every nation who swear in every language and haul at ropes and pulleys to every song in every cadence. One sees the emigrants each carrying his bed, and the indifferent, the bravado or the tear-worn faces. Then the great ships set down in the dry docks with dozens of men who cling all round their huge sides. They bang with hammers and rivet the iron plates till the noise is that of hell turned loose. Each and all does his little bit and sees his little end. Yet the prodigious might and power and courage of man stands out unthought of probably except by me among them all. Yet I was doing nothing.'

That visit aroused a family interest in the sea, which later played a significant part in his research into means of protecting those who serve at sea.

Leonard qualified well in 1890. Writing to his future wife, Janet, he explained that three choices were then open to him. 'The first would lead to wealth and power, which his friends urged him to take. That was to become a medical consultant with a two horse chariot and a heavy butler gained by honest practical work and a holy regard for respectable conventionality. The second was to set up his plate in the East End of London and serve the poorer classes. The third he described as 'the search after that path, which when found saves the millions rather than alleviate the few hundreds for the passing moment.'

Whether he had any real choice is doubtful. His heart and soul were in research and what he could do to alleviate the sufferings of mankind from what were then multitudinous illnesses. He chose the third path and successfully applied for the Sharpey Scholarship at University College. On completing that scholarship, he moved to the Waynflete department of physiology at Oxford. There, in 1891 aged twenty-five years, he married Janet Alexander. That same year, he returned to University College to serve under the great physiologist Edward Schafer. In 1895, the London Hospital in Whitechapel appointed him their lecturer in physiology. This became a professorship when the London Hospital established the Chair in 1912.

Thus, Leonard embarked on a life of medical research and married Janet. They settled in Hampstead and first resided in a small cottage close to the heath by the White Stone Pond. Here their first child and son, Martin (the author's father), was born in 1893. They moved to Jasmine Cottage in Frognal. There a second son, Brian, was born in 1896 followed by a third son, Austin Bradford, in 1897 and a daughter, Margaret, in 1899.

Brian, sixty years later, described his earliest childhood recollections thus:

'My parents rented a small eighteenth-century house in Frognal called Jasmine Cottage on a turn in that steep winding lane. We lived there until I was nearly six, so all my earliest memories date from this Hampstead era.

'I still recall vividly grouped together on the doorstep of Jasmine Cottage. Nannie with the push-cart in case I got tired. My brother, Martin, dressed in a jersey and knickerbocker as befitted the dignity of six years. Myself his still unbreached junior dressed in a flowered frock and both of us wearing wide straw hats.

'We turned our backs on Grove Cottage where our two old cousins, Ellen and Constance, (daughters of Frederic and nieces of

169

Rowland) lived. We made for the High Street and shops on a treasure hunt to find presents for our father's birthday. This may have been tobacco for my father still smoked a pipe at the time. Otherwise, perhaps, it was a paint brush or tube of paint for he was an enthusiastic Sunday painter.

'The small back garden in which we played was shut in by high walls and thus a little dark. We envied the bare footed urchins who followed the water-carts down Frognal and paddled in the spray they scattered behind them. Another childish interest was the arrival at our front door of the various itinerant hawkers melodiously calling their wares.

'The knife grinder and scissors sharpener brought the whirring wheel from which the sparks flew. The chair mender entangled himself like a cocoon in seemingly endless lengths of cane. The muffin man rang his hand bell with his green baize-covered tray poised precariously upon his head. The buy a broom woman and the slatternly gypsies selling heather also came. We gave the latter short shrift. Sometimes, the organ grinder visited us with a shivering monkey perched on his instrument.

'In those days of unemployment and no dole, ragged men hung about the London railway stations ready to run a mile or two after a cab. They hoped to earn a few coppers for helping to carry the luggage into the house at the end of the journey. How clearly I remember the scowl on the face of one such unfortunate when they sent him off with a brisk "We want none o' you. Off you go!".Had he run all the way from Euston or Paddington up the Hampstead hills to that end?

'Following his appointment to the London hospital in Whitechapel, my father was finding the daily journey from Hampstead by a horse drawn bus fatiguing. Also, my parents needed more room for a growing family. In March 1902, two large horse-drawn vehicles arrived at Jasmine Cottage. We stood at the gate while a procession of men in white or baize aprons went to and fro with our cherished possessions. The next morning, we awoke to all the surprises of a new home and its seemingly endless garden of about an acre and a half.   We had moved to Osborne House facing the High Road in Loughton on the fringe of Epping Forest. Although only eleven miles from central London, Loughton was and remained for twenty years a rural village. Here a fourth son, Maurice, was born in 1905 and a second daughter, Nanette, in 1908. The garden was large with stables, so that the large family could run wild and indulge their interests in pets from grass snakes to tame owls. It remained for twenty-five years the family home.'

Respiratory tuberculosis interrupted Leonard Hill's pleasure in this new home probably caused by his research work. He took an extended leave of absence, which he spent in the milder climate of the west country at St. Ives and Lyme Regis. He overcame the infection and gave up smoking.

Leonard Hill's early researches at University College and at the London Hospital Medical School largely concerned the circulation of the blood. They led to his first book *The Physiology and Pathology of the Cerebral Circulation* published in 1896. His work and experiments on various conditions that might influence the blood pressure led him and a colleague to develop the now customary armlet method for measuring blood pressure.

He relied upon his blood pressure measurements to support his belief in the doctrine of early to bed and early to rise. Thus, in 1898 he wrote:

'We record the arterial pressure at 8.45 p.m. sitting after dinner overcome with sleepiness and at 7.30 a.m. horizontal in bed engaged in mental work. However, the most noticeable rise in pressure was between eight and nine in the evening reading an exciting book at great speed.'

Leonard Hill soon became an accepted authority in the field of circulation. In 1900, Schafer invited him to contribute a section on that subject in the latter's great text book of physiology. That same year, he was elected to the Royal Society at the early age of thirty-four.

Leonard also researched into the causes of caisson disease in deep sea divers better known as the bends. He concluded that slow uniform decompression, which allowed time for the excess of oxygen to escape from the body through the lungs without forming bubbles, would avoid this condition. He successfully decompressed himself after an exposure to six atmospheres allowing twenty minutes for each atmosphere. The work that he carried out on deep sea diving led him later to research into problems of escape from wrecked submarines. He was largely responsible for the Admiralty's decision to equip submarine crews with the Davis escape apparatus.

Concurrently with this work, Leonard Hill was researching into the regulation of breathing and the effects of breathing pure oxygen. Thus, he showed that filling the lungs with oxygen enabled holding of breath for longer periods. Further that forced breathing of oxygen could suppress symptoms of hyperventilation. As part of his experiments, he gave oxygen to the local milk horse. In his words:

'It set off on its daily round and, when it came to a hill up which it habitually walks, it trotted up to the top and effectively winded me. I was following on my bicycle, and I had omitted to fill myself with oxygen before the start.'

Leonard's research work led him on to investigate the effects of sunlight, temperature and humidity on human environment and health. He turned largely to environment and health when, in 1914, he left the London Hospital to become Director of applied physiology in the National Institute of Medical Research.

The reader will recall that the pre-Raphaelite painter, Arthur Hughes, was a close friend of Birkbeck Hill and his family. They exchanged much correspondence, but unfortunately little of that correspondence now remains. However, later letters written by Arthur Hughes do show his fondness for the family of Birkbeck Hill and their way of life.

The first, dated 1st February 1891, relates to Leonard:

'An old friend, Dr. Birkbeck Hill, has a lot of children with whom I have always been in the habit of corresponding with nonsense rhymes. Now they are all grown up and, as they get married, they buy of me a little picture as their first art treasure. Just now one son, who has taken gold medals in his medical career, wrote to say he had sold his medals to buy one of my last year's Cornish sketches! Upon which I scolded him, but it was too late and he was very obstinate and I had to give way. So

172

then I sent this nonsense about Physicians:'

Physician of my soul
I look not in the face,
He thumps out my disgrace
He leaves me in a hole....

Physician of my body,
He gives me filth to drink,
I cast it down the sink,
I take a little toddy.

Physician of my pouch,
He cures me all my ills,
I go and pay my bills
Sweet sleep comes to my couch.

So, lover of blue seas,
Believe me yours till death,
And would sweet helpful breath
Could waft to you from these.
Alas! poor mimic seas.

The second, dated 28th August 1895, relates to Norman. The reference to Kew is to the home of Arthur Hughes.

'I have lately sold three little Cornish landscapes. Rather romantically, I think. Long ago, I used to visit dear friends, the Birkbeck Hills, whose children then were small but very good friends. These are now grown into men and women doing famously in the world. Now and then they, one or another, come to see me. They buy a very small picture of Cornwall sketches, which I made a few years ago. Yet, this last incident crowns all. For one, a Liverpool Solicitor, has such a grateful client that the said G.C.must needs make my young friend a present. He wished this to be in the form of 60 pounds worth of electroplate. This so horrified them that by some means they made Grateful one to know that what they would

173

like most of all would be landscapes by A. H!!!. The 60 pounds are to come to Kew in consequence.'

The third, dated 17th October 1897, he addressed to his daughter Agnes from No.3. Ashfield Road, Aigburth, Liverpool where he was staying with Norman and Mary:

'I have been trying to get a letter off to you for a long time. Yet, with painting three sisters in one picture and paying visits to surrounding friends my small head has been too full.

'I am all the same having a most pleasant experience. It is only delightful staying with these: Norman just the same as of old but with the added glories of his career. Mrs. Norman is most interesting and the children just what we might expect. All my sitters are beautiful and for kindness and sweetness everything they could be. I think my work will go thro' happily, but I wish it would go faster. They like it every step. One day Mrs. Norman asked a lot of folk to afternoon tea because I was there she said. Yet I wish I had not been so sort arter tho I did know one or two a little.

'I had next evening to dine and sleep at Gray Hill's and spend next day with Mrs. G.H. All their houses are most lovely and interesting and filled with most lovely treasures. The Gray Hills live at Birkenhead across the Mersey. It is very pleasant to go by the steamer across the river with all the various shipping and other sights of the Port.

'I feel as if I were in a foreign town with the advantage of being able to communicate with the inhabitants. There is an overhead railway too. Close by is a beautiful Park. It has a lake and streams and waterfalls and stepping stones. It also has a fairy Grotto with rocks and peacocks, Swans and Cygnets and other fowl, and a Palm House and Sculpture. I take a morning walk there seeing Norman part of his way to town and an evening walk also. They allow me to smoke everywhere in the house, tobacco being quite understood. So you see I am altogether in clover, but for all that a little bit homesick too. I wish I could do something in my picture to produce others. It would be a pleasant place in which to have a few clients.'

The fourth letter dated 6th March 1903 and likewise

George Birkbeck Hill

Sir Maurice Hill

Sir Norman Hill

Sir Leonard Hill

Sir John Gray Hill, President of the Law Society

addressed to his daughter Agnes, is a sad one:

'Dear old Birkbeck Hill died ten days ago after a long illness. I did not know of it and was always hoping to go and see him. Margaret wrote to me that Lucy was worn out with nursing. They buried him beside Mrs. Hill at Aspley Guise, where she lived and died. I should like some day to go and see it. They were of the worthiest of all I have known.'

Margaret and Lucy were the daughters of Birkbeck Hill.

CHAPTER 9

NIGHTMARE SCENARIO

Gray Hill had built a second home upon the Mount of Olives overlooking Jerusalem, which he described thus:

'Ras Aba Kharoub is a unique place. I chose the site as the highest on the hills that stand about Jerusalem. We have thirty to thirty-five acres of land in all. We built and added to the house, made the great cisterns, and planted every tree and plant there. We are much attached to the place, which has cost a very large amount. Yet we are only able to pass a few months there every year. The cisterns hold about six hundred thousand gallons. We have found them more than ample for all our purposes. That includes watering trees, additional building operations, and some giving away to poor people.'

Both Gray Hill and his wife, Carrie, wished to spend more time in this second home. In December 1891, he arranged for Carrie to travel there alone and for himself to follow in March for a stay of six weeks. He wrote to his P & O friends explaining that his wife would be travelling on the P & O *Brindisi Express* and the SS. *Bokhara* to Alexandria. Further that, as she was of delicate health and would be travelling alone, she required a comfortable sleeping car on the train and a comfortable cabin aboard the ship.

References by Gray Hill to Carrie's delicate health are surprising in circumstances of their adventurous travels in Syria. She clearly suffered some weakness caused by the damp of Liverpool, which the dry air and warmth of Syria and Jerusalem banished.

Gray Hill was suggesting to the P & O:

'Now that the railway is opened from Jaffa to Jerusalem, is it not worthwhile the P & O sending their Brindisi-Alexandria & Naples-Alexandria boats on to Jaffa durng the tourist season? It is only about twenty minutes steam from Alexandria, and many passengers go to the Holy Land either direct from England or after

176

a stay in Egypt.'

In January 1895, Gray Hill wrote to the British Consul in Damascus. He sought confirmation that the Turkish Government then had military forces in Madaba, Kerak and Ma-an that could provide an escort for him and his wife to visit Petra that spring. He referred to a new ferry at the South end of the Dead Sea and enquired whether the best route was via that ferry and Kerak and Ma-an. Finally, he expressed his annoyance to learn that nothing could be done to obtain redress of the money and property taken from him by the Sheik of Kerak.

From the end of the century, Gray Hill and Carrie were looking to winter in their Mount of Olives home or in further exploration of Syria. Thus, longer periods of absence and increased activities outside the office resulted in Gray Hill spending less and less time on legal affairs. He remained at the centre of activities, but was leaving ever more of the daily legal work to his partners and, especially, to his nephew Norman.

The latter was an extremely hard worker. As Secretary of the Liverpool Steam Ship Owners Association, he was much involved in the shipping industry and questions of maritime safety. Additionally, he was handling much maritime legal work. A declaration made before him by the Quartermaster and sole survivor of the 5640-ton Antwerp steamship *Noranmore* shows the ever present dangers of the sea even for the larger vessel.

This witness, after describing how the vessel turned turtle, went on:

'I was thrown out into the sea but got on board the one lifeboat launched. It was full of water and five members of the crew were already in it. At daylight the next morning, we found ourselves within a few yards of the *Noranmore*, which was then lying bottom up with the seas washing over her. We took into the boat two members of the crew whom we found floating on a plank but could see no others.

'I remained four days without food in the boat, which was full of water, until rescued by a Turkish Brigantine. During the period while I was in the boat, all the other men perished. Some were washed overboard and others threw themselves overboard. I am quite unable to account in any way for the loss of the vessel. None of the men who were with me in the lifeboat could do so.'

In 1901, Gray Hill was elected a member of the Council of the Law Society especially to express the views of Liverpool. Two years later, he was elected President of the Society. The following year, 1904, King Edward VII conferred a Knighthood upon him for services to his profession. He assumed the style Sir John Gray Hill. Reference to him will continue as Gray Hill.

Another outside interest of Gray Hill was that of a patron to the great Shakespearean actor of the day, F. R. Benson. Gray Hill sought subscriptions for the performance of Benson's company in Liverpool.

He wrote to prospective subscribers critical of the stage of his day, which criticism appears equally applicable to much modern television:

'The work Mr. Benson is doing is of a most important character from a public point of view. I have always felt a great interest in drama and hold a strong opinion as to its importance concerning education. The present state of the Stage is a very degraded one with little but what is trivial, unwholesome or meretricious being presented at our theatres.

'Mr. Benson is an enthusiastic artist devoted to the poetical drama and activated by the best motives. I feel that it is very important that we should support his efforts. With his well-trained company, he could arouse public interest and revive the love of the great works of Shakespeare and our other great dramatists of the past time. A generation is growing up which feeds on the contemptible plays of the day and knows nothing of the great past. The effect on the minds of the young must be of a very serious nature. Let us do our best to get some opportunity given for them to choose the best and pass the other by. Now they have no choice.'

The expanding commerce of Liverpool in the opening years of the twentieth century led to busy commercial courts and a strong bar. Many great lawyers of the day began their careers in Liverpool as did the two nephews of Gray Hill. Maurice Hill later became a leading Admiralty Silk and later still the Admiralty Judge. Leslie Scott became Solicitor General and later a Lord of Appeal.

However, that was then in the future.

In 1908, Gray Hill was advising his young nephew, Leslie Scott, in a way then regarded as wise counsel but, in later times, a nephew might regard as impertinent:

'I hear that you are thinking of building a house and borrowing money on a mortgage. I hope that you will not do anything so extremely imprudent. You should be content to begin as Aunt C and I did and as Norman and Mary did in a small house and in a small way. The Speaker of the House of Commons and Mrs. Gully lived in lodgings in Liverpool for three years, and you need not be ashamed to do what they did.

'It seems to me the height of imprudence for young married people to tie a load of debt about their necks. Especially, to launch out in expenditure before they have a substantial sum earned and put by. I would never buy anything with borrowed money. I think and so does Norman that it would be much easier for you to live for the present on the Liverpool side. Much better connections from a business point of view are to be found there.

'Now my dear Leslie do be content to begin in a quiet unostentatious way and above all things do not build. I have had enough experience of building to know that the cost always far exceeds the estimates, while an attempt to do a thing cheaply always ends in disaster.'

Gray Hill, like his father before him and those of the Hill family to follow, had much empathy with those serving or aspiring to serve at sea.

In December 1907, he was writing to Shipowners N H Potter & Sons:

'I am interested in a boy now in the *Indefatigable* named John Woods whose father, now deceased, was my head gardener. Woods is seventeen years old but young for his age. He has been about two years in the *Indefatigable* where he has become a first class petty officer. The Captain of his ship gives him a very good character.

I want to apprentice him for say three years if I can without a premium. However, I am willing to be guarantee for say twenty-five pounds if he should not complete his service under Indentures. Would you be prepared to take Woods?

The reply was 'yes.'

Gray Hill was President of the Lancashire and Sea Training Home for Poor Boys. He took a keen personal interest in all its boys and their future. He was advancing monies to purchase land for building a Home at Liscard. Yet, economic storm clouds were then gathering over the head of Gray Hill. He was to find himself entrapped by those very investment problems against which he had so strenuously warned others.

The reader will recollect that he was a shareholder in the Law Guarantee Trust and Accident Society. A company established by solicitors to provide guarantees including for ships bail. From 1895 onwards, the Society was issuing guarantees of mortgages secured on licensed premises. By 1907, Gray Hill held 3650 ordinary shares that he had purchased for £4160. He was also Vice-Chairman of the Company.

That year the Chancellor of the Exchequer imposed a new tax on beers and liquors. This resulted in a serious depreciation in the value of public houses, so that valuation of that class of property was no longer possible. The Company faced a serious deficiency on its guarantees and an inadequate capital base from which to meet that deficiency. Failure of the Company would lead to substantial further calls on shareholders. The Company resolved upon an increase in its share capital by an issue of new shares.

As its Vice-Chairman, Gray Hill felt under moral duty to do his utmost to save the Company. He subscribed for new shares and increased his holding from 3650 to 6100 ordinary shares and 6000 preference shares. Additionally, he and Carrie took up 2350 preference shares into their marriage settlement. In May 1909, the Company made a further call upon the ordinary shares. They appointed a new Chairman from outside to revitalise the Company.

Unfortunately, these measures proved inadequate to save the Company in circumstances of its increasing deficiencies. In 1909, the Directors submitted a resolution for winding up of the Company.

An accompanying complex and lengthy report by the Chairman explained:

'A very large part of the deficiency arises from the enormous shrinkage that has taken place in the value of public houses. In guaranteeing mortgages on such public houses, the Board only did what every Brewer and every Banker in the City of London did during the years 1896 to 1900. No-one at that date could have had the least idea of the enormous shrinkage in value that would take place within ten or twelve years in that type of property.'

On 11th August 1911, Gray Hill wrote to the Liquidator requesting additional time to pay calls on his shares while he realised other assets. He refers to a loss on his shares of £57,400 including cost and additional calls. That loss compared with a valuation of his personal assets at £39,194. Those assets included his Mount Olive home and the furniture and pictures at Mere Hall together valued at £9,500. Also the assets of the marriage settlement including Mere Hall valued at £32,439 and Carrie's personal assets valued at £5,925. These sums may appear low in circumstances where Gray Hill owned a mansion furnished with old Masters and antiques. Nevertheless, the monetary values of the day were low. He had lost a fortune.

Gray Hill's initial thoughts were that he had realised his worst nightmare and that all his assets were to be swept away in an overwhelming catastrophe. However, his nephew Norman gave much support to his uncle in restoring stability to his affairs. He arranged for Christies to auction portraits and other pictures and antique furniture from Mere Hall. The pictures included three Constables sold for about thirty pounds each. He arranged for the sale of investments including some forming part of the marriage settlement. In the result they saved Mere Hall and the Jerusalem property with some investment income.

Despite his own troubles, Gray Hill found time to write a personal letter to Lloyd George, then Chancellor of the Exchequer, whom he knew him well through his political affiliations.

He wrote as President of the Lancashire and Sea Training Home for Poor Boys:

181

'I trust that in your Budget you will not forget the Charitable Institutions that train poor boys for the sea service. You will remember when you were President of the Board of Trade visiting the Sea Training Home at Liscard near here. You made a speech in which you said the Government ought to help in the work. Then you may remember later, when you became Chancellor of the Exchequer, that you told me personally you were ready to grant funds. We have waited long and patiently, but not a sixpence has reached us.

'The output of boys from the Institutions to the Mercantile Marine is about six hundred. That is excluding the boys from the training ship *Exmouth* and excluding boys trained in Reformatory Institutions whether in hulks or on shore. The British shipowner does not want little criminals. Thus the latter class of boy, when he goes to sea, generally goes on a foreign ship.

'The annual cost of maintenance of a boy (putting down nothing for rent, interest or cost of land, equipment or buildings) is at least thirty-five pounds a year. I do not ask the Government to pay it all, only about half. What is that amongst the millions with which you are dealing?

'Speaking for my own Institution, we give each boy a sea kit; get him a berth in a good ship returning to Liverpool; meet him on his return; take him back to the Home (protecting him from the land sharks); make him repair his kit; and ship him again. We keep a record of every boy, and the result is our boys keep at sea and are very well reported. Do I pray you not forget the poor sailor boy again.

'I may tell you that the Kents Navy League has inspected all the Institutions and found the Liscard Home the best. It has collected three thousand pounds with which to build an additional home on our land to hold another 100 boys. Yet how are we to fill it without help. I personally have given a great deal to our home, but I have not the means now to do so. Any number of boys are waiting to go to sea. The demand on us by shipowners to supply well-trained boys is much greater than we can satisfy. It is pitiable that a lack of funds should stop us in the works. Pray forgive the warmth of my appeal and my addressing to you a private letter.'

In 1914, then aged seventy-five, Gray Hill was planning to visit again his much loved Mount of Olive home. His letter of instruction to George Mabbedy is the last entered in his private letter book. On 14th June 1914, he died suddenly leaving a grieving Carrie. So ended the life of a kind and distinguished gentleman of much wisdom. He had lived his life to the full. Yet, in his closing years, those very circumstances against which he had so direly warned others had entrapped him.

CHAPTER 10

SIR NORMAN HILL & THE TITANIC

In 1893, following his appointment as secretary of the Liverpool Steam Ship Owners Association, Norman Hill became increasingly involved in public work relating to the shipping industry. Thus, in his early days, he was involved in the reform of light dues charged on shipping for maintaining lighthouses. That reform ended the practice of making a profit out of the lighthouses.

Later, he was closely involved in two major Acts of Parliament of 1906 relating to shipping. The first, the Marine Insurance Act 1906, codified the law relating to marine insurance. It continues today as the primary source of that law. The second Act amended the Merchant Shipping Act 1894, which had codified and extended earlier legislation relating to construction and equipment of British vessels and their stowage and load lines.

British shipowners had long been complaining that the freedom of foreign vessels from this earlier legislation hampered fair competition. The 1906 Amending Act largely remedied that grievance by applying the bulk of the British safety regulations to foreign ships visiting United Kingdom ports. Additionally, the Act substituted for obsolete and inflexible rules provisions for general supervision including by the Corporation of Lloyds. The Act further set up a Merchant Shipping Advisory Committee to advise the Board of Trade on regulations relating to shipping. The Committee comprised shipowners, shipbuilders and seamen under the chairmanship of Norman Hill, which position he held for the next thirty years.

As described under the Liverpool Steam Ship Owner's centenary history, Norman Hill under the Association's annual reports expressed strong opinions on pertinent matters of the day. These opinions were expressed in a most literary style and widely read and regarded. They included strong criticism of Government and Parliament for judging questions affecting the very existence of the

British Mercantile Marine on party political grounds and not on their true merits.

Later, members of the Association sought to criticise Norman Hill for issuing in his personal capacity a pamphlet on fiscal questions of the day. He replied that he must be free to form and state his personal opinions as he pleased. Otherwise, he could not continue to act as secretary of the Association. The threat was enough to end that unjustified criticism.

In 1911, Norman Hill received a knighthood for services to Government concerning shipping. His style was Sir Norman Hill.

He received many congratulatory messages including one from the family artist friend Arthur Hughes:

Dear Sir Norman,

And it gives me much pleasure to write it as above. It is only the other day that I was commiserating with Maurice on having to wear silk and the possibility of accidentally sitting upon a bramble in some fishing excursion. But there is no such alloy in the title attached to you and a little of the glory of which comes to the insignificant friends that are proud of you both. Worthy descendants, as all of you are, of my own old very dear friends of so long ago.

Allow me also to congratulate respectfully the new Lady Hill, and remember me.

Affectionately yours,
Arthur Hughes

The opening years of the twentieth century saw the beginnings of mechanisation within offices. In 1909, Sir Norman had a lift installed to serve his offices. Telephones contained in padded cells or telephone boxes followed. Clerks were responsible for answering the instrument and conveying messages to the recipient. They were repeatedly complaining that the instrument was extremely indistinct and must be put right. Machine reproduction by an early form of the typewriter was replacing handwritten letters and copies.

Men continued to provide back up services as clerical and office assistants and as typists. The female invasion of the office was still to come. Generally, ladies remained at home either married

185

or preparing for marriage. What mattered most was to find the right husband. Those lower down the social scale earned a living as domestic labour. The female intellectual or professional woman of the day known as the blue stocking was generally despised. Such a reputation could spoil the prospects of a good marriage. Those of good education but little money sought positions as governess or genteel shop girl while awaiting a husband.

Electric telegraph was providing a prompt means of communication over long distances where cable could be laid. Wireless without need for cable or wire was enabling ships to communicate one with another and with the shore by means of a key and the Morse code. The Marconi Company was providing skilled wireless operators.

Passenger ships of ever increasing luxury and speed were sailing the Atlantic reducing the separation of Europe from the new world of America. They included the luxury White Star vessels owned by the Oceanic Steam Navigation Company Limited. That latter company was British registered and had a paid up capital of £750,000 and three directors, namely the chairman, Mr. Bruce Ismay, the Rt. Hon. Lord Pirrie and Mr. H A Sanderson. The International Mercantile Marine Company of New Jersey held a majority share holding in Oceanic Steam and in other British registered companies sailing the Atlantic.

The White Star passenger ships were luxurious floating hotels and, as such, provided impeccable service, cuisine and entertainment for its first class passengers. In 1912, the addition of the *Titanic* increased the White Star fleet to thirteen ships. The Oceanic employed them all in carrying passengers, mail and cargo from Southampton, Cherbourg, Plymouth and Queenstown to and from New York. They believed them to be unsinkable by reason of their bulkhead construction.

The *Titanic* had three propellers each individually powered. The three engines together were capable of developing 55,000 horse power. The Titanic was 852.5 feet in length, 92.5 feet in beam, and of 46,328 tons gross and 21,831 tons net register. Bulkhead construction comprised fifteen transverse watertight bulkheads dividing the ship fore to aft into sixteen separate compartments. The bulkheads extended up to at least the E boat deck that was a continuous steel deck from end to end of the ship.

The reader may be interested to compare measurements of the *Titanic* with those of the modern *Queen Elizabeth 2*. The latter are 963 feet in length, 105 feet in beam, and of 66,450 tons gross and 39,881 tons net register. Thus the *Titanic* was only a little less in her length and beam than the *Queen Elizabeth 2*. The reader may also be interested to compare the measurements of the *Titanic* with those of the first Cunard steamship *Britannia* built some seventy years earlier. The latter were 207 feet in length, 34 feet in beam, and of 1155 tons gross and 619 tons net register. A difference that illustrates the extraordinary developments in shipping during the nineteenth century.

The *Titanic* was fitted with the then latest wireless telegraphy system worked by a Marconi 5-kilowatt motor generator with emergency batteries. That system comprised two complete sets of apparatus of which one was for transmitting and the other for receiving. The vessel was also fitted for receiving signals from submarine bells laid at depth by the Submarine Signalling Company. These signals were picked up by microphones positioned inside the vessel's hull on the port and starboard sides below water level and wired to receivers in the navigation room. Thus, the navigation officer was readily able to establish the true position of the vessel.

The *Titanic* was fitted with every luxury for the comfort and entertainment of her first class passengers, which included electrical lighting and heating and three electric passenger lifts. The sumptuous first class restaurant and its orchestra matched the best of London hotels.

On Wednesday 10th April 1912, a proud *Titanic* sailed from Southampton on her maiden voyage bound for New York. She called at Cherbourg and then at Queenstown. She sailed from the latter port on the afternoon of Thursday 11th April. The *Titanic* carried 1,316 passengers of whom 325 were travelling first class, 285 second class and 706 third class. First class passengers included the Owners managing director, Mr. Ismay. Second class passengers included eight bandsmen on board to entertain the first class passengers. The crew numbered 885.

The White Star Company had invited Sir Norman Hill as legal adviser and friend and his wife, Mary, as their guests and first class passengers on the return voyage to New York. Sir Norman had declined. He held strong views against accepting such hospitality from clients. Had he gone, then like friends and colleagues, he might not have returned. His daughter, Rosalind, recalled that her father and mother had a foreboding sense of impending doom.

On Friday the 15th April 1912, the world awoke to learn from its press that the *Titanic* had sunk. The Cunard vessel, *Carpathia*, had come to her rescue but had saved only 703 out of a total of 2201 persons aboard. The Board of Trade ordered an immediate formal Investigation. This opened on the 2nd May 1912 before the Wreck Commissioner, the Rt. Hon. Lord Mersey, assisted by Marine Assessors.

The Investigation was a meticulous one. It occupied thirty-six working days from 2nd May to 3rd July 1912. Counsel for the Board of Trade included both the Attorney General and the Solicitor General. Three leading Counsel instructed by Hill Dickinson & Co appeared for the Titanic and her Owners, namely the Rt. Hon. Sir Robert Finlay KC MP, Mr. F. Laing KC and Mr. Maurice Hill KC assisted by junior Counsel, Mr. Norman Raeburn. Other interested parties appeared by Counsel. The transcript of the Investigation comprises one thousand pages. To read that transcript places the reader back on board the *Titanic* in the midst of the sinking.

The Statement of Case ordering the formal Investigation simply stated:

'The *Titanic* left Queenstown for New York on or about the 11th day of April 1912 with a crew of about 892 hands all told and about 1316 passengers. On the night of Sunday the 14th day of April 1912, the vessel struck ice in or near latitude 41 degrees 46 Mins. N. longitude 50 degrees 14 Mins. W., North Atlantic Ocean. And at about 2 a.m. on the following day, she foundered in about the same locality and loss of life thereby ensued or occurred.'

Most of the witnesses at the Court of Inquiry were survivors from the *Titanic*. They had harrowing tales to tell, but also tales of great heroism and devotion to duty.

As was said by the Attorney General:

'My Lord, one cannot peruse the evidence given in this case without, I think, being very much struck by the discipline and behaviour of the crew taken as a whole. To take one instant and I think a very striking one, I call to attention the evidence of Dillon and Cavell, trimmer and fireman. They had been on deck and were ordered with others down below in a vessel that they knew was in great jeopardy. All these men knew perfectly well that they were in grave peril. Yet they went down without any question to work below at a time when the water was coming into No.4 boiler room. They remained until the water was up to their knees, when they were ordered back on deck. They then found that all the boats had gone except the one collapsible. These were not even seamen. I do not think we say a word too much when we say that the behaviour of these men was heroic.

'Not one Engineer was saved. This is not uncommon. They are right down in the vessel and during a time of peril they do not come up. They did not come up in this case until, if at all, all hope of safety had disappeared. Another striking fact is that eight ship boys were on board the vessel and every one of them was drowned. They might very properly have sought to be treated as juveniles, but they did not do so. They went down as part of the crew of the ship.

'My Lord, with the rarest of exceptions, everybody on board, although in the gravest peril and imminent danger of losing their lives, behaved with calmness and devotion to duty. I hope we will always remember this to the credit of those who sail on board British vessels. One should also remember the passengers and the accounts which witnesses have given us of the women who refused to leave their husbands. Who took their chance knowing perfectly well what it meant, but preferring to remain with their husbands to going on board the boats. We must also not forget that the men on board generally did not attempt to leave the vessel. They knew that accommodation was not even sufficient for the women and children on board. In one case, two men got into a boat because they thought no more women were available. When they saw women, the men got out and the women were placed in the boat and saved.'

Nevertheless, an Officer in charge of loading the boats drew a revolver and fired two shots to prevent a number of foreign men forcing their way on to a lifeboat. In doing so, he was acting pursuant to the moral code of the day that gave absolute priority to saving women and children to the prejudice of men. Perhaps, to an age grown accustomed to the equality of the sexes in all things that code may appear an odd one. Its enforcement on the *Titanic* coupled with an unjustified fear of overloading the davits and falls led to the crew launching lifeboats below their fully laden capacity. That failure and boats subsequently lying too far off the *Titanic* for fear of suction when she went down resulted in fewer survivors than the boats could have taken.

The facts of the sinking found by the Court of Enquiry reveal that on 14th April 1912 the *Titanic* received three wireless messages reporting ice on her route. Yet the *Titanic* continued at her full speed of twenty-two knots. That was in accord with then general practice. In the words of Sir Robert Finlay, the evidence is absolutely overwhelming that no-one in the Atlantic trade lowers speed in consequence of reported ice.

However, the circumstances encountered by the *Titanic* were abnormal in two respects. First, the sea was calm without any of the swell that ordinarily shows as a distinct ripple at the foot of the iceberg. Second, the iceberg presented a black side to the approaching *Titanic*. That resulted in an absence of the warning lighting over the top of the iceberg normally caused by the luminous effect of white ice.

As was put by Sir Robert Finlay:

'The absence of swell is proved to have existed. The presence of the black berg is proved to have existed. It is proved that each are most unusual phenomena. The combination of the two was extraordinary. There was a fatality about this, which might not occur in a hundred years. It was that which led to this berg not being seen until it was close upon the nose of the ship.'

Evidence given as to distance and speed on first sighting the iceberg was one quarter of a mile distant at a speed of twenty-two knots. This speed would have resulted in a rate of movement through the water of seven hundred yards a minute to cover the distance in a little over half a minute. In a futile attempt to avoid collision, the officer of the watch immediately ordered the wheel of the *Titanic* hard to starboard (a porting movement).

Then, as put by the Attorney General:

'First you have the blow struck in the fore peak tank. There is an undoubted puncture of the skin there - penetration. Then you have it further in Nos 1, 2 & three holds. Then you have a very serious blow struck in the fireman's passage penetrating through the outer skin and the inner skin of the fireman's passage. That was a distance of 3 ft. 6 ins. Thus, one can form some conception of the force of the blow caused by some spur or something of that nature on that iceberg, which was under water. It opened up the fireman's passage through which the water was coming in such gusts. Later we have the evidence of the blow struck between No.6 and No.5 boiler sections. That blow penetrated both before the after bulkhead of No.6 section and abaft that bulkhead to hole both Nos. 5 and 6 sections.'

The Court found that the collision took place at 11.40 p.m. on the 14th April and caused damage and holing to the *Titanic* over a length of three hundred feet. That was to her fore peak, Nos.1, 2 and 3 holds and Nos 5 and 6 boiler rooms, all of which were opened up to the sea. The Court further found that, as the ship was moving at more than twenty knots, she would have covered the three hundred feet in less than ten seconds. So that all the damage was done within that time.

Thus from that moment, the unsinkable *Titanic* was a doomed ship, although this was not immediately apparent to those on board.

As found by Lord Mersey, the Wreck Commissioner presiding at the Investigation:

'I am advised that the *Titanic* as constructed could not have remained afloat long with such damage as she had received. Her bulkheads would have enabled her to remain afloat with any two compartments open to the sea. In fact any three of the four forward compartments could have been flooded by the damage received without sinking the ship to the top of her bulkheads. Even if the four forward compartments had been flooded, the water would not have got into any compartments abaft of them and the ship would have remained afloat. But she could not remain afloat with the four forward compartments and the forward boiler room No.6 also flooded with consequent successive overflowing of after bulkheads.

'It has been shown that water came into these five forward compartments to a height of about fourteen feet above the keel in the first ten minutes. This was at a rate of inflow with which the ship's pumps could not possibly have coped. Thus, the damage done to these five compartments inevitably sealed the fate of the ship. The damage done to the boiler rooms Nos. 5 and 4 was too slight to have hastened appreciably the sinking of the ship. The rate at which water came into No.6 boiler room makes it highly probable that the compartment was filled in not more than an hour. After that, water overflowed the bulkhead between Nos. 5 & 6 boiler rooms.'

Thus, the damage to No.6 boiler room sealed the fate of the *Titanic*. She finally went down at 2.20 a.m. on the 15th April. That was some two and half hours after striking the iceberg.

Sir Robert Finlay referred to the fatality of these events. Individual stories given in evidence tell how death or survival was a matter of pure chance with the dice loaded in favour of women and children. Thus:

Alfred Crawford, 1st class bedroom steward gave evidence relating to Mr. and Mrs Strauss:

'I helped passengers to put on their life belts. I then went to my boat, No.8 and assisted to get ladies into that boat. Mrs. Strauss refused to leave her husband and they were left behind. Captain Smith asked me how many crew were in the boat and I replied two. He then told me to get into the boat as it was being lowered.'

Thus Mr. and Mrs. Strauss were left behind and lost. Alfred Crawford was more fortunate in being ordered to crew the boat.

Mrs. Annie Robinson, first class stewardess:

'Seven ladies and one maid and a governess were under my charge. All us stewardesses on E deck were doing the same thing. That is looking after our lady passengers, and all were saved too. We were put into No.11 boat and left the *Titanic* about forty-five minutes before she went down. The band was still playing as we left the ship.

Charles Joughin, chief baker:

'I was assigned as crew to No.10 boat. I went to that boat. When I arrived, they were getting the boat ready for the passengers. The Chief Officer, Mr. Wilde, shouted out for the stewards to keep the men back, but that was not necessary. The men kept back themselves, and we made a line and passed the ladies and children through. Discipline was splendid. We got the boat about half full, and then we had difficulty in finding ladies for it. They ran away from the boat and said they were safer where they were. I myself and three other chaps went on the next deck and forcibly brought up women and children. They did not want to go but were all squatting down on the deck. We brought them up and threw them into the boat.

'Eventually, the boat was pretty well filled. According to standing orders, I was captain of this boat. An Officer ordered two sailors and a steward to get in as crew. I was waiting for orders to get into the boat. The officer evidently thought it full enough, so I did not get in it. As far as I could see, only women and children were in the boat apart from the three crew. I went below for a drink.'

The following questioning by cross-examining Counsel is of interest about that drink:

Question 6248. 'A drink of what? ..... Spirits.'

The Commissioner: 'Does it matter very much what it was?'

Counsel: 'Yes my Lord. This is very important because I am going to prove, or rather my suggestion is, that he then saved his life. I think his getting the drink had a lot to do with saving his life.'

The Commissioner: 'He told me he had one glass of liqueur.'

Question 6249. 'What kind of glass was it?'
'It was a tumbler half full.'
Question 6250. 'A tumbler half full of liqueur?'
'Yes.'
Charles Joughin then continued his evidence:

'I went back on to the boat deck. All the boats had gone, so I went down on to E deck. I threw about fifty deck chairs overboard to give something to cling to when the boat went down. I then went to the deck pantry for a drink of water, and heard a kind of crash as if something had buckled and a rush of people overhead.

'I went back to the boat deck. The people had gathered on the port side in one bunch. I got down towards the well of the deck. As I did so, the vessel gave a great list over to port and chucked the people over : many hundreds of them. Eventually, I got to the starboard side of the poop and got hold of the rail outside of the ship. I was just wondering what next to do, when the vessel went and I found myself in the water. It did not drag me down, and I do not believe my head went under the water at all.

'I was in the water for a long time. I should say for over two hours. I was just paddling and treading water until daylight broke, when I saw some wreckage. I swam slowly towards it and found it was a collapsible boat on its side. An Officer and about twenty or twenty-five men were standing on the top of it. No room was on it for me. A cook recognised me and held out his hand and helped me. Eventually, a lifeboat came in sight. They sang out that they could only take ten. I swam to it, and they took me in.'

Thus, this chief baker managed to survive in freezing water for more than two hours without suffering hypothermia or other ill effect. Can there be any other explanation than that the half tumbler of neat liqueur saved his life?

Charles Herbert Lighttoller, the second Officer, after giving evidence about getting the life boats away, continued:
'I went across to the starboard side of the Officers Quarters to see if I could do anything on the starboard side. I saw the First Officer, Mr. Murdoch, working at the falls of the starboard

emergency boat with a number of crew helping. Then the vessel seemed to take a bit of a dive, and I walked into the water that was intensely cold. I was swimming out towards the head of the ship, the crow's nest, and turned to swim across clear of the ship to starboard.

'The next I knew, I was up against a blower and grating on the forepart of the funnel held by water rushing down the grating. Then, a rush of air from down below the funnel blew me away from the grating, and I was dragged below the surface. When I surfaced, I found myself alongside a collapsible boat still shut up bottom up. I held on to it by a piece of rope. Then the forward funnel fell down within three or four inches of the boat. The boat was lifted bodily and thrown about 20 feet clear of the ship as near as I could judge.

'I remember next being alongside this collapsible boat again. About half a dozen were standing on it. I climbed on and looked at the ship. The third, if not the second funnel, was still visible. The stern was clear of the water. After the ship reached an angle of fifty or sixty degrees or something about that, I heard a rumbling sound. I attributed this to the boilers leaving their beds and crashing down on or through the bulkheads. The ship then became more perpendicular and finally attained the absolute perpendicular. She then went down very slowly until the end. Several people were in the water round about us. They swam towards our boat and got on to it during the night. We could not paddle the boat. It was absolutely waterlogged.'

Eventually, a lifeboat picked up this witness.

Thomas Patrick Dillon:

'On the night of the accident, I was on duty in the engine room. I felt a slight shock when the ship struck the iceberg. We remained working below until about quarter past one, when we received the order: All hands on deck. Put your life preservers on. I went up on to the well deck. Some passengers were there: men and two women. Crew were singing out from the boat deck that the last boat was leaving and were there any more women. We chased these two women up the ladder to the boat deck. I was on the poop with many others. We saw no women. I remained on the poop until the vessel went down. As she did so, I shoved myself away from her into the water. I was sucked down about two fathoms and then seemed to get lifted to the surface. Many people were in the water: about a thousand. I was swimming about twenty minutes, when I was picked up by No.4 life boat.'

Charles Hendrickson, Fireman.

'I was in my bunk asleep when the accident occurred. One of my mates in the room, D. Ford, awaked me and pulled me out. I was dead asleep when he did so. My mate was later drowned.

'I went up on deck. The iceberg was just abaft the engine room. I saw much ice on deck, but I did not think the position serious. I returned below intending to turn in again, when the same man, Ford, came back and said water was coming in down below. On looking down the spiral staircase, I saw water rushing in and reported this to the Second Engineer.

'Eventually, they gave an order: We want a leading hand. All hands get life belts and get up on deck. I went on deck and assisted in getting the boats away. The Bosun told me to give a hand with a boat on the after side of the bridge. We started firing rockets. Two women were there who they put into the boat with three gentlemen. Then the Officer called out: Are there any more women here? He told me to jump in, and four fire fighters got in beside myself. That was all on the boat deck. The Officer told one of the seamen, Symons, to stand off a little way and come back when called.'

George Symons:

'I was relieved at ten o'clock when I went below and turned in. A grounding sound on the ship's bottom awakened me. I thought at first that the vessel had lost her anchor and chain and it was running along the bottom. Others got up, but I did not get up immediately as I thought nothing was wrong. However, another seaman, Hobbs, told me that I should get up. As I was dressing, the order came to all hands to stand by.

'I helped with the boats on the starboard fore-end numbered

3, 5 and 7. The Chief Officer, Mr. Murdoch, ordered me to boat No. 1 and to jump in and see that the plug was in place. Two ladies asked the Officer if they could get into the boat and he told them to do so. Then three gentlemen came running up. They asked also if they could get into the boat and the Officer told them to do so. Mr. Murdoch then looked around for more. As nobody was in sight, he gave the order to lower away. Plenty of room was available in the boat. As we were being lowered down, we got hung up by a wire guy. Someone came down on the next deck and chopped it away. The Officer ordered that I stand off and await orders. I really expected an order to return to the ship and land the passengers aboard again.

'After the ship had gone down, many people in the water were calling out for help. We had moved away from the vessel. I gave the order to pull back to the scene of the disaster, but by that time I could hear and see nobody.'

Mr. Murdoch, the Chief Officer, was drowned.

Sir Cosmo Duff Gordon, Passenger:
'My wife woke me at a quarter to twelve. I went up on deck and saw two or three men there. They said that we were supposed to have run into an iceberg but it was all right. One of these men was another passenger, Colonel Astor, who went down with the vessel. I went back to my cabin and told my wife to dress. Then I went back on deck and saw men stripping the lifeboat and went back to my cabin and dressed myself. A steward came to the cabin. He said that the ladies were to put on life belts and to go up to the boat deck.

'Miss Francatelli, my wife's secretary, accompanied us. We all went up to the boat deck together to the starboard side. We found that they were filling or lowering one life boat. They were only taking women into that boat. I saw two other life boats lowered, namely the next two forward. They filled the first one with women and children. They partially filled the next one with women, and with men when they could find no other women. My wife and Miss Francatelli were standing with me at this time. The Officer had asked them two or three times to get into a lifeboat. My wife refused to go without me.

'We then heard the order Man the emergency boat. I spoke to the Officer who gave that order and said may we get into the boat? He replied: "yes I wish you would." No other passengers were at all near us then. He put the ladies in and helped me in. Two Americans, who came running along the deck, joined us. I think he told two or three firemen that they might just as well get in. Then he put one man Symons in charge of the boat. I think we had got about 1000 yards away from the *Titanic* before she went down. We heard the explosion first and then a wail of one confused sound of the people who were drowning.'

Sir Cosmo was subjected to much rumour and criticism at the time. Some described him as a wealthy gentleman who had escaped from the *Titanic* in an under laden lifeboat that did not return to rescue those in the water. The fireman, Hendrickson, suggested that Sir Cosmo and his wife objected to going to the assistance of the drowning people because of the risk of suction from the sinking *Titanic*. Others in the boat did not support these statements. Sir Cosmo and his wife vehemently denied them. Other criticism related to Sir Cosmo promising five pounds to each of the crew in the boat. He did this on their telling him that the Owners would not compensate them for loss of their possessions. Yet again some suggested that this was a form of a bribe.

Joseph Bruce Ismay, Chairman:

'I am a member of the firm of Ismay Imrie & Co. That company owns the Oceanic Steamship Company Limited, which in turn owns all the White Star Line steamers. I was a passenger on board the *Titanic* on the fateful day of 14th April 1912. The impact awakened me. I stayed in bed a little time and then got up and went to the bridge. Captain Smith was there and told me that we had struck ice. I asked him whether he thought the danger was serious. He replied that he thought it was.

'Later, I rendered what assistance I could in getting out the boats and putting in the women and children. I saw numbers 3, 5, 7 and 9 boats lowered on the starboard side. At this time, I thought the vessel was in a very serious condition and sinking. We got all the eight wooden boats on the starboard side away. I then helped with the collapsible boat and getting in the women and children. After we had put all the women and children and those on deck into this collapsible boat, I myself got into the boat as it was being lowered away.'

Mr. Ismay was vigorously cross examined by Counsel representing the members of the Dock & General Workers Union. Mr. Ismay admitted that, when he got into the boat, he thought that the *Titanic* was sinking. Further, that he knew that some hundreds of people on the ship must go down with her. Counsel suggested to him that, as Managing Director, it was his duty to remain aboard the vessel until she went to the bottom. Mr. Ismay replied that no more passengers were waiting to get into the boat that was then being lowered away.

Thus, Counsel was suggesting that, as managing director, Mr. Ismay had no more right to save his life than the Captain while any other person remained aboard his doomed ship.

In answer to that contention, Sir Robert Finlay, Counsel for the White Star, submitted:

'The question comes to this. Was it Mr. Ismay's duty to remain there, although by doing so he could save no other life and could have done no good to any human being? My Lord, if Mr. Ismay had felt then impelled to commit suicide, the same kindly critics who are now attacking him would still have done so. They would have said instead that he went to the bottom because he did not dare to face an enquiry that he knew must follow.

'I submit to your Lordship that there is no observation of an unfavourable nature to be made from any point of view on Mr. Ismay's conduct. He was not under that duty, which the Captain always feels to go down with the ship if anyone else remains on board. Mr. Ismay did all he could in the way of helping the woman and children. It was only when the boat was actually being lowered and that place was empty that he got into it. I submit to your Lordship that Mr. Ismay violated no duty nor any point of honour. I will put it as high as that.'

In his findings, Lord Mersey addressed the contentions thus made against Sir Cosmo Duff Gordon and Mr.Bruce Ismay:

'The very gross charge against Sir Cosmo Duff Gordon that, having got into No.1 boat, he bribed the men in it to row away from the drowning people is unfounded. I have said that the members of the crew in that boat might have attempted to save the people in the water. Further that such an attempt would probably have been successful. Yet I do not believe that any act of Sir Cosmo deterred the men from making the attempt. Nevertheless, I think that, if he had encouraged the men to return to the position where the Titanic had foundered, they would probably have tried to do so. In that event, they could have saved some lives.

'The attack made upon Mr. Bruce Ismay was that the position of Managing Director of the Steamship Company imposed some moral duty to remain on board until the vessel foundered. I do not agree. Mr. Ismay, after rendering assistance to many passengers, found C collapsible, the last boat on the starboard side, actually being lowered. No other people were there at the time. Room was available for him and he jumped in. Had he not jumped in, he would merely have added one more life, namely his own, to the number of those lost.'

A number of witnesses gave expert evidence. They included:

Sir Norman Hill, in his capacity as Chairman of the Merchant Shipping Advisory Committee, gave evidence of studies by the Committee on various matters. These included increasing the then existing lifeboat scale for vessels of more than 10,000 tons, the best type of lifeboat, and the subdivision of vessels into watertight compartments. He then gave interesting statistical information regarding the then safety of sea travel:

'In the last twenty years, we find thirty thousand voyages made by passenger ships across the Atlantic or an average of sixteen hundred voyages a year. We find twenty-five casualties either resulting in loss of life or resulting in total loss of a ship without loss of life. That is less than one in a thousand. In those twenty-five casualties, the lives of sixty-eight passengers and eighty crew were lost making a total of one hundred and forty-eight lives lost. That is excluding the *Titanic*. I am not able to say how that percentage of loss of life at sea compares with land travel.'

The following remarks under cross examination of Sir Norman Hill by Counsel show the reputation that Sir Norman enjoyed in shipping:

Sir Norman Hill: 'I think you must remember that the members of the Committee are all experts. We do not have to examine witnesses - at any rate I do not. I am the Chairman.'

Counsel (Mr. Scanlen): 'Just a question on that. You say that the members of the Committee are all experts. I will begin with the Chairman. You belong to the honourable profession of the law, do you not?'

Sir Norman Hill: 'I do, but since 1894 I have devoted a very great deal of my time to all matters affecting shipping. I do really consider I am an expert on the statistics of shipping but not on the building.'

The Attorney General: 'I can vouch for that.'

The Commissioner: 'You are not likely to persuade me, Mr. Scanlen, that Sir Norman Hill is not an expert on this matter. I know him to be an expert.'

Guglielmo Marconi, the inventor of wireless telegraphy, gave evidence of his system fitted on the *Titanic*.

'That system was first fitted on a large liner in 1900. Namely on the Kaiser Wilhelm de Grosse owned by the North-German Lloyd Company. In the following year, 1901, wireless equipment was fitted in the *Lusitania* and *Carmania* and in a number of other vessels.

The wireless installation on board the *Titanic* was our property under contract. It was what we call a 5-kilowatt installation. It was of a very modern type guaranteed for a distance of about 350 miles and can carry a great deal farther. The *Titanic* carried two operators. The wireless apparatus was in duplicate. It had a spare battery by means of which the operators could still use it if flooding of the engine room cut off the current from the ship's dynamos. A distress signal takes priority over everything else.

Since the *Titanic* disaster, I have given much thought to making the wireless apparatus ring a bell on its receiving warning that a ship in danger needs assistance. It would require the danger signal to contain a long impulse or sequence of waves that would last for fifteen, twenty or thirty seconds. This would cause the bell to give a prolonged ring like that given on shore by a fire alarm.'

Sir Ernest Shackleton, the Arctic explorer, gave evidence about ice conditions. Especially, that normally an iceberg can be sighted five miles distant.

On being questioned by Lord Mersey why they did not see this iceberg until so late, he replied:

'I think it is an abnormal case entirely. The next time somebody might see it a little earlier.'

The findings of the Court of Inquiry comprised seventy-one pages. Essentially, the Court found that the *Titanic* struck the iceberg at a speed of twenty knots. That in less than ten seconds severe damage was done to her bottom extending over a length of about three hundred feet. That the *Titanic* could have remained afloat if they had been able to confine the damage and flooding to her first four compartments. That No.6 boiler-room and to a lesser extent No.5 boiler-room were also open to the sea. That, with all six compartments open to the sea, water rose steadily in all these compartments. That the *Titanic* was a doomed ship and nothing could have saved her.

Unhappily, although those on board gave evidence of the sighting of lights of another vessel, none came to her immediate assistance. She sank with a loss of 1,490 persons including the Captain, Chief Officer and First Officer and all Engineer Officers. As described by Sir Robert Finlay, there was fatality about this sinking that ought readily have been avoided but led so relentlessly to her sinking.

Doubtless, a Court today would find the speed of the *Titanic* in the prevailing circumstances and conditions of ice as excessive if not positively foolhardy. In case of such a finding, the Court would award substantial damages for injury and loss of life. However, in 1912, the crew as employees were entitled to compensation only as prescribed by the Workmen's Compensation Act 1906. Compensation for death was a sum equivalent to three years' earnings but not less than £150 nor more than £300 and for injury something less. The terms of the passenger ticket precluded passengers from making any claim against the ship and her owners. Their only compensation was under such insurances as they might have taken out for the voyage.

The effect on families was traumatic both in the unexpected loss of loved ones and the consequential change in their material circumstances. The Titanic Disaster Fund provided some relief. Yet dependants of the crew faced severe monetary problems as shown by the following two letters written by Hill Dickinson & Co:

'The Secretary, Titanic Disaster Fund.

This man was a storekeeper on the S.S *Titanic*. He leaves a young widow having been married only eighteen weeks. His mother called upon us and asked what we could do for her. We told her that, if she claimed to be interested in the monies payable under the Workmens' Compensation Act, her claim would rank against that of the young widow. The mother replied that she did not want to deprive the widow of any compensation money. The mother is suffering from a bad heart and her doctor had advised her to give up her business. The son had promised to help her if she did so. We told her that we would mention her name to you.'

Solicitors representing a claimant.

'From what you tell us, it appears that the deceased's wife and five children and his mother and sister were dependent on his earnings. If this is so, the mother and sister will participate with the wife and five children in whatever compensation money is payable into Court. The Judge will decide questions of how much each of the mother and sister are entitled. If the mother wishes to participate in the compensation money, please send us her marriage certificate and the birth certificate of the deceased and of his invalid sister.'

The firm received claims by aged parents committed to the workhouse. Also in respect of a fireman's widow committed to the Rainhill lunatic asylum and in respect of his son.

The part played by fate, when it came to deciding life or death, was to repeat itself two years later in the sinking of the *Lusitania* by German submarine attack.

The Titanic strikes the iceberg

"All the News That's Fit to Print."

The New York Times.

VOL. LXI...NO. 19,582.

NEW YORK, TUESDAY, APRIL 16, 1912.—TWENTY-FOUR PAGES.

ONE CENT In Greater New York, Jersey City, and Newark. | TWO CENTS Elsewhere.

THE WEATHER.

Unsettled Tuesday; Wednesday, fair, colder; moderate, southerly winds, becoming variable.

☞ For full weather report see Page 11.

TITANIC SINKS FOUR HOURS AFTER HITTING ICEBERG; 866 RESCUED BY CARPATHIA, PROBABLY 1250 PERISH; ISMAY SAFE, MRS. ASTOR MAYBE, NOTED NAMES MISSING

Col. Astor and Bride, Isidor Straus and Wife, and Maj. Butt Aboard.

"RULE OF SEA" FOLLOWED

Women and Children Put Over in Lifeboats and Are Supposed to be Safe on Carpathia.

PICKED UP AFTER 8 HOURS

Vincent Astor Calls at White Star Office for News of His Father and Leaves Weeping.

FRANKLIN HOPEFUL ALL DAY

Manager of the Line Insisted Titanic Was Unsinkable Even After She Had Gone Down.

HEAD OF THE LINE ABOARD

J. Bruce Ismay Making First Trip on Gigantic Ship That Was to Surpass All Others.

The admission that the Titanic, the biggest steamship in the world, had been sunk by an iceberg and had gone

Biggest Liner Plunges to the Bottom at 2:20 A. M.

RESCUERS THERE TOO LATE

Except to Pick Up the Few Hundreds Who Took to the Lifeboats.

WOMEN AND CHILDREN FIRST

Cunarder Carpathia Rushing to New York with the Survivors.

SEA SEARCH FOR OTHERS

The California Stands By on Chance of Picking Up Other Boats or Rafts.

OLYMPIC SENDS THE NEWS

Only Ship to Flash Wireless Messages to Shore After the Disaster.

LATER REPORT SAYS 866.

BOSTON, April 15.—A wireless message picked up late to-night,

PARTIAL LIST OF THE SAVED.

Includes Bruce Ismay, Mrs. Widener, Mrs. H. B. Harris, and an incomplete list of others, suggesting

Special to The New York Times.

CAPE RACE, N. F., Tuesday, April 16.—Following is a partial list of survivors among the first-class passengers of the Titanic, received by the Marconi wireless station this morning from the Carpathia, via the steamship Olympic:

Mrs. JACOB P.
Mr. HARRY ANDERSON.
Mr. ED. W. APPLETON.
Mrs. ROSE ABBOTT.
Mr. W. E. MINAHAN.
Miss P. P. CASSEBEER.
Mr. WM. M. CLARKE.
Mrs. E. G. CROSBIE.
Miss E. R. G. CROSBIE.
Miss JEAN HIPPACH.
Mrs. HY. H. HARPER.
Mr. ALEX. HALVERSON.
Miss MARGARET HAYS.
Mr. BRUCE ISMAY.
Mr. and Mrs. ED. KIMBERLEY.
Miss EMILIE KENCHEN.
Mr. F. A. KENYMAN.
Mr. P. D. FOGLEY.
Mr. A. F. LEADER.
Miss BERTHA LAVOIT.
Mr. ERNEST LIVER.
Miss MARY LINES.
Mr. SIGRID LINDSTROM.
Mr. GUSTAVE J. LESNEUR.
Mrs. GIORGETTA A. MADILL.
Mrs. MELICARD.
Mrs. TUCKER and maid.
Mr. J. B. THAYER, Jr.
Mr. HENRY WOOLNER.
Miss ANNA WARD.
Mr. RICHARD N. WILLIAMS.
Miss HELEN A. WILSON.
Miss MARY WICK.
Mr. WILLARD.
Mr. GEO. D. WIDENER and maid.
Mr. J. STEWART WHITE.
Miss MARIE YOUNG.
Mr. THOMAS POTTER, Jr.
Mrs. EDNA S. ROBERTA.
Countess of ROTHES

Mr. C. ROLMANE.
Mrs. SUSAN P. ROGERSON. (Probably Ryerson).
Mrs. E. R. ROGERSON.
Master ALLISON and nurse.
Miss N. ANDREWS.
Miss XANETTE PARKHART.
Miss E. W. ALLEN.
Mr. and Mrs. H. BISHOP.
Mr. H. BLANK.
Miss A. BASSINA.
Mrs. JAMES BAXTER.
Mr. GEORGE A. BRAYTON.
Miss C. BONNELL.
Mrs. J. M. BROWN.
Mr. and Mrs. R. L. BECKWITH.
Miss M. C. BOWEN.
Miss ELLA THOHI.
Mr. and Mrs. E. Z. TAYLOR.
Mr. GILBERT M. TUCKER.
Mr. J. B. THAYER.
Mr. and Mrs. H. B. HARRISON.
Mrs. M. ROTHSCHILD.
Mrs. MADELEINE NEWELL.
Mrs. MARJORIE NEWELL.
Miss HELEN W. NEWSOM.
Mr. BEHR.
Mr. K. H. BEHR.
Mr. F. C. OSERE.
Miss HELEN R. OSTBY.
Mrs. BRAHAM.
Miss LUCILLE CARTER.
Mr. WILLIAM CARTER.
Master CARTER.
Miss FLORENCE WARE.
Miss ALICE PHILLIPS.
Mrs. PAULA MUNGE.
Mrs. FANE.
Mr. WILLIAM O.
HOWARD B. CASE.
Miss BENTIKA.

Mrs. WILLIAM BUCKNELL.
Mr. O. M. BARKWORTH.
Miss M. H. B. STEFFASON.
Mrs. ELSIE BOWERMAN.

The Marconi station reports that it missed the word after "Mrs. Jacob P." in a list received by the Associated Press this morning this morning, suggesting that the name of Mrs. John Jacob Astor is included. This supposition is strengthened by the fact that the words "Mrs. L. J. Astor, Astor in the only "Ay" in top "A," column of to-day's passenger list attended by a maid.

NAMES PICKED UP AT BOSTON.

BOSTON, April 16.—Among the names received at the Marconi station by wireless from the steamer Carpathia here to-day were the following:

Mr. and Mrs. L. HENRY,
Mr. A. HOOPER.
Mr. MILK.
Mr. J. FLYNN.
Miss ALICE FORTUNE.
Mrs. ROBERT DOUGLAS.
Mrs. HILDA SLAYTER.
Mr. J. SMITH.

CAPT. E. J. SMITH,
Commander of the Titanic.

Continued on Page 2.

Special to The New York Times.

CAPE RACE, N. F., April 15.—The White Star liner Olympic reports by wireless this evening that the Cunarder Carpathia reached, at daybreak this morning, the position from which wireless calls for help were sent out last night by the Titanic after her collision with an iceberg. The Carpathia found only the lifeboats and the wreckage of what had been the biggest steamship afloat.

The Titanic had foundered at about 2:20 A. M., in latitude 41:46 north and longitude 50:14 west. This is about 30 minutes of latitude, or about 34 miles, due south of the position at which she struck the iceberg. All her boats are accounted for and about 655 souls have been saved of the crew and passengers, most of the latter presumably women and children.

There were about 2,100 persons aboard the Titanic.

The Leyland liner California is remaining and searching the position of the disaster, while the Carpathia is returning to New York with the survivors.

It can be positively stated that up to 11 o'clock to-night nothing whatever had been received at or heard by the Marconi station here to the effect that the Parisian, Virginian or any other ships had picked up any survivors, other than those picked up by the Carpathia.

First News of the Disaster.

The first news of the disaster was received by the Marconi wireless station here at 10:25 o'clock last night [as told in yesterday's New York Times]. The Titanic was first heard giving the distress signal "C. Q. D.," which was answered by a number of ships, including the Carpathia.

The sinking of the Titanic

CHAPTER 11

WAR and LUSITANIA

In 1913, King George V and Queen Mary came to Liverpool to open the Gladstone Dock. The Liverpool Steam Ship Owners Association arranged a marine display in the river Mersey. This comprised more than a hundred vessels forming a ten-mile line. Few clouds were then visible on the international horizon, though the military and naval strengths of Germany had for long caused grave uneasiness in many countries including Great Britain. The following year, hostilities and the Great War burst upon the world with horrific suddenness and probably by accident.

Britain then possessed, in carrying power and speed, the finest merchant fleet the world had ever seen. A fleet created by the individual enterprise of diverse British shipowners. It served not only a great Empire, but carried half the overseas trade of the world. Great Britain was at the very pinnacle of her greatness, and so was Liverpool as the home of the fleet.

The 1913 United Kingdom Register of Shipping shows that fleet to have comprised 8,587 steamers of 100 tons upwards totalling in aggregate 18,893,000 gross tons. It had an estimated book value of £164,500,000 and comprised 41.6 per cent of world tonnage. Inclusion of steamers registered in the overseas dominions and colonies increased that tonnage to 20,524,000 tons or 45.2 per cent of world total. Sail had all but disappeared in overseas trade. Manning of this great fleet gave employment to 292,000 men and boys. They included nearly 47,000 lascars and more than 32,000 foreigners of various nationalities.

Before the war, Sir Norman Hill served on a sub-Committee of the Imperial Defence Committee. Its terms of reference were to devise a scheme of war risk insurance of ships against war losses. At Sir Norman's instigation, the sub-Committee recommended a scheme of war risk insurance brought into effect on the outbreak of war. That scheme visualised shipowners setting up their own mutual associations to insure members' ships against war perils with the Government reinsuring 80 per cent of losses. Thus, shipowners could continue trading knowing that they had fully insured their ships against war losses.

Shipowners instructed Sir Norman Hill to set up the Liverpool and London War Risks Association under the chairmanship of Bruce Ismay of the White Star Line. They appointed Sir Norman as its manager. A committee of shipowners met weekly during the war.

The Minute Book No.2. of the Association covers the first year of the war. An early entry read:

'The Association thanked Maurice Hill QC and Roger Lawrence QC for their prompt and effective help in August 1914 in settling the War Risks Insurance forms. This enabled the Association to bring the Scheme into operation immediately on the outbreak of war with Germany. The Association instructed the Secretary to expend 100 Guineas each in purchasing plate or some other gift to be presented to each of the above named gentlemen.'

Another early entry related to compensation paid under the scheme for a seaman killed or injured by enemy action. That compensation, as decreed by the Government, was £500 for the death of a Master, £400 for a Chief Officer or Chief Engineer and £300 for any other seaman. Compensation for partial disablement was one pound per week. However, if the disablement continued for more than a year, the compensation was one half that payable on death less that already paid in weekly allowance. Even by the monetary values of the day, that was a poor return for the ultimate sacrifice. Subsequently, the Government decreed that the Associations should uplift the scale to the naval scale.

One example of the many minutes of the Association that revealed great personal courage read:

'The Association recorded its high appreciation of the seamanlike skill and courage shown by Captain L.M. Bevan of the S.S. Thesius. He avoided, by successfully manoeuvring his ship, capture by a German submarine off Bishop Rock on the 29th March 1915. He did so, although for three and a half hours the submarine repeatedly fired upon his vessel. The Association resolved that he be voted the sum of 100 Guineas in recognition of his services.'

Many minutes relate to the loss of the *Lusitania*. She was one of the great passenger liners of the day owned by The Cunard Company and sunk by torpedo. The Cunard Company claimed and the Association paid One Million Pounds in respect of her loss. Many entries relate to individual claims for death and injury of the crew.

The Government ordered a formal Inquiry into the loss of the *Lusitania*. A loss then described as the most infamous of the war. Lord Mersey again headed the Court of Inquiry assisted by naval and nautical advisers. Two Kings' Counsel, instructed by Hill Dickinson & Co., appeared for the Cunard Company. Various Counsel appeared for other interested parties. The proceedings continued for five days. The Court examined many witnesses including the Master, First Officer and other surviving members of the crew and some passengers.

Witnesses gave evidence that the *Lusitania* sailed from New York bound for Liverpool on the 1st May 1915. She carried 702 crew and 1,257 passengers. The passengers included 440 women and 129 children of whom 39 were infants. The vessel carried a general cargo as described under the ship's manifest. Part of that cargo comprised five thousand cases of cartridges stowed well forward in the ship on the upper and lower decks.

Before the vessel sailed from New York, the German authorities there published warnings that German submarines would attack the ship and not to take passage in her. Passengers did not take these threats seriously. They did not believe that the German government could seriously contemplate an atrocity, which would cause many civilian deaths including American deaths.

On the 7th May 1915 shortly after 2.00 p.m., the *Lusitania* was going up the Irish Channel. Passengers were at or finishing lunch. At 2.15 p.m., those on the bridge observed a torpedo on the starboard side coming towards the ship. The torpedo struck between the third and fourth funnels.

These witnesses further gave evidence that a second torpedo

struck on the starboard side and that a third torpedo fired from a submarine on the port side missed the ship. Further, that the submarines gave no warning at all nor afforded any opportunity for escape nor rendered assistance after the sinking.

The stricken *Lusitania* listed heavily to starboard. She sank in less than twenty minutes. Lives lost totalled 1,198 of whom 785 were passengers comprising 421 males, 270 females and ninety-four children. This latter category included thirty-five infants out of a total of thirty-nine infants carried. The passengers included 124 Americans.

Like the *Titanic*, the evidence revealed great personal heroism.

Mr. Butler Aspinall QC on behalf of the Cunard stated under his final address to the Court:

'We have it that the first consideration of the officers and the Master was the women and children. What happened? As this great vessel goes down, where do we find the Captain? Where would you expect to find him? On the bridge of his vessel.

'Time is short. The vessel has a list that means, of course, that practically all the boats on the port side are out of action. By some great good luck some of those boats did reach the water. Yet most were damaged in being lowered and rendered useless for saving life. Not only was the time short and half the boats put out of action. The ship had a great list and never lost her headway. Considering the height from which the boats had to be lowered and the difficulty of lowering them with the ship in motion, extremely good work was done in handling them.

'Unfortunately, passengers, actuated by the best of intentions to save the lives of others and their own, took charge of certain boats on the port side with catastrophic results. Bumping against the ship's side damaged those boats that reached the water, so that they were then leaking. Lowering of other boats threw the unhappy passengers and occupants of those boats into the water.

'By way of illustration, I refer to the part played by Leslie Morton. He was a boy aged eighteen. He was thrown into the water. He and another man saw a collapsible boat with its cover on. They ripped off the cover, got in, and succeeded in saving some fifty lives. They put them in a smack. Then, with the help of others, they returned to the wreck and saved more lives. Mr. Jones, the First Officer, in the same way told us that was the sort of thing he did. I have no doubt that many similar deeds, of which we have heard nothing, were in fact done.'

Under the findings of the Court, Lord Mersey singled out Leslie Morton as deserving a special word of commendation:

'He was only eighteen years of age, but he seems to have exhibited great courage, self possession and resource.'

Leslie Morton's evidence read:

'I was an Able Seaman on the *Lusitania*. On Friday 7th May 1915 during the two to four watch, I was an extra lookout on the forecastle head. I had instructions to keep a good lookout for periscopes.

'At ten minutes past two, I looked at my watch. Putting it into my pocket, I glanced round the starboard side. I saw a big burst of foam about five hundred yards away four points on the starboard bow. Immediately after, I saw a thin streak of foam making for the ship at a rapid speed. Then I saw another streak of foam going parallel with the first one and a little behind it. I reported to the bridge: Torpedoes coming on the starboard side. I said to my mate: "They have got us this time."

'It seemed to me that they fired the torpedoes at right angles to the ship's course. About twenty-five to thirty seconds after seeing the streak, the first torpedo struck between numbers two and three funnels. The second one struck just under number three funnel, as far as I could judge from my position forward. The shock knocked me off my feet. The ship gave a continual quiver.

'I picked myself up and made for the forecastle to go down below to call my brother who was asleep at the time. As I was running towards the forecastle, I saw what seemed a conning tower just submerging. It looked like the top portion of a silk hat just going under the water.

'After awakening my brother, I went up on to the port side of the boat deck. I looked at the port boats and saw that they were useless. They were swinging inboard owing to the heavy list. I went to the starboard side to my boat No.13 the emergency boat. I got into my boat and put on my life belt. Next, I knocked off the patent screw and released the boat from the davit falls, so that she was all ready for lowering. Passengers mostly women and children and some men were getting into the boat. When the boat was full and ready for lowering, I went to assist at the next boat No.11 and helped to fill that boat.

'Then I saw my brother in a boat alongside the ship. I went down the davit fall into that boat. The boat filled with people. We pushed the after end off. We called to the passengers to push the forward end off. Some people seemed as if they could not let go. The boat turned over and sank. I swam for it.

'When I got to where I thought far enough away, I turned on my back and looked at the *Lusitania*. She was just going down by the head on the starboard side. The last thing I remember was Captain Turner on the bridge just by the signal halyards. There seemed an explosion as she sank that dislodged No.3. funnel.

'I saw a collapsible boat empty and climbed into it with a sailor named Parry. We ripped off part of the cover and tried to set up the sides. We picked up many people and must have got more than fifty in the boat. We made for a fishing ketch about 5 miles away, landed our passengers and dropped astern of the fishing smack. We took some twenty or thirty people off a lifeboat that was sinking. By this time the minesweeper *Indian Empire* had reached us, and they took us out of the collapsible boat.

'My brother was saved and is in Court.'

The following extracts of the evidence demonstrate the atrocity and the heroism shown. Again fate largely determined those who were to live and those who were to die.

William Thomas Turner - Master.

'I was Master of the *Lusitania* when on a voyage from New York to Liverpool that started on the 1st May 1915. The vessel was unarmed without any weapons at all. When struck, she was about 15 miles out off the Old Head of Kinsale. That is distant 250 miles from Liverpool. My watch showed 2.15. It stopped at 2.36 1/4. The weather was fine and clear and the sea smooth.

'The Second Officer called out: "A torpedo coming, sir." I went across to the starboard side and saw the wake. Immediately afterwards, an explosion occurred and then a second concussion. A large volume of smoke and steam came up on the starboard side between the third and fourth funnels counting from forward. I headed the ship for land.

'I ordered the boats to be lowered down to the rails and to get the women and children in first. The vessel had a lot of way on her, so I told them to hold off lowering the boats until the way was off the ship a bit. I put the engine telegraph to full speed astern without response and concluded that the engines were out of commission. I told Staff Captain Anderson to lower the boats when he thought the way was sufficiently off.

'The vessel had a list of about 15 degrees to starboard. The boats on the port side caught on the rail and capsized some people out. Other boats on that side were let go on the run. Some of them fell inboard on the decks and hurt some passengers.

'About eighteen minutes elapsed from the time the torpedo struck until the vessel sank. My watch stopped at 2.36 1/4. I remained on the bridge until she went down under me. It seemed a long time that I was in the water. I was picked up by one of the ship's boats. They transferred me to the trawler *Bluebell* and landed me at Queenstown. I am very sorry to say that Captain Anderson was lost.'

Hugh Robert Johnson - Quartermaster

'I was at the wheel when the *Lusitania* was torpedoed. The vessel took a list of 15 degrees to starboard. She stopped at 15 degrees for just a couple of minutes. Then she started to go further over. I sang out what she was doing - 20 and 25. When I sang out that she had 25 degrees of list, the Captain told me to save myself.

'I got a life buoy that was in the starboard wing of the bridge. As I put on the life buoy, the water had come up to the bridge and the starboard side was well under. The Captain was on the port side of the bridge that is the high up side. I simply had to go wherever the tide took me and was washed right across the ship.

'Eventually, through a bit of luck, I was swept among some wreckage some of which was a boat turned upside down. I managed to get on it and was picked up by a trawler.'

Andrew Cockburn - Senior Second Engineer.

'After seeing that the watertight doors were closed, I put on a life belt and went back to the engine-room. I found the Chief Engineer and the Second Engineer who were on watch at the time. All steam had gone and everything was stopped in the engine room. The place was in darkness. I could hear water flooding into the ship. The boat was listing heavily to starboard. Absolutely nothing could be done.

'I went on deck. The ship appeared to be sinking. I got to the rail and took hold of the netting on the ship's side and went down with her. I got on to an upturned boat and was saved.'

Robert Leith - Wireless Telegraphist

'I felt some shock or other. I thought it was a boiler explosion and went immediately to the wireless cabin. The other operator, McCormick, was there. I sent out an S.O.S. followed by ..... Come at once big list and gave the position ..... A wireless coast station immediately acknowledged the signal. I repeated the message practically continuously. We sent the messages by ship's power until that gave out and then by the emergency power supply in the wireless cabin.

'I remained in the cabin as long as it was possible until just a few moments before the ship sank. I jumped from the ship into a boat that was full of water. I have no recollection from where I jumped. Three or four people were in the boat. The ship's funnel appeared to be coming down on the top of me. I sprang from that boat to another one.'

Arthur Roland Jones - First Officer

'At the time of the disaster, I was in the first class dining saloon and heard an explosion. I got up and went on deck and got to my boat about four minutes after the explosion. The vessel then had a list of between 30 and 35 degrees. I could not stand on the deck and had to hang on to the rail. I put about sixty-five into No.13 boat and got her away safely. Then I put over eighty into No.15 boat and got her safely into the water. I went down the fall into that boat. A matter of fifteen seconds later, the ship went down. She started with her head to starboard and then went down by the head.

'After the ship had sunk from under us, the Marconi aerial wire came down across the top of our boat and very nearly took us down with it. The boat was in very disturbed water for two or three minutes. We were in very great danger.

'I observed a boat that appeared to me to have two or three people in it. How it got adrift like that, I do not know. When we got out of this terribly disturbed water in safety, I immediately ran forward of my boat's head for that empty boat. When I reached her, I gave the boatswain's mate (a seaman) and the assistant purser and about ten stewards orders to form a boat's crew. I counted out about thirty passengers also and put them into this other boat. I directed the boat to go back to the wreck to save more lives. I took my own boat back too and picked up quite a number into my boat. Fewer than I had before, but I filled her with fifty-five or fifty-six.

'I pulled off then to the *Bluebell*, a little fishing smack about 5 miles in the offing. I put the passengers on the *Bluebell* and made to go back to the wreck. About halfway back, we met with a broken collapsible boat in a bad condition with about thirty-five inside it. Some of these people were lying exhausted in the bottom of the boat and some were injured, so I took them all on board my boat. Shortly afterwards, the trawler *Indian Empire* came along and stopped. I put all the injured people aboard her. Then she took me in tow. I remained in the boat until we reached the last scene of the wreck.

'I pulled off then and think we saved about ten more people. At least, we pulled them out of the water. Two of them died before I could get them ashore. Others were in a very weak state. We put these people on a Queenstown tender, *Flying Fox*. It was then about eight o'clock. We were really exhausted without food and water and could do no more. A number of cruisers and destroyers and patrol boats were then on the scene. They had handy little boats, whereas my big boat takes some pulling. We got on board the *Flying Fox* and reached Queenstown about eleven o'clock.'

Mr. John Freeman - Passenger
'I and my wife were sitting on the promenade deck looking at the coast of Ireland, when the explosion occurred. It was in front near the first funnel. I said to my wife That is a mine thinking we were running on to a mine. I did not think that they would torpedo us without any warning. We stood looking. Immediately a second explosion occurred followed by hot water and steam and it seemed cinders as well. The second explosion took place near to the first one.

'My wife suffers very much from the cold, and I thought it useless to get a life belt for her as our berth was in the lower deck. We had already arranged that in an emergency we would make immediately for the promenade deck and the boats. People were going to the port side. I said to my wife: We will go the other way. We lost our footing and slid down the side of the vessel. We got to our feet. However, the list was so great that we fell down again. I held on to the railing and supported my wife. I got her into a lifeboat that some sailors were preparing to lower. No great crowd was getting into the lifeboat then, so that I thought she would be all right.

'Next, I went to collect a life jacket for myself. I went back to the second class part of the vessel. I found no panic whatever. People were just standing there, and I saw a young man and young women with no life jackets. I went to E deck. It was in darkness except a little light through port holes. I managed to find a life belt and went back to the promenade deck. I had got some life jackets and given them to one or two people. I went to see how my wife's boat was getting on. She was saved.

'I returned to the stern of the vessel and saw that the vessel was sinking rapidly. I jumped overboard just before she went under. Then I saw two collapsible boats caught together one on top of the

214

other and swam towards them. I obtained some help in separating them and pulled about a dozen people from the wreckage on to one or other of the boats. It was about three hours before I was picked up.'

Mrs. Mabel Rate Leigh Royd - Passenger

'I was in my cabin lying down after lunch when I heard a crash. My husband and I had no doubt what had happened. I gathered a few things together, which took two or three minutes. I then went up with my husband on deck. When we reached the top deck, we realised that we had come without our life belts. We returned for them. On our return to the deck, the staircase was very difficult to ascend as the list was becoming more marked. Mounting the staircase was so difficult that we thought as we took three steps we might fall back four. A steward helped by pushing us up on to the top deck. I should like to say that I think their behaviour was most excellent and self sacrificing. That applies to stewards and stewardesses.

'The list was so strong that we could not walk down the deck. We had to sort of rush down clinging to the railing that at the time was nearly under water. We sort of tumbled into the boat assisted by passengers and seamen. No sooner had we got into the boat than it was lowered with another boat on top of us and a broken funnel falling. The upper boat actually struck our boat and turned our boat over. We went down under the water. I had a life belt on and was underneath for a few seconds. Then I came to the surface.

'I thought I was in the water about a quarter of an hour or twenty minutes when I was picked up by some stewards who were on an upturned boat. I asked them to look round to see if they could possibly see my husband in the water as I had only been a few minutes in the water. One replied: "Oh, I think you have been longer than that as it is now by my watch after three o'clock, and the ship went down a quarter past two."

'I never saw my husband again.'

Frederick Tootal - First Class Passenger:

'I was talking to a lady who was waiting for the lift and another gentleman who was travelling with me when a loud explosion took place. We both took the lady by the arm and started going up the stairs. We got on to the next deck, the C deck, on the port side. Then we went aft with her to the companionway leading up to the boat deck where a big crowd had collected. They were taking the women and children first, so we left the lady there.

'We went up to the boat deck on the starboard side aft. There we found a boat quite empty swung out from the ship's side about five feet, and my friend and I jumped in. We could just reach the hands of the people on deck. We helped many women into the boat. They started to lower us, when other people jumped in. The man who was looking after the four davit ropes could not control them. The boat was tilted forward and threw us into the water. When I came up, I saw another boat about 30 yards away. I swam towards it and they took me in. Afterwards, I was picked up by a trawler.'

Miss Alice Lines - Passenger:
'I was a nurse on board to the children of Major Warner Farrell. When the torpedo struck, I was on E deck. I rushed for the baby and boy and took them up on A deck as quick as possible. I had difficulty in standing and was thrown inwards with a hill to climb to get into the lifeboat. The baby was in my arms and the little boy of five hanging to my skirt. I got them into the boat on the port side. We went down in the boat quite easily, but it was rather difficult to get away. I and both the children were all right except a few bruises.'

It appears that this was the only boat to get safely away from the port side.

Francis Bertram Jenkins - First Class Passenger:
'When the torpedo struck, I was at luncheon in the first class saloon with a Mrs. Crichton. I took her and another young lady to a boat on the port side. Having got Mrs. Crichton partly into the boat, I was standing one foot on the deck of the *Lusitania* and the other foot on the boat. A rope broke and the boat went into the water. I

seemed to go down a long way. When I came up, I was under the boat. It was bottom upwards.

'I saw an open port hole about 2 feet above me and clutched it but could not hold on. Then I saw a rope hanging down and got hold of it. Some twenty others took hold. We seemed to be sinking and some could not swim. I let go and seeing a champagne case swam for it, but let go and swam for an oar. I then saw a long piece of wood some distance ahead of me to which I swam and reached it in an exhausted condition. Ultimately, I was picked up about four o'clock and must have been unconscious some two hours. I was picked up by a lifeboat in which were some eighty other passengers. Mrs. Crichton was unfortunately drowned.'

Lord Mersey specifically mentions one other witness. The relevant extract of his report read:

'One witness described himself as a French subject from the vicinity of Switzerland. At the time of the explosion, he was in the second class dining room in the after part of the ship. He stated that the nature of the explosion was similar to the rattling of a Maxim gun for a short period. He suggested that this noise revealed the secret existence of some ammunition. The sound he said came from underneath the whole floor.

'I did not believe this gentleman. His demeanour was very unsatisfactory. His story was not confirmed. He had threatened the Cunard Company that, if they did not pay him some immediate compensation, he would have the unpleasant duty of making his claim in public. Further, in that event, he would be producing evidence, which will not be to the credit either of your Company or of the Admiralty. The Company had not complied with his request. Leith, the Marconi operator, was also in the second class dining room at the time of the explosion. He speaks of but one explosion. I do not believe that an explosion occurred in any part of the cargo.'

The essential findings of the Court, which Lord Mersey gave after the hearing the evidence were thus:

'At 2.15 p.m. on the 7th May 1915, the *Lusitania* was ten to fifteen miles off Old Head of Kinsale. A torpedo struck her on the starboard side between the third and fourth funnels. The weather was clear and the sea smooth. The blow broke No.5. lifeboat to splinters. A second torpedo, fired immediately afterwards, also struck the ship on the starboard side almost simultaneously.

'A German submarine fired both these torpedoes from distances variously estimated at from 200 to 500 yards. They gave no warning. It is also in evidence that another submarine shortly afterwards fired a torpedo on the port side of the *Lusitania*. This torpedo did not strike the ship. I mention the circumstance only to show that more than one submarine was taking part in the attack.

'The Captain was on the bridge at the time his ship was struck. He remained there giving orders until the ship foundered. His first order was to lower all boats to the rail. They obeyed this order as far as it possibly could be. He then called out: "Women and children first."

'Leith, the Marconi operator, immediately sent out an S.O.S. signal and later another message: Come at once, big list, 10 miles south Head Old Kinsale. He repeated these messages continuously, which were acknowledged.

'Some witnesses made complaints about the manner in which the crew launched the boats and about their leaky condition when in the water. I do not question the good faith of these witnesses, but I think their complaints were ill founded.

'Three difficulties presented themselves about the launching of the boats. First, time was very short and only twenty minutes elapsed between the first alarm and the sinking of the ship. Secondly, the ship was underway the whole time with the engines put out of commission almost at once, so that they could not take off the way. Thirdly, the ship instantly took a great list to starboard. This made it impossible to launch the port side boats properly and rendered it very difficult for the passengers to get into the starboard boats. The list threw the port side boats inboard and the starboard boats inconveniently far outboard.

'Besides these difficulties, the frightened passengers made well meaning but probably disastrous attempts to help in the launching operations. These passengers attempted to push some boats on the port side off the ship and to get them to the water.

'Some of these boats caught on the rail and capsized. One or two did reach the water, but the evidence shows that they became seriously damaged in the operation. They were lowered a distance of 60 feet or more with people in them. They must have been fouling the side of the ship the whole time. In one case the stern post was wrenched away. The result was that these boats leaked when they reached the water. Captain Anderson was superintending the launching operations and did the best that could be done in the circumstances. Many boats were lowered on the starboard side, and no factual evidence showed that any of them leaked.

'The *Lusitania* sank in less than twenty minutes after being struck with the loss by drowning of 1,098 men, women and children.

'Sir Edward Carson (the Attorney General) in opening the case described the German Government as acting contrary to international law and the usages of war. Further, that their action was a deliberate attempt to murder the passengers. This statement is I think true and made it in language not too strong for the occasion. The defenceless creatures on board, made up of harmless men and women and of helpless children, were done to death by the crew of the German submarine. They, in turn, were acting under the direction of the officials of the German Government.

'In the question submitted by the Board of Trade, they ask me: What was the cause of the loss of life? The answer is plain. The effective cause of the loss of life was the attack made against the ship by those on board the submarine. It was a murderous attack because made with a deliberate and wholly unjustifiable intention of killing the people on board. German authorities on the laws of war at sea establish beyond all doubt that sometimes the destruction of an enemy trader may be permissible. Further, that is subject always to the obligation first to secure the safety of the lives of those on board.

'The German Government has said that the *Lusitania* was a vessel equipped with masked guns and supplied with trained gunners with special ammunition. Further, that she was transporting Canadian troops and was violating the laws of the United States. These statements are untrue. They are nothing but baseless inventions. They serve only to condemn the persons who use them. The steamer carried no masked guns nor trained gunners nor special ammunition. Nor was she transporting troops or violating any laws of the United States.

'At the request of the Attorney General and in the public interest, we took part of the evidence in the Inquiry in camera. This concerned advice given by the Admiralty for avoiding submarine attacks. In some respects, Captain Turner did not follow the advice given to him. Some may think (though I seriously doubt it) that had he done so, his ship would have reached Liverpool in safety. After seeking the guidance of my Assessors, I conclude that we should not blame Captain Turner.

'The advice was for his most serious and careful consideration, but not intended to deprive him of the right to exercise his skilled judgment in the navigation of his ship. That he did for the best.'

The advice given by the Admiralty, considered in camera, was to steer a mid channel and a zig zag course. The submarine's slow speed would then much reduce the risk of a torpedo striking the vessel. In fact, the ship was struck when taking a fix off Kinsale for which purpose she was no longer continuing her zig zag course.

Britain and America denounced the sinking of the *Lusitania* as a bestial criminal act. It played a part in ultimately bringing the USA into the war.

Writers and historians have subsequently referred to the evidence and log of one German submarine apparently involved. This stated that the submarine fired only one torpedo, which struck the liner on the starboard side between the third and fourth funnels. These writers further refer to German allegations that the *Lusitania* was carrying contraband. Namely shells and other munitions of war that exploded and caused the vessel to sink so rapidly.

Cunard's own history refers to the torpedo striking the liner amidships on her starboard side followed by a second explosion inside the hull forward of the first funnel. That second explosion

The Lusitania. Taking to the lifeboats

The sinking of the Lusitania. May 7th 1915

resulted in the destruction of the watertight bulkheads allowing thousands of tons of water to flood into the vessel. The history adds that this second explosion remains a matter for conjecture.

If living today, Lord Mersey would need carefully to consider this later evidence from the submarine of only one torpedo. If he accepted that evidence, then he would need further to consider how such substantial damage was done to the *Lusitania* and her bulkheads to cause such rapid sinking.

It seems inconceivable that the *Lusitania* was carrying contraband without the knowledge of the USA Authorities, her master and officers, and, especially, her Owners. For her to have done so knowingly would have been illegal under USA law and would have avoided the ticket and transit conditions and her insurance and limits of liability. Thus, it is unthinkable that the Owners would have agreed to carry contraband without first having obtained special indemnities from the Government under the advice of Sir Norman Hill. No evidence exists that they did so.

The sinking of the *Lusitania* effectively ended any pretence of chivalrous conduct between the combatants at sea. This is not surprising having regard to the carnage that was taking place under the appalling conditions of trench warfare and the hatred thus created between the combatants. By 1917, the Germans had introduced unrestricted submarine warfare coupled with the command Sink without trace intending to starve Britain into submission.

Britain needed to give top priority to combatting this submarine menace. Surprisingly, in circumstances of the great ship building capacity of the country, no protective force of fast light ships was available. Instead, measures taken included dummy battle ships floating at sea to confuse the enemy. Q ships or naval vessels disguised as cargo ships and often sailing under foreign colours that sought to entrap and sink German submarines. British merchant ships, armed and often flying the American or other foreign flag, ready to fire upon and sink the enemy.

At the time, Sir Norman Hill, as Secretary of the Liverpool Steamship Owners Association, was advocating his ideas for a convoy system. At his suggestion, the Association set up a Convoy

Committee to classify members' vessels voyaging in the Atlantic according to speed and cargo capacity. The intention was to form groups of ships able to retain their position in convoy voyage after voyage.

In June 1917, the Association published a resolution sent to the Prime Minister and other members of the Government and to local Members of Parliament:

'expressing our grave concern at the very serious and continuing losses of ocean going steamships. They take place in areas where, during the voyage, vessels become concentrated under the direction of the Admiralty, but where the Admiralty provides no adequate protection.'

The history of the Association records:

'Shortly after passing of this resolution, the Admiralty adopted the convoy system. Its introduction was, in fact, very largely brought about by the Association. Yet it had first to overcome considerable opposition from the Admiralty based on doubts as to its ability to operate the system. Once that system came into existence, the outcome quickly proved its value. .....The convoy system in 1917 proved the turning point in the most intensive and dangerous assault this country has so far had to meet in its history as a maritime power.'

Thus, the convoy system originated in the mind of Sir Norman Hill. Coupled with appropriate naval protection that system played a large part in combatting the submarine menace of the two world wars and in each contributed to ultimate victory.

Another important role played by Sir Norman Hill in war torn Britain was that of Chairman of the Port and Transit Executive Committee. The war time Government vested the Committee with wide powers over all questions relating to flow of traffic through the ports of the country. The Government asked Sir Norman Hill to provide an estimate of the probable deficiency in available shipping for the year 1917. That report was so alarming that the Government immediately appointed a Committee under Lord Curzon to report on the whole question of imports.

The result was a prohibition or severe restriction on the import of luxury and non essential goods into the country that saved imports of nearly six million tons a year. That saving allowed for the forecast heavy decline in carrying space without reducing essential imports. Sir Norman Hill had been urging the Government to adopt that restriction since 1915 as the most effective means of ensuring essential supplies. Remarkably, the Government allowed those non essential imports to continue so late into the war.

Thus, during the Great War, Sir Norman Hill played an essential part in securing sufficient merchant shipping to overcome the extreme peril then facing the nation. His brother, then the highly reputed physiologist Professor Leonard Hill, played an equal part in the war effort. He served on a number of Government committees and was a member of the Army and Navy Medical Advisory Boards and the then Medical Administrative Committee of the Air Board.

He was especially concerned with the health of the nation and its munition workers and the diet of the population generally. When the Government first introduced food rationing, he advised that they should ration meat and not bread. They accepted that advice, and bread remained freely available.

The Government also consulted Leonard Hill about the ventilation of the dugouts constructed in the front line trenches and the medical aspects of gas warfare. This required that he visited the battle area in France. During this period, he suffered a second attack of respiratory tuberculosis. Most likely caused by his poison gas researches, when he may have breathed in a little poison gas. Again, he spent quite a long time recuperating during which he worked and sketched at West Bay in Dorset and at home in Loughton.

On resuming work and following the war, Leonard Hill developed the kata thermometer to help him measure the influence of temperature, humidity and air movement on human comfort, health and work capacity. This instrument was a simple alcoholic thermometer. Immersion in hot water drove the alcohol in the bulb up the stem on which he marked 100 and 95 degrees Fahrenheit. The mean of these temperatures corresponded to man's body temperature. He recorded by stop watch the time taken to fall between these two figures under differing environmental conditions.

By these simple means, he sought to obtain the cooling power of the environment from convection, radiation and evaporation in a single figure. The interpretation of that figure for purposes of human comfort required many observations in real life outside the laboratory in homes, schools, factories and offices. Those observations were subsequently set out in Leonard Hill's great work *The Science of Ventilation and Open Air Treatment* published by the Medical Research Council in 1923.

That work dealt with the physical and chemical characteristics of the atmosphere and their influences on the respiratory membrane and thus on such diseases as the common cold. He discussed the effects upon man of sunlight and open air as opposed to the smoke pollution of cities. Further, he discussed the deleterious effects of inadequate ventilation and stagnant heating of dwellings and workrooms and the overclothing, overeating and under exercising of their inmates.

In his words:

'Our modern populations have purer water and more food. They are clothed better and are much less drunken than a generation ago. Yet the ventilation of their workplaces and homes is very little better and, perhaps, in some respects, is worse than it used to be. Under the conditions of natural life, man is blown upon by every wind and wet with every shower. The heating and ventilating engineers have aimed at giving us in our buildings a uniform summer temperature unchanged by wind or calm, warm sunshine, or cool shadow of the clouds.'

His thesis was that the ideal method of warming and ventilating rooms was by radiant heat, a warm floor, and an agreeable movement of cool air. In short, they should provide the conditions of a sunny spring day out of doors. He emphasised the benefit to national health that would result from proper ventilation indoors, the prevention of smoke pollution, and, more generally, from an open air life and proper food.

He wrote:

'It is manifest that draughts acutely affect some people and therefor draught is popularly considered the chief cause of colds. Nursery and family tradition rules habit, and tradition is usually at

224

least half a century behind science. The room is shut up. Science may beat against the door, but tradition holds it fast.'

Throughout his life, Leonard practised what he preached. For many years, all the year round, he would arise at six in the morning and bicycle two or three miles through Epping Forest to bathe in a forest pool. He was a vigorous walker in any kind of weather, which he continued to the end of his life.

CHAPTER 12

BETWEEN THE WARS.

The Great War ended suddenly in November 1918. By then much of the flower of British manhood had perished in the fields of Flanders. Few families had not lost a husband and a father or a son or both. Great sadness and tragedy prevailed throughout the land. Men had returned from the trenches determined that this had been the war to end all wars. They sought a life of security for all. Yet, little had changed in post war Britain.

Many returning from the war faced problems in obtaining employment as illustrated in the following reply of Sir Norman Hill to Mrs. Leyland. In explanation, she was seeking on behalf of her husband, Geoffrey, a capital payment out of family trusts established by the shipowner, Freddie Leyland.

'I quite agree that Geoff must get regular and constant employment. Yet, apart from poultry farming, he has had no training. I do not know what employment is open to him. Tens of thousands of men are coming back from the Army and seeking employment that requires no special training. In competition with these men, I do not think that Geoff would have any chance. As to yourself, you must remember that a very great deal of the work that has been open to women during the war is no longer obtainable. Very fierce competition will apply to all the posts left. I do not know your plans. Still, you must bear in mind that it will be as difficult for you to obtain paid employment as it will be for Geoff to earn a salary.'

Solicitors had established a national War Memorial Fund to help those returning who wished to enter the profession. They appointed Sir Norman as chairman.

A typical advice to the secretary read:

'As far as I can judge, the case is one in which we should give help. I am inclined to think that, if it were possible, the best chance for Mr. Leak would be to get him into the office of Mr. Bracewell at Barnoldswick. If this is not possible, then I think the best course would be to give him a couple of years training in a country conveyancing office. During that time, he can get through the examinations. You will note that Mr. Leak is almost at the end of his resources. I would suggest that we give him some immediate help while we are making arrangements.'

Sir Norman was also advising those wishing to follow a career at sea that they should seek a place on the training ship *Conway*.

Nevertheless, he continued:

'I know they have been very full, and you may have to wait. If you cannot get into the *Conway*, then I think you should seek appointment as an apprentice in one of the Lines. Here again most of the Lines have long waiting lists, and you may be kept waiting.'

Thus, men returning from the war and their families were finding life very difficult without gainful employment. Social security and grants did not then exist nor did any general provision of health or care by the State. Those in need could only look to charity for help.

In that regard, Sir Norman played a leading part in the provision by charitable donation of the War Memorial Cottage Hospital at Neston Wirral where he lived.

The Hospital appointed him a trustee in which capacity he wrote:

'The hospital will accommodate twelve patients. It will provide one private ward for which it will make a charge of three guineas a week. The hospital will expect the other patients to contribute up to say ten shillings a week according to their means. Nevertheless, it will need to treat a number without charge.

'Besides treating ordinary cases, we are arranging for massage treatment for men injured in the war. The Ministry of Pensions will pay us for providing this treatment. On the best estimates, we shall have at the start to provide about twenty treatments a week.

'A paid matron with Red Cross volunteer help as nurses will run the hospital at the start. The hospital will employ two servants in the house, and an outdoor man two or three days a week. Patients will pay the doctors' fees, if any, and each doctor will be entitled to attend his own patients. The Medical Officer of the hospital will act as a volunteer. We are budgeting on the keep of the staff and on the patients costing about fifteen shillings a week. We anticipate our total expenditure including salaries, coal, petrol, rates, taxes, etc. amounting to about £800 a year.'

Sir Norman was also a trustee of a charitable home for feeble minded (mentally deficient) girls. His wife Mary was chairman of the committee of management.

Sir Norman wrote to the general manager of Cunard:

'My wife is Chairman of the Management Committee of Ashton House Parkgate for feeble minded girls. The girls, who are generally twenty in number, contribute to their own support by working in a Laundry attached to the Home. Recently, the Trust has purchased a house at Oxton and is to move the Home there. The Committee are wishful to get expert advice as to the equipment of the Laundry in the new Home. Funds are limited but, to the extent that they will serve, the Committee want to introduce in the new Home appliances that will lighten the work of the girls. Further, they want to make the new Home as far as possible self supporting from the work, provided they do not overburden the girls. The Committee seek expert opinion as to the best way of equipping and running the Laundry in the new Home. Would it be possible for the officials of the Cunard Laundry to advise?'

Besides his charitable activities, Sir Norman participated in many local activities. He was always ready to help local people with their problems particularly with officialdom.

Thus, he wrote to the Military Service Civil Liabilities Department that was responsible for making grants to returning servicemen for damage done to their property while away on active service:

'My neighbour, T. Robinson of Swifts Cottages, Parkgate, Cheshire has shown me your answer to his request for help. That is in repairing the damage done to his fishing boats, nets and sails whilst he was on active service. Robinson is a hard working man with a wife and six children. He tells me that the military granted him leave to look after his boat the *Catherine* that storms had damaged. Yet, without money Robinson has never been able really

228

to recondition the boat.

'If, as I understand, the Department has rejected the claim merely because he put it in out of date, I would venture to ask for further consideration. Robinson has great difficulty both in understanding written instructions and stating his case. If the Department has rejected the claim for want of satisfactory evidence, then I shall be ready to have full detailed documents prepared and submit them to you.'

Subsequent correspondence reveals that his intervention was successful.

He also wrote to the Ministry of Fisheries following refusal to grant a salmon fishing licence:

'The Dee Fisheries have granted William Fewtrell, a regular fisherman working from Parkgate, a Salmon Draught Net Licence on and off over the last twenty-five years. He has applied for the licence in those years in which the Deep is on the Wirral side of the river. This year, on his application, the Clerk to Dee Fisheries has told him that he is too late and that they have granted all licences. Yet, they displayed no notice at Parkgate as to allotment of licences and, in the result, have granted no licences this year to Parkgate fishermen. The case is a hard one. Fewtrell's son served in the Navy, and he invested all his savings in nets and gear for the Salmon fishing before they applied. The withholding of the Licence means the savings all being wasted. Fewtrell has been a fisherman at Parkgate all his life. He is a steady working man with a wife and a big family of young children.

'As I understand the Order, it is a condition precedent to the selection of applicants for the Licences that the Fishery Board shall publish due notice. I submit that they have given no such notice to the Parkgate Fishermen. In the circumstances, I submit that the case is one in which the Parkgate Fishermen are entitled to appeal to your Ministry for protection of their rights. In particular, I, on their behalf, ask that Dee Fisheries may forthwith grant a Licence to William Fewtrell.'

Again the intervention of Sir Norman proved successful, and they granted a licence. Today, Parkgate is no longer a fishing village, but a pleasant suburban village serving Liverpool and Birkenhead as a dormitory.

Sir Norman was much interested in education and self education of the day. He arranged for the tutoring of his own son, Gray, largely at home.

He expressed his views on the law examinations of the day thus:

'I regard as folly the setting of examination papers which students are unable to answer, although they have diligently followed the work of the office supplemented by reading and lectures. I regard the coach as a parasite brought into existence by the forms of questions that are now put at both the Intermediate and Final Examinations.'

In 1919, King George V conferred a baronetcy upon Sir Norman Hill for services to his country and, especially, to shipping before and during the 1914-18 war.

However, those services had taken their toll as shown in a letter of the 24th November 1919 addressed to Sir Norman by the then Prime Minister, David Lloyd George:

'I duly received your letter of the 6th inst. asking to be relieved from your duties on the Port and Transit Executive Committee. Reports have been submitted to me from time to time of the excellent work that you have done. While I feel, under the circumstances, I must accept your resignation. Yet, I desire to put on record my sincere appreciation of your great services to the State during a prolonged period that required from you constant and exacting labour. I trust that your proposed holiday may restore you to a full measure of health and strength.'

During 1919, Sir Norman, as Chairman of the Liverpool Law Society, proposed a revision in the manner in which they calculated solicitors' fees. He proposed that such fees be commensurate with the nature and value of the work done and in his words:

'In place of priced and artificial items on the 6/8d basis contained under a detailed bill as presently required by the Solicitors Act 1843. This magnifies the importance of the manner in which

230

the work is done. It thus offers a premium to the practice of red tape and routine and exposes the profession to ridicule and distrust. The doctor no longer covers his fees in the price at which he sells bottles of medicine. The surgeon most certainly does not charge for the length of time he takes over the operation. Architects, Auctioneers and Stockbrokers have their scales based on values and not on time occupied.'

Sir Norman was not successful in his efforts. Nor has the basic premise altered much over intervening years. Emphasis is still placed on hourly time sheets and the volume of letters and documents resulting in ever more paperwork.

Sir Norman was Chairman of the Liverpool Committee of the Russian Famine Fund. He urged the Fund that they must satisfy Liverpool both of the urgent need for assistance and that the Fund would only use that assistance to support those in need.

Later, he wrote:

'We are clear that Great Britain, with or without the help of other nations, must help in re-establishing the economic position of Russia. However, we have grave doubts whether the granting of credits to the existing Russian Government would help towards bringing this about. Probably, it would embarrass the Prime Minister if the businessmen in this country took the opportunity for emphasising that the nation should not give credits to the existing Russian Government. He could more conveniently deal with that issue by carrying his point and getting the whole question referred to an expert committee sitting at the Hague.'

As earlier described, Sir Norman Hill was an acknowledged expert in maritime law. Following the war, he played a leading part in the formulation of the Hague Rules. Namely, a set of rules adopted by international convention at the Hague in 1923 to regulate the contractual terms of carriage of goods by sea.

Nations party to the convention agreed to apply the Rules compulsorily to all outward bills of lading from their ports that acknowledged goods for carriage overseas. The Rules replaced many differing terms of carriage that had previously absolved the shipowner from responsibility for damage done to the goods during their carriage. The Carriage of Goods by Sea Act 1924 gave the Rules legislative effect in the United Kingdom.

Sir Norman Hill, having played his part in formulating the Rules, pleaded that lawyers of all nations interpret them as traders and shipowners everywhere understood them.

Yet the eminent commercial lawyers, Lord Justice Scrutton and Mr. Justice MacKinnon, vehemently attacked that plea, which they described as a terrifying prospect and continued:

'How are English judges and lawyers charged with administering English statute and common law to ascertain how the traders and shipowners of all nations understand an English Act of Parliament?'

Subsequently, Sir Norman replied to that question under a foreword to Hodgesons Carriage of Goods by Sea Act. This followed a House of Lords judgment in the Ixia that gave effect to his own thinking.

His reply read thus:

'In the past seven years, English judges and lawyers have devoted time and energy to bringing the Rules into conformity with English statute and common law. Yet the aim and object of the Act were to make effective an international convention for the unification of certain rules relating to Bills of Lading. Rules intended to bring certainty and uniformity to Bills of Lading in clear and unambiguous terms and to confer clearly defined rights upon every holder of the bill of lading.

'It was on that footing that the Liverpool Steam Ship Owners Association welcomed the Rules in 1923. The judgments now given in the House of Lords in the Ixia case emphasise that is how the Courts will interpret the Act of 1924. They will not interpret it as an attempt to codify English law. Can the responsibility of thus interpreting the Act really present a terrifying prospect to even the most timid of English judges?'

Such insular and narrow treatment by these earlier eminent commercial judges will surprise modern day marine lawyers. Particularly, now that the Hague Rules and their modern equivalent, the Visby Rules, largely receive universal adoption and interpretation.

232

Following the death of John Gray Hill in 1914, his widow, Caroline Emily (Carrie), during and after the war, had continued to reside at Mere Hall. Of course, the war had precluded any travels on her part and, especially, to her beloved Jerusalem and to her second home on the Mount of Olives.

Writing in reply to congratulations that she had received from an old friend, Mr. Benas, concerning the baronetcy awarded to Sir Norman, she described her later years thus:

'Norman cares little for honours but we of his kindred do, and dear Sir John would have been so proud. It is nice to know you understand what he has given up here and done for his country. I have had much neuritis of late owing to servant worries. This I believe due to the unrest of the world, but they take up too much of one's time and strength when I have less to give.

'However, I have had many orders for pictures from strangers in Durban all so longing for a sight of Syria. So I have been a bit happy with doing these. Altogether fifty have gone, and now ten more are sent for. I seem to get far away from this place when I am painting, and it brings back the happiest part of my life. Yet, it is sad when alone and without dear Sir John's constant love and sympathy.'

During the war, the Turks allied to the Germans had occupied Caroline's Mount Olive home. In March 1918, she received news in a letter (now at Bruce Castle, Tottenham) from General Allenby of the Egyptian Expeditionary Force:

'I have investigated the condition of your house upon Mount Scopus. As soon as possible after the troops entered Jerusalem, the General Officer in command of the 60th Division examined the house. He saw no sign of the two sealed rooms to which you refer. Doubtless, they were broken into by the Turks and the furniture looted or destroyed.

'Walls have suffered in three or four places by gun fire. The floors and ceilings are sound and, without doubt, the building is structurally solid though, unfortunately, little more than a shell. The gardens are overgrown and not cared for and the pergolas have lost their wooden cross beams. British troops have occupied the buildings

233

until recently, but they are now vacant. I am therefore arranging that they shall lock the outer doors and make a periodical inspection.'

After the ending of the war, the Zionist Organisation offered to purchase both the house and the outlying land for fifteen thousand pounds. They wanted it for building the Zionist University of Jerusalem. The offer was acceptable to Caroline on terms that she might retain a life interest in her Jerusalem home.

Subsequently, in May 1920, Sir Norman wrote to those representing the Zionist Organisation:

'On the sale, I reserved Lady Hill's life interest hoping that it would be a consolation to her that she could go back to live in the house anytime. Though I was doubtful whether she would ever avail herself of this right. The fact that we have sold the outlying land to the Zionist Organisation has led to Lady Hill receiving letters and protests and offers. Thus, the property is proving a cause of worry and not of consolation. In the circumstances, I am prepared to advise Lady Hill to concur in the surrender of the life interest, provided the Zionist Organisation now pays the full purchase price.'

On 3rd July 1920, Sir Norman completed the sale of all the Jerusalem property. Four years later, Caroline was dead. She was born at a time when the railway was expanding as the alternative to the horse, and when steam was replacing sail at sea. She died when the combustion engine was replacing the horse, and sea travel had become comfortable and for the first class passenger luxurious with virtual disappearance of sail.

Caroline was a talented artist throughout her life. Pictures painted by her hang at the Walker Art Gallery, Liverpool and at the Williamson Gallery, Birkenhead. Two of her desert scenes hang at the home of the author's daughter, Elizabeth Hill, who also has much affection for Arabia and the Arab people.

St. George's Cathedral at Jerusalem provides final testaments to the lives of Gray Hill and his wife Carrie. The cathedral was first consecrated in 1898 and was completed in 1910. The Gray Hills dedicated one bay of the cloisters in memory of their parents as recorded on a tablet within the cloister. Adjoining tablets are to the honoured memory of John Gray Hill and his beloved wife, Caroline

Emily.

To revert to Norman and Mary Hill, they rented their house at Neston. They owned a second home Greenplace at Stockbridge in the Test valley, Hampshire. A home sometimes visited by the author in his childhood days and revisited in later years. A lovely house in a lovely garden surrounded by beautiful views and countryside where they spent as much time as they were able. Over the fireplace stands the carving:

ELLEN MARY STRATFORD HILL WIFE OF ARTHUR NORMAN HILL
BUILT THIS HOUSE 1906.

In 1921, Sir Norman purchased the Manorial rights of Stockbridge. From then on, he played an increasingly active part in the affairs of the district and its inhabitants and, especially, the Court Leet. He administered the rights of the tenants in copyhold of the Manor. To that end, he appointed a local solicitor, Mr. Talbot of Andover, as his Steward of the Manor and wrote to him:

'I have recently purchased this Manor, and I am writing to ask if you will please hold a Court Leet as Steward on my behalf. The Manor is of very little value to the Lord. Yet I am anxious to secure the observance of the Manor Customs in as far as they are for the benefit of Commoners generally. They have valuable rights of pasture over the Borough Marsh. The Parish Council of Stockbridge has asked that I enforce the customs in regard thereto.

'To enable this to be done, it is advisable that I appoint a Hayward. The one and only purpose of holding the Court Leet is to give the Commoners the opportunity of selecting a person to fill that office. If they want help, then I am ready to help them in maintaining old customs. Dollar, the Town Crier of Stockbridge, should summon the Court and he should cry it three times. The cry will be: By Order of the Lord of the Manor and Borough of Stockbridge, a Court Leet will be held at the Town Hall Stockbridge on Monday the 18th April at seven o'clock of the evening.'

Also, he wrote to local auctioneers:

'I am wishful to see the Annual Sheep and Lamb Fair

maintained. Can I do anything as Lord of the Manor to increase the usefulness of the fair to sellers and buyers or to you as the principal auctioneers there?'

In July 1923, Sir Norman wrote to the tenant of Manor Cottage who was seeking a tenancy of the Stockbridge Downs for training horses on the Downs:

'I am ready to give you a sole right to train on the Down with liberty to keep down the rabbits, so that they may not interfere with the gallops. Yet I do not think that I should let the Down to you. As you know, some farmers have the right to turn sheep on to the Down and the people of Stockbridge may walk on the Down. I am bound to protect these rights in which regard I shall be coming to live at Green Place.'

Sir Norman was then sixty years of age. The war years had taken their toll. He suffered from severe bouts of asthma and had decided upon an easier life and to move to Green Place. Thus, in 1923 after thirty years as Secretary of the Liverpool Steam Ship Owners' Association, he retired.

The Association immediately appointed him an honorary Member and declared of him:

'To express adequately to those outside the shipping industry what his service to the Association has meant during that long period is impossible. Yet those who are intimately acquainted with the work of the Association know that he carried out the ordinary duties of the office with unparalleled ability and industry. Additionally, he brought the farsighted wisdom of the statesman to bear on the great questions where the interests of the Association became interwoven with national and international policies.'

Sir Norman's advice and help remained freely available to the Association who frequently called upon it. He continued the senior partner of his firm, but acted principally in a consultancy capacity. His nephew, Martin Spencer Hill, succeeded him as secretary of the Liverpool Steam Ship Owners' Association.

Martin Hill, as he preferred to be known, was the eldest son of Leonard Hill who had articled him before the war to the marine solicitors, Thomas Cooper & Co, in London. Following his return from the trenches, Martin had achieved honours in his Solicitors Final Examination and had joined his Uncle Norman as an assistant solicitor in December 1919.

In 1929, the growing importance of London as the centre of British shipping resulted in Martin Hill moving to London. The intention was more fully to represent the Liverpool Steam Ship Owners' Association in its growing relations with the Chamber of Shipping. Additionally, the move expanded the already extensive maritime and commercial activities of Martin Hill and his firm, Hill Dickinson & Co., into London. The move proved a rewarding one in cementing existing close relations with the shipping industry nationally and internationally.

These were hard times for the country. The general strike of 1926 had involved all the miners, railway and transport workers' unions with the resultant need to import twenty-one million tons of coal. More particularly, it had caused much hardship and division within the country. Worse was to follow with the great depression of the 1930's continuing over the first five years of the decade.

This had appalling repercussions on the United Kingdom shipping industry. At the end of 1930, The Liverpool Steam Ship Owners Association reported that British shipowners had laid up six hundred and fifty-nine ships of an aggregate 2,513,000 gross tons. This led to attendant difficulties of finding sufficient lay up accommodation. Those liners still at sea were operating only to about half capacity of their available cargo and passenger space. Many were operating at a loss to preserve established trades.

Many loyal officers and seamen found themselves unemployed with little prospect of finding alternative employment. This was a personal catastrophe with no compensation for loss of employment and often no entitlement to a pension from the employer.

Dole was payable at a weekly rate of twenty-six shillings (£1.30) plus two shillings (10p) for each child during the first six months of unemployment. A national retirement pension of ten shillings (50p) weekly was payable on attaining sixty-five years of age. That was often the only reward of masters and officers in a great British Merchant Marine who had served the nation so bravely during four years of a devastating war.

Some more enlightened employers had established company pension schemes following the 1921 Finance Act. That act allowed contributions by the employer and the employee to such schemes approved by the Inland Revenue to rank for full tax relief. Martin Hill and his firm were among the first solicitors to obtain such approval for its many commercial and shipping clients.

In 1937, representatives of ship owners and merchant navy officers headed by Arthur Cauty of Cunard and Captain Coombs of the Officers Union approached Martin Hill. They sought his advice on a proposal to establish a shipping industry pension scheme for the provision of pensions to retiring merchant navy officers not already within a Company Scheme. The Merchant Navy Officers Pension Fund was thus born. Over following years, Martin Hill took a great personal interest in this pension scheme for which he acted gratuitously or for nominal fees.

Like his uncle Norman before him, Martin Hill had a profound knowledge of maritime law. He was a member of the British Maritime Law Association made up of ship owning and cargo underwriting interests. That Association played a large part in bringing about a sensible interpretation of the Hague Rules.

During 1937, Lloyds' Recoveries Department approached Martin Hill. They asked him whether he would be prepared to take on the legal work of recovering marine claims paid by Lloyds Underwriters. Properly he declined due to a conflict of interest because of him and his firm representing so many shipowners against whom underwriters would be claiming.

Instead, he recommended his young brother, Maurice Hill. The latter had practised as a barrister for a few years, but, finding that this was unprofitable, he had left the bar to become a solicitor. He had joined with a Mr. Clyde to establish the marine practice of Clyde & Co in London. Lloyd's Recoveries accepted the recommendation, so giving to Maurice Hill and this young and thrusting firm a valuable connection into marine insurance.

In 1939, Martin Hill received the Order of the British Empire for services rendered to Shipping. In that same year, he moved his firm's London office into the new building constructed by the then rapidly growing Chamber of Shipping in St. Mary Axe. The intent was to increase cooperation between the two organisations. The subsequent appointment of Maurice Hill (son of the Judge) as General Manager of the Chamber of Shipping enhanced this purpose.

An articled clerk Lesley Adam who joined the Liverpool office of Hill Dickinson in 1932, later wrote of these times:

'The office was as class conscious as the country generally. I was very happy to get the benefit because articled clerks formed a class of their own. Clerks and partners alike treated us with respect. To the one we would one day be their masters and to the other their equals. To reach our special status, our fathers had paid a premium of three hundred pounds on our being articled and eighty pounds in stamp duty on our articles. They kept us and paid all our fees and expenses for five years. The fact that we frequently had no money in our pockets made no difference, because they were the days of the Great Depression and no-one else had any either. Three million unemployed were much worse off than we were.

'The tempo of life was slow. We had time for the *Times* crossword and tea at the *Kardomah*. However, a consequence of the slower tempo of life was that we worked long hours. In particular, Mr. Goffey, a senior partner, frequently kept his clerks at the office until 10.00 p.m. and on Saturday afternoons. Articled clerks were not exempt from this regime. One Saturday, the partners allowed me to go rowing in the afternoon provided that I was back in office properly dressed by 7.00 pm. Overtime was unknown, but clerks received one shilling and sixpence tea money if they worked after 8.00 p.m.

'Conveyancing was a comparatively leisurely pursuit for those who enjoyed probing such mysteries as springing and shifting uses, but was not a subject for the DIY enthusiast. Our clients borrowed money only from their bankers or from each other. I did not see a building society mortgage until after the war.

'Mr. Goffey was a bachelor and eschewed social life. He had a capacity for hard work and endless patience in teaching articled clerks. He often told me of the great queues that formed from the Ismay offices situate below those of the firm to the Pier Head. They were relatives anxiously awaiting news of the *Titanic*.

'In 1932, the Great War was only fourteen years past. Wounded men were commonplace. They included Mr. Goffey with the Chief Clerk, Herbert Peever, and the lift man, Tranter, and no doubt others within the firm also. Female staff comprised two female telephonists and one female typist.

'Herbert Peever used to tell us of the days when as an office boy every evening he carried Sir John Hill's bag down to the landing stage. He crossed on the Birkenhead Ferry and carried the bag to Mere Hall reversing the journey the next morning. When he was particularly flush with money, he treated himself to a penny train ride. When George Dickinson went to his estate at Red How in Cumberland, he would send Herbert Peever to sit in a corner seat until Mr. Dickinson arrived.

'At my then age of sixteen, all the clerks seemed very old to me and probably were. Mr. Bruce, the senior costs clerk, wore stiff wing collars and looked more like the senior partner than any senior partner I ever knew. Mr. David Baty, the cashier, was a most dignified figure wearing his tie through a gold ring with a solitaire diamond inset. He kept the Firm's books by hand almost as they had been kept for 100 years.

'When I was admitted as a solicitor in 1937, I received a salary of two hundred pounds per annum. The cashier, David Baty, used to come round at the end of each month with three one-pound notes, one ten-shilling note, three shillings, one threepenny bit and one penny. This he pressed into my hand when nobody was looking with the invariable remark "wish it were more." However, I was fortunate in that the articled clerk sitting on my left at Gibson & Weldons, the law tutors, went on the dole on passing his law finals. The one on my right went back to his firm to work for nothing.'

The war brought an end to this form of life. Lesley Adam was a territorial officer. He went to France, and the Germans captured him at Dunkirk. He spent the next five years as a prisoner of war in Germany.

PART 2
ROY GRAY HILL - AN AUTOBIOGRAPHY

CHAPTER 13   BOYHOOD

I was born into an interlude of peace between two major world wars. My birth on 5th January 1922 coincided with the beginning of great technological change rooted in the petrol engine and electronics. The motor vehicle had made its appearance at the turn of the century and increasingly was becoming an alternative mode of travel. The first powered flight had taken place in 1903 by means of a twelve-horsepower petrol engine fitted in a biplane that remained air born for fifty-nine seconds. In 1910, a much improved version had made the first two-way crossing of the English Channel. Other and improved types of aircraft had served the combatants during the Great War as spotter and reconnaissance aircraft. Nevertheless, the motor car, aeroplane and wireless were all in their infancy.

Divisions existed within the growing industrial centres where increasingly powerful and militant trade unions were seeking improvement in the pay and working conditions of their members. Their demands often led to acrimony between mediocre management and militant trade unionists much aggravated by archaic class divisions.

Life in the rural areas continued little altered based on agriculture and a life within each village community going back to feudal days. A tranquil life centred around the village church, school, inn and shops and where the villagers took pleasure in their own social activities. A life varied only by periodic visits to the market town. All knew each other and each others affairs. This created greater sympathy and understanding between those of the village and a desire to serve the village community to the best of one's ability.

I was first born to my father, Martin Hill, known for his intellect and humour and to my mother, Vena, admired for her beauty and generosity. I inherited the family characteristics of a good memory, analytical mind and common sense with some puritan sympathies. Not I hasten to say in the religious sense, but in my manner of living. I dislike over indulgence in any form and that which is ostentatious and vulgar. At leisure, I enjoy the simple life of physical and open air activity combined with music, opera and good literature.

Earliest recollections include the fascination of my father for the then emergent touring motor car. I remember how he took me out aged four on a winter's day in his open Morris motor car wrapped up warmly in blankets with hot water bottles. We journeyed into North Wales and up the then notorious and difficult Horse Shoe Pass at Llangollen. It all seemed so steep and impassible. Yet up we went and reached the top where we drank from thermos flasks. This to me then was all very exciting. Though I do recall my mothers' protestations that she would never seek to drive such an abominable machine as the motor car.

I recall my father's love of music and his gramophone with winding handle and side horns. From this emerged the powerful tones of Wagner, Beethoven, Brahms and Sibelius. He exchanged this during the 1930's for the then latest technological marvel: the Marconi radiogram fitted with an automatic change of eight 78 records. He much enjoyed the new experience of sitting in his armchair and listening to a complete symphony or opera without moving to turn over a record.

I recall summer holidays at grandfather Leonard's retreat at Corton in Suffolk. I recall further the wondrous walks there along the cliff path with its fragrant scent of wild flowers and the beautiful butterflies flitting hither and thither. The tranquillity of the place has remained with me from childhood with the scenes that my grandfather so happily painted on to canvas. Then, when I was aged nine, came the Corton holiday and our visit to the fair at Great Yarmouth and the excitement of the merry-go-round and distorting mirrors. Especially, we enjoyed the travels by boat as it passed through mysterious tunnels with their shrieks and skeletons and other horrors. What a good time we had, but what a bad time was to follow.

A few days later, I succumbed to a bad attack of chicken

pox and had to wear gloves to avoid harmful scratching. I remember clearly the night of terrible thirst, of going to the kitchen for water and of a severe pain in my right ankle. So bad that I could only crawl back to my bed and to sleep. The next morning, I was unable to move. Serious illness dims further recollection. I had been struck down by osteomylitis: namely a form of tuberculosis of the bone. A disease that in those days, before the coming of antibiotics, frequently proved fatal.

I owe my life to my grandfather, then Sir Leonard Hill knighted for his services to medical research. He, the great physician that he was, recognised the symptoms in their early stage. He summoned appropriate medical skills to the then remote village of Corton and to a bungalow still lit by oil lamps and served by well water. They found osteomylitis in both the right ankle and behind the right ear. They decided that immediate surgery was imperative to save a child so ill that they could not move him to a hospital.

The surgeon carried out the operation on the kitchen table. I recall the smell of chloroform, a mask placed over my face, the instruction to count slowly, and the great drumming in my ears as I passed into unconsciousness. Later, I awoke in the main bedroom to readings by my mother who seemed so sad. Now seemingly so unreal as I passed in and out of consciousness. My mother subsequently confided to my wife that she believed there to be no hope for me and that she prayed for my early release. She saw my face swollen up like a football, my strength ebbing away, and as she thought in great pain. I have no recollection of great pain but only of an overwhelming desire to sleep.

Subsequent recollections are of return home and later to school. I recall studies in geography and of an atlas that showed one quarter of the world's surface coloured in red as representing the British Empire. Particularly interesting were studies of darkest Africa and of cannibals and pygmies and of a continent still not wholly explored by the white man. I enjoyed the description of the meeting between Mr Stanley and Dr. Livingstone

My father purchased a new home. Namely, a large Georgian house called Devon Lodge contained in two acres of productive

243

garden in Rydens Road Walton-on-Thames. The area was then rural. I recall the small farm up the road and accompanying my mother to collect milk. She never locked the house on these occasions. One day, asking my mother why she did not lock the door, she replied: "Why, no-one will enter while we are out." Looking back over the years, what a sad change has come about. Still those were the days of imprisonment with hard labour, the birch, the cat of nine tails for violence, and hanging for murder. Those punishments were a real deterrent to the criminal.

Living in domestic staff then comprised a Norden trained nanny, a maid and a gardener. The latter was a former miner. My father paid him fifteen shillings (75p) a week with his keep. He paid the maid something less. The gardener was an intelligent man with whom I had lengthy discussions on future space travel. He deserved something better, and today he would probably achieve a university place.

Understandably after the traumas of my illness, my mother preferred an alternative to Corton for our family holidays. Thus, we went to farms in Devon and Cornwall. This was much to the delight of myself and my sister Betty. We lost no time on arrival in getting to know the farmer and his farm and, especially, his animals. We had great excitement in mounting the big cart horses and riding them about the farm and along the narrow and deserted lanes. All the family enjoyed the delicious farm food consisting of poultry, game and pies, and great picnics by the sea. This was all for three pounds a week and half for us children.

However, those were days of cheap prices with beef at a shilling a pound, cod at four pence a pound and butter at eighteen pence. Cigarettes cost eighteen pence for twenty and a bottle of whisky twenty-five shillings. The three bedroom bungalows that were springing up in the district were selling for £395. The purchase price of a new car was little more than one hundred pounds and sometimes less. A reasonable second hand car cost little more than twenty pounds. Nevertheless we saw few motor cars on the roads, which enabled the family to while away long journeys by each counting differently coloured cars. We did not allow black as the predominant colour.

One memorable Easter, father took us all to the Valley of Rocks Hotel at Lynton, which was then a most elegant hotel. Especially, I recall the afternoon teas served by waiters wearing black ties and white gloves. They were serving the most delicious cakes from a trolley that they wheeled from guest to guest as plates were emptied. I recall with less enthusiasm the object of our visit.

That was to cheer on a variety of noisy and dirty sports cars that were competing in their attempt to climb the notorious Beggars Roost hill. This hill had severe gradients and hairpin bends and a muddy surface. Clearly, my father would have been overjoyed to participate with his keen interest in the sports car. He then owned a Silver Jaguar SS II, which with its long sleek bonnet and elegant lines I now regard as the most pleasing of all he ever owned.

In 1933 when aged eleven, I suffered another attack of osteomylitis in the left thigh that resulted in my admission to Guys Hospital London for further surgery. Three months' convalescence in the open air and sunshine followed under the advice of grandfather Leonard. Only books and the wireless were available to fill the hours of the invalid. Of necessity, I had become an avid reader.

Moreover, with an enquiring mind I had reached the age when I was questioning what we are and from where we come and what the future might hold. I found H.G. Wells fascinating. The Time Machine offered much fertile ground for thought as did *The First Men on the Moon* and *The War of the Worlds*. Then *Scoops*, the fictional scientific magazine of the day, offered fascinating thoughts on life at the end of the century and into the 21st century. Much of that forecast, which then seemed so outrageously imaginative, has now happened.

George Bernard Shaw was another favourite. His beliefs in the life force appealed more to me than the cruel and vengeful God of the early testament. I was questioning the beliefs of heaven and hell and everlasting life, which were then still largely held. I was asking myself in what form might we reappear at the resurrection and at what stage of our life? How would we recognise each other and how would the line be drawn between those destined for heaven and those for the everlasting torments of hell?

A stay with my grandfather Leonard and my grandmother Janet at their home in Chalfont St. Peter further shaped my thinking. They believed in the Victorian principles of thrift and make do and more so did their Aunt Polly. She invited my grandmother and me to take afternoon tea with her. I was first warned that, in good Victorian tradition, she regarded young people as there to be seen and not heard. I met this remarkable old lady dressed all in black with a black bonnet. She was well into her 90's and thus born into the 1840's. She produced a remarkably good tea interjected by the cheeky remarks of her parrot.

My grandfather was then in his early sixties and to me both old and very wise. He repeated the folly of overeating and obesity. He deprecated white bread, which he regarded as the waste that remained after extracting the nutrient of whole wheat flour. 'Rubbish,' he would say to me, 'they would be better on a diet of milk, brown bread and nuts.' His brother, my great-uncle Norman, shared those views. He would exclaim: 'I am prepared to work myself to the death for my clients, but I am damned if I am going to eat myself to death for them.'

My grandfather was the epitome of the absent-minded professor. His reputation as a physician was unsurpassed. Yet he was of so little financial logic that my grandmother insisted that he entrusted the family finances to her. Otherwise, he would have given away all that he possessed on hearing the first hard-luck tale however improbable. My grandmother recounted how she once had to point out to him that he was preparing to leave for the hospital in his underpants.

During my stay, I much enjoyed accompanying my grandfather in his leisure activities. I watched in awe the rapidity with which he painted scenes of animal, flower and country bordering the little brook that then flowed through the Chalfont valley. Looking back, he was remarkably good. While he painted, I listened intently to his discourses on the meaning of life and how we were all of one universal source and power that were themselves indestructible.

In 1930, he had published in booklet form titled *The Philosophy of a Biologist* a paper that he had first read in 1915 to the British Institute of Philosophical Studies. The preface to that booklet contained the essence of his thinking as expressed to me. Thinking, perhaps, which was not pleasing to the orthodox Christian of the day, but based on his own faith and certainty that scientific knowledge would extend human life and happiness.

It read:

'Modern science has brought us to the conception of a power eternal, infinite, unknowable, energizing all in the universe, the dead no less than the quick. A power that is equivalent to the purest conception of God stripped of all dogma and superstition. A power that is in all and through all, from where we came, of which we are a part, and where we return after death. A power that is active in all atoms of matter comprising the nebulae, the stars, the dust, and the living cell and determines every action and reaction in the eternal evolution of the universe, the earth and life upon earth.'

Subsequently:

'They tell us that the number of the stars in the two million nebulae of the universe is such that, if the stars were grains of sand, the grains would cover England hundreds of yards deep. Our earth is one millionth part of one such grain. Yet we bother ourselves over questions of social rank. Man must reconcile himself to the humbler position of the inhabitant of a speck of dust and adjust his views on the meaning of human life accordingly.'

Because of illness, I had lost a year's schooling, but I had benefited from enforced absence by reading and listening in my formative years. Yet long and enforced absence from preparatory day school vexed me. Although remarkably named Wallop, the school was a kindly place and forward looking in its educational thinking. It encouraged a desire to seek out knowledge by its pupils. It still enjoys a special place in my memory. In particular, having recovered from illness and encouraged to exercise, I gained a first in the school sports to receive the prize of my first camera.

Unfortunately, boarding at public school was not so agreeable and is the one period of my life to which I do not look back with any pleasure. Situate in the then rural area of Chigwell and so named, its pupils reached the school by a slow steam train that meandered through the then open Essex countryside. The school's best feature was the then scenic walks through the Roding river valley lying between Chigwell and Buckhurst Hill.

Archbishop Harsnett had founded the school in the 1600's. It appeared to me to have progressed little in the intervening period. Like most schools of the day, prowess in sport was all important. School life was a more civilised resemblance of that description of the public school given by my great-grandfather Birkbeck Hill. Moreover, it appeared to me a system directed to educating future leaders of the great British Empire on the playing field and in prayer cloistered like medieval monks. That might have been appropriate to the 17th century, but not to my thinking into the 1930's.

Education primarily centred on the classics. Teaching of the sciences was virtually nonexistent. Teaching of history and geography and even the scriptures was directed to absorption of dull fact. The school did not try to present life and thinking of time or place or to pursue questions of how and why. The all prevailing influence of the old Archbishop was stifling. Chapel services were compulsory for all both in the early morning and late evening with Sunday mid-morning service at the local parish church.

The lasting effect on me, or perhaps innate within me, was a dislike of football and cricket whether as participant or spectator. In my later school days, I learned the art of attending roll call but avoiding participation in those activities. I thus found time to self teach the education for which my parents were paying.

Exercise was available to me in the voluntary pursuits of cross country running, walking and swimming all of which I enjoy. The school swimming pool was in the open, sparse and without heating. Still, I find cold water exhilarating and it has never deterred me. The school taught the younger boys to swim under supervision. I remain grateful for that tuition. Experienced swimmers swam during designated hours. I never understood why football and cricket should have been compulsory. Yet, the really important subject of swimming left to the volunteer.

During my boyhood, I developed a keen interest in electronics.

Consequently, I occupied much of the school holidays in constructing wireless sets and amplifiers and various alarm systems. I installed a telephone line connecting our home to that of a neighbour using a reel of galvanised wire with amplifiers and loudspeakers at each end. At first, hearing music over the amplifiers mystified me. However, I accounted for this by the length of wire used coinciding with the wavelength of the BBC Home Service.

I was also constructing matchbox crystal sets that by appropriate adjustment of a whisker to crystal received wireless programmes by earphone without need of a battery. These were very popular among school inmates as enabling them to listen to wireless programmes after lights out.

During the 1930's, refrigerators were making an appearance. My mother purchased a Frigidaire model. We all looked upon this as miraculous in keeping food cool and fresh and producing copious quantities of ice cream. Until then, my mother had kept perishables in a fly protected container forming an extension of the larder out into the open air. She had made ice cream in a large drum like utensil into which she placed broken ice obtained from the local fishmonger. She filled an inner compartment with a mixture of cream and the juice of fresh strawberries or raspberries or whatever other flavour she required. It made superb ice cream at a time when we regarded cream as an essential to good living.

The 1930s were also days of developing aircraft, of air pioneers circling the world, and of civil air lines for travel by the more adventurous. Sea travel remained dominant. Bigger and more luxurious liners were appearing and flying the red ensign. Cunard and the White Star Line had merged. The new company, The Cunard White Star Line, introduced the *Queen Mary* on to their transatlantic service followed by the *Queen Elizabeth*. These vessels commanded the seas as the most luxurious form of travel afloat. Cunard and the British flag were prestigious.

To my delight, Cunard invited my father and mother on the shake down voyage of both these great vessels. Other guests included HG Wells and George Bernard Shaw. I entrusted my autograph book to my father. He returned it with both signatures and many other famous signatures of the time. Unfortunately, it has long since been lost.

In 1937, my father was engaged in drafting long documents at home. He explained that they were for setting up a scheme to provide pensions on retirement to merchant navy officers. He further explained that many officers on retirement only received the State pension of ten shillings weekly. Then and still today, it horrifies me to think how masters and chief officers retiring from our great merchant marine with little opportunity for saving managed to live on so paltry a sum.

From these beginnings, in 1938, the Merchant Navy Officers Pension Fund became established. Initially served by a small and devoted staff, the Fund has grown to rank today among the larger pension funds. It has been my privilege in later days to play a part in that development.

Two events from my school days stand out in my mind as if of yesterday. First, in 1936, the head master summoned us to the Great Hall to hear over the wireless the abdication speech of King Edward VIII. In a quiet voice, he made clear that he was unable to continue as monarch without Mrs. Simpson, the American divorcee, at his side. We all found this quite extraordinary at a time when the nation held the monarchy in such high esteem and the guilty party to a divorce in such contempt. How, in such circumstances we asked ourselves, could the King be justified in abdicating his duties and giving up the Crown.

Second, my friendship for the wealthy German Jewish boy, Neuman, who warned us so frequently that Hitler intended war and that he had geared his economy to war. We preferred not to believe him. Like all the nation, we had an overwhelming desire for peace. Both Neuman and I left school in the summer of 1939. He returned to Germany, and I entered articles as a solicitor.

In May 1939, my father sold his home at Walton-upon-Thames to a developer to escape encroaching development. We moved to a newly constructed and smaller house at West Byfleet in the beautiful Surrey countryside. My father named the house Beggars Roost. He thus displayed both his sense of humour and his enjoyment of the motor hill climb of that name, which we had attended at Lynton. The move was to prove fortunate in that domestic staff would no longer be available following the outbreak of war.

Again, I recall clearly the 3rd September 1939 and the announcement over the wireless at 11.00 a.m. by the Prime Minister, Neville Chamberlain. Germany had failed to meet the ultimatum to withdraw from Poland and, accordingly, we were at war. Shortly afterwards, we heard the eerie sounding of the first air raid alarm, but this was a false alarm. None sought war, but all realised that no alternative was available. I heard nothing more of my school friend, Neuman. I must assume that, like so many of his race, they put him to death in those satanic concentration camps.

CHAPTER 14

THE SECOND WORLD WAR

In the days leading up to the war, Martin Hill took a leading part in negotiating terms for State requisition of British shipping. I recall his lengthy drafting of the relevant requisition form of charter party known as T99A. Thus, on the outbreak of war, the relevant arrangements were in place for the nation to employ its merchant fleet in the best interests of the war effort. Owners continued to operate their fleets but to the direction and account of the Government for which they received an agreed requisition hire.

The centenary history of the Association describes how, from the outset of the war, the enemy attempted to cripple the country's overseas supply lines. How, as in the 1914-18 war, they employed tactics of organised piracy in which they flagrantly violated every rule and practice of war at sea. This began on the first day of war, when the liner *Athenia* was sunk without warning. Sinking on sight by submarine and aircraft followed. It mattered not whether the ship was carrying passengers or cargo or of what nationality, and was done without any consideration for those on board whether passenger or crew.

The history further describes how, in the opening weeks of the war, everything was in the enemy's favour. British ships were at sea on their normal peacetime vocations. They were unarmed and unescorted. The enemy had planned the war and had placed their submarines in readiness along the ocean highways.

The Association again set up its convoy committee to liaise with the Shipping Defence Advisory Committee and the Navy, which reintroduced the convoy system. Liverpool became the shore headquarters of the Western Approaches. A Government War Risks Insurance Scheme was already in place modelled on that of the 1914-18 war. The Government first reinsured 80% of losses and later 96%. The participating associations included The Liverpool and London War Risks Association then managed by Martin Hill.

*Signing deed establishing the Merchant Navy Officers Pension Fund
Martin Spencer Hill (far left)*

Martin Spencer Hill

Roy Gray Hill joins the Royal Air Force

In 1940, the latter received the Order of the British Empire for his services to shipping.

As further described under its history, the Association sought the best possible means of protection against the elements for those sunk and adrift in lifeboats. They consulted my grandfather, Sir Leonard Hill, as the leading authority in the scientific and physiological problems involved. He participated in the design of an ingenious protective suit. This provided protection not only against the cold winds and waters of the North Atlantic but also against the blistering effect of the tropical sun. The authorities issued these protective suits throughout the merchant navy and they proved invaluable in saving life.

On the outbreak of war, I was seventeen years of age. I had matriculated and was exempt from the Solicitors' preliminary examination. Accordingly, I made an immediate start upon articles with the intention of promptly passing the Solicitors' intermediate examination and joining the Royal Air Force Volunteer Reserve. I hoped that the Law Society would then allow subsequent war service to count under articles. In those days, admission as a solicitor still generally required five years' articles with a premium of £300 paid on articles. The articled clerk received no salary.

I was attending lectures and studying for the Intermediate Examination. I joined the local Home Guard and was part of a night guard on a local electricity substation. At first, we were without arms but later had rifles. We would have stood no chance at all against a trained enemy.

The first nine months of the war were without movement. Talk was of this phoney war and even of the possibilities of peace. However, the invasion and fall of Belgium, Holland and France followed with the retreat of the British Forces to Dunkirk. There a multiplicity of vessels met and miraculously brought back many to England.

I was going from West Byfleet up to London daily by train. All talk was of when and where the Germans would invade and what we could do to protect ourselves. We feared the coming of parachute troops followed by invasion from the sea and tanks across the Home Counties and encircling London. We stood alone, yet few believed that we faced defeat.

The summer of 1940 was a glorious one with day after day of fine sunny weather. A neighbour and I dug out and constructed an air raid shelter. We prepared for the worst. Then came the German planes both fighter and bomber with our own Hurricanes and Spitfires weaving above and the dogfights and machine gun fire. Churchill never spoke a truer word when he said of their pilots "Never have so many owed so much to so few." Against all the odds, they had won the Battle of Britain and so thwarted the invasion.

The battle of London followed with its nightly unrelenting bombing. Its inhabitants sought protection in underground stations and other air raid shelters. Frequently, I passed through these stations at dusk to see the population preparing with Thermos flask, baggage and night attire to spend evening and night there. They were well aware of what was about to happen above, but their cheerfulness and good humour always impressed me.

Later, I arrived home at West Byfleet some 30 miles west of London. I watched the night sky glow as it was lit up by the bombing and burning of London. Looking back, it is a wonder that any cheerfulness survived such an ordeal. Yet it did and triumphed. The bombers turned their attention elsewhere. London had survived and was to enjoy some relief from its ordeal.

My father continued to travel daily up to London during the battle of London. He did not know if and when he would arrive and what he would find on arrival. Nor did he know how he would return. He had sad tales to tell of the famous places that the bombers had destroyed overnight.

The Germans were employing fire bombs. Not dangerous in themselves, if promptly extinguished, but lethal when mixed with high explosives. Yet, office staff formed fire teams on a rota basis to extinguish fire bombs and resultant fires. My father was serving on such a rota one or two nights a week. I had much admiration for these volunteers who faced such dangerous conditions to save London from burning. Many perished in the attempt.

During this period, I had stayed back at home to complete

final revision for the Solicitors' intermediate examination, which I took and passed in June 1941. Then, I immediately volunteered for service in the Royal Air Force. To my surprise, as I wore spectacles, they accepted me for aircrew. However, because of my young age, this required the written consent of my parents. Looking back, perhaps not unexpectedly in view of my earlier illness, they were not prepared to give this. I was disappointed at the time, but medical opinion from within the RAF subsequently supported their decision.

Instead, the immediate consequence was a series of IQ tests. An interview with a senior officer followed which opened with a warning of secrecy. The officer explained that the RAF then possessed a new technological weapon. This could plot the position of approaching enemy aircraft for the direction of our own fighters. He further explained that the RAF was short of skilled personnel who could maintain the equipment. They would send me on a wireless course. If I scored 80%, they would train me in this new equipment. This was all very exciting to me with my interest in electronics.

First, however, I had to undergo a month of intense physical training and so called square bashing. Unlike most of my fellow recruits, I did not find this particularly irksome. Perhaps, it appeared the easier after the rigours of public school. A wireless course followed this and then a radar course of some twelve weeks in all. The RAF then posted me to Ventnor Isle of Wight. This was the southernmost radar station of the radar protection chain around Britain. A chain that I then realised had played such an essential a part in winning the Battle of Britain. A chain largely operated by the young women of the W.A.A.F.

The camaraderie of those days, forged in the desperate need to defend the country against a vicious enemy, set aside all barriers of class and sex. At war, Great Britain and its Empire and Dominions was at peace unto itself as never since. All were coming to the assistance of the mother country. I remember with affection those in the RAF coming from Canada, Australia, New Zealand, India, South Africa, Rhodesia, Barbados and from all corners of the Empire.

At this time, radar stations were well distinguished by their 80 ft. aerial masts. Many such masts stood at Ventnor with resultant enemy air attacks. Fortunately, during my period at Ventnor, little damage was done to the installation and none to the aerials. However, before my arrival and during the Battle of Britain, serious damage had been done but speedily repaired.

Considerable excitement arose at the time because of a commando raid on a German encampment on the cliff top north of Le Havre. We knew that the Germans had some form of radar. The purpose of the raid was to bring back equipment to compare with our own. The commando's achieved that purpose with certain vital components brought back.

Information was that the Germans were going to reciprocate by attacking a British radar station possibly Ventnor. We went on night watch armed with sten guns and locked into our underground radar bunkers. I suspect that these would have offered little protection against a determined enemy using grenades and other high explosive devices to gain entry. Nevertheless, we were prepared for the worst with the RAF regiment keeping watch outside. We were relieved when the morning arrived with nothing untoward having occurred overnight.

During the winter of 1941/42, a new device installed at Ventnor for measuring the height of enemy aircraft failed. At the time, an enemy attack was in progress and information was vital for passing on to our night fighter pilots. The device was essential for that purpose. Immediate investigation revealed to me that the aerials at the top of the mast were defective. This meant I had to climb the mast upright ladders at night under storm conditions to investigate and hopefully repair the aerial.

I made my way up the mast holding tightly on to the ladder against the savage gusts of wind that were howling through the swaying mast. The thought that an essential part of the system was inoperative during enemy attack spurred me on. I got up the mast very quickly for its height. I then encountered problems in finding the defective aerial in the black out while having to hang on to the ladder with one arm crooked around its side. More than once, I thought that the howling wind was going to break my grasp and pluck me from the ladder. However, I managed to hang on and replace what was an aerial bar dislodged by the storm force winds. I scampered back down the mast. I was most relieved to find that we were back on the air and that the whole operation had occupied less than fifteen minutes. It had seemed a lifetime.

Another vivid recollection is the shooting down at night of a German bomber over St. Catherine's Down with the taking of one prisoner and three corpses. The station matron dampened down our excitement at this event in exclaiming: 'Still, never forget that each of those dead men is some mother's beloved son.' A truism that could not more emphatically emphasise the depravity of war.

Little did I know at this time that my future wife, Norah, and her two brothers were taking an active part in this event. The brothers brought in two corpses by wheelbarrow. They also played a part in the apprehension of the survivor who was found sitting on a gate exclaiming "English swinehund." Next morning, Norah found the survivor's parachute and some partially burned documents hidden under a rhododendron bush. These included a snapshot of the crew.

After some twelve months at Ventnor, the RAF posted me first to Cranwell in Lincolnshire and then to Yatesbury in Wiltshire to lecture recruits in radar. This was a disappointing move after the excitement of the radar chain and its absence of military discipline.

However, some twelve months later early in 1943, the RAF sent me to the radar headquarters of Telecommunications Research Establishment (TRE) at Malvern College. They had evacuated the pupils of this well-known public school to Harrow. The course that I attended there was an exciting one. It related to a new scientific development the magnetron, which enabled reduction of pulse wavelengths from metres to centimetres. That, in turn, enabled aircraft radar to scan the terrain below onto a horizontally positioned radar screen.

Bombers were being fitted with this new equipment. I led a team responsible for setting up demonstration equipment on Bomber Command stations. This equipment showed what the crews would observe on the radar when flying over the target area. Thus, for Hamburg, the first city they targeted, the radar clearly showed the river estuary, lakes and railway marshalling yards with the adjoining buildings and approach roads. The radar further showed the point of bomb impact by a white dot of light.

This new aid to navigation and its precision bombing much impressed the bomber crews. I recall, as if yesterday, the crews in their bomber jackets and fur lined boots climbing aboard their aircraft and the roar of departing Wellingtons and Lancasters into the night. We had many anxieties about whom and how many would return the following morning. We were fighting, so they preached, for the future of our children and our children's children. Let them since born reflect upon their worthiness for the supreme sacrifice made by so many that they might enjoy their way of life.

As the war progressed, my father was telling me that losses inflicted upon our merchant ships and their crews by enemy submarines were becoming unbearable. They threatened our supply lines and very survival. He feared that, despite all convoy and naval protection, the submarine menace would starve us into defeat.

Yet the development of the magnetron and fitment of airborne radar into coastal command aircraft was to result in a dramatic change. It enabled these aircraft to find and attack the enemy submarines often at night when they surfaced to charge their batteries. We had turned tables, so that the enemy was losing submarines faster than they could replace them. We had won the Battle of the Atlantic, but only at the tragic cost of so many brave seafarers. Had it not been for them, the fascist regime would have triumphed and you, the reader, would not be enjoying your present way of life.

The development of the magnetron also resulted in airborne radar being fitted into our fighter aircraft. This enabled the night fighter pilots, following a first direction from the ground, to close and attack enemy aircraft. The success rate at night was so good that, in explanation, the RAF put about the story that they were feeding the fighter pilots carrots to improve their night vision. Thus, although the RAF could not acknowledge it at the time, the invention of the magnetron played a large part in ultimate victory.

Towards the end of 1943, I found myself posted back to Yatesbury to lecture officers on the technicalities of on board radar.

At this time, London and the southeast faced a new menace, namely the rocket bomb. The first to appear was the V1. A small pilotless plane laden with explosive timed to cut out its engine over London and to drop. We heard and saw its approach. Frequently, it was shot down. Otherwise, when we heard the engine cut out, we would dive for cover. It was not a serious menace and the subject of some ribaldry.

The second to appear the V2, was much more serious. It was a true rocket with a heavy bomb load. We did not hear it before an explosion. I feared for the safety of my father who was at his London office and travelling about London. Civilians were truly in the front line. Heavy bombing of the rocket sites was taking place. All were looking for an early invasion of France to stop this increasing menace.

The second front opened on 5th June 1944 with the invasion of Normandy. Shortly afterwards, the RAF posted me back to the Isle of Wight and to a small radar station at Bembridge employing the magnetron within the Ventnor network. This proved an easy going period for me. The RAF billeted us out in former holiday boarding houses. I was fortunate in having as my landlady a kind and motherly lady appropriately named Mrs. Holiday.

Life was seemingly so peaceful and the bathing beaches so pleasant that I arranged for my parents to join me for a long weekend with Mrs. Holiday. I obtained the necessary military passes for them to visit the Isle of Wight. I envisaged that the visit would give them some holiday in war torn Britain and my father some relief from the rocket attacks on London.

Unfortunately, it proved a bad choice of weekend. We were machine gunned by two enemy dive bombers while sunbathing on the beach. We were fortunate that they did not hit us. The planes missed the radar station and dropped their bombs on the town and departed. During my parents return home, the Germans heavily bombed Southampton. Fortunately, my parents were returning via Portsmouth, although it was a difficult crossing with much anti aircraft fire and dog fights above.

Not long after my arrival at Bembridge, our small but essential radar unit went off the air at midnight. Group command immediately requested particulars of the cause and likely period of failure. I reported a suspected failure of the magnetron and that no spare was available on the Island. Group asked me to reconfirm that diagnosis as magnetrons were in very scarce supply. I reconfirmed, when Group informed me that they were seeking a replacement.

At noon that same day, Group advised that they were dispatching a replacement under police guard and instructed that I personally meet the transport at the ferry terminal. I did so and collected the new magnetron and fitted it. The diagnosis proved correct and we were back on the air. Happily, whilst we were off the air, little activity was taking place over the channel.

During this period, I had met my future wife, Norah, a local girl from Chale of a farming family. When we first met, she was home from Plumpton in Sussex where she was teaching. We both enjoyed dancing and walking over the Island together. We found we had the same interests. She brought out many farm goodies to me then hard to find such as cream, eggs, butter, and excellent cakes made by her mother.

At this time, I had purchased an ancient bicycle to get about the island. I was enjoying visits to her family and their farm and their way of life. They were spoiling me with excellent farm food and its cooking at a time of scarcity. The old adage the way to a man's heart is through his stomach was to prove right. In the earlier words of my great-great uncle Gray Hill, I had met the kind and tender helpmate in whom throughout life I could place complete trust and reliance. However, at the time, I regarded myself fortunate in having then met a very pretty and jolly girl of twenty years with whom I could share many interests. Love and marriage were to follow.

The rapidity of the advance into France led to hopes that the war with Germany would be over by Christmas 1944. However, that was not to be. In May 1945, after six years of terrible war, it was suddenly all at an end. The lights were on again.

V.E. (Victory in Europe) day was a public holiday. Great rejoicing and dancing took place in the streets. Strangers were kissing one another. It was a day of intense excitement and relief. I have not and shall never know another such day. We had endured such terrible perils and survived. Instantly feelings of the most intense joy replaced all the tribulations, anxieties and fears for loved ones of the past six years. Words cannot convey to those who were not then born or who were in their infancy the intensity of those feelings. Such feelings included themselves as our children and our children's children whose future we had preserved.

The next morning was one of more sober thoughts. We were still at war with Japan. Many brave men would not return. There remained much to be done before we were truly at peace. Little did we then know that the ending of the war with Japan was so near. On 6th August 1945, American aircraft dropped the atomic bomb on Hiroshima. Four days later, they dropped a second bomb on Nagasaki. The war with Japan was over. We were truly at peace. We celebrated V.J. day similarly to V.E. day, but it lacked the same intensity. The shadow of the atomic bomb had come to stay.

Let those who are now our children and our children's children and future generations never forget the sacrifices made for their now comfortable way of life. Those sacrifices were truly appalling. Many brave men and women died, and some under the most appalling conditions of agony. The nation required terrible decisions taken at a time when it appeared that the enemy might defeat us or that continued war would result in unbearable injury to the nation. Leaders of the day have since come under criticism for the actions that they then took. Most, if not all who went through the war, would regard that criticism as grossly unfair. However unhappily, we all participated and agreed in what was done at the time to defeat so evil a regime. That included the essential bombing of enemy cities.

Throughout the war, I had continued my legal studies with the aid of armed services correspondence courses. I had obtained special dispensation from the Law Society to take the Solicitors' Final Examination in March 1945. Most of my fellow candidates were elderly and mostly solicitors' clerks who had decided to seek qualification. Two others in uniform were army officers. Seventy-nine candidates sat the examination, and forty-nine passed with six distinctions including myself.

Demobilisation of the armed forces proved a lengthy process. A year elapsed before my own demobilisation in July 1946. Meanwhile, the RAF closed down Bembridge radar station and posted me to Royston in Cambridgeshire to participate in a like closure. I decided to take further correspondence courses first in economics and then in philosophy.

I was interested in the latter subject of philosophy in circumstances where I had survived earlier illness and now this terrible war. Was this by fate alone? What of my grandfather's views as he had expressed them to me in earlier days. Were we each part of something greater dying and being replaced like the individual cells of our own bodies? So that as individuals we were the temporary abode of everlasting life? If so, were all religions mere superstition based on the individual's desire for his own everlasting life, when life itself was everlasting? Alternatively, were all religions part of a composite whole expressed in differing forms? If so, how had they caused so much hate and suffering? Was this the birth pangs of an ultimate life on earth beyond our present comprehension as I preferred to believe? Unfortunately, my studies in philosophy added little to that thinking.

German bomber crew shot down

CHAPTER 15

AFTERMATH OF WAR

On 26th July 1946, the RAF demobilised me and I gladly exchanged my uniform for an ill fitting suit and trilby hat. I returned to a civilian life of severe and continuing shortages in every commodity and high taxation. Labour had won the election on a wave of popular support centred on returning service men and women. They were looking for a new dawn in the conception of one nation and equality for all. They had sympathy for the Russian ally and its ideas and made humorous demands with a modicum of idealism for Joe (Stalin) as king.

The new labour administration was in tune with this thinking. It achieved much good in providing social security from the cradle to the grave. Real deprivation as had previously existed was to become a past evil. Unfortunately, those who comprised this new administration were blinkered. They rightly saw the need for protecting the weak and providing equal opportunity and security for all. Yet they failed to distinguish between an egalitarian society and one of equal opportunity for all. Thus, their policies were to benefit the shirker to the detriment of the conscientious. Over following years, successive governments continued to give effect to these policies. They drained the energies of the nation by their penal taxation and unrestricted welfare benefits near to collapse.

Moreover, this labour administration failed to appreciate the effect of their indiscriminate nationalisation and replacement of enterprise management by bureaucratic control. They failed to see that this would stifle enterprise and result in a decline and loss of profitability and increasing subsidies. They disliked the very thought of profit, which they displayed by closing the profitable Liverpool Cotton Exchange and thus throwing away a Liverpool and national asset. Similarly, they had an aversion to anything connected with the nation's imperial past. In truth, they were too idealistic in failing to see the effect of their policies.

Thus, their term in government coincided with the decline of the British Empire and all for which it had stood. A decline destined to alter the British people and their behaviour over the second half of the twentieth century. A decline and a transformation in which Liverpool would be at the fore as it had been at the fore of its development.

It is debatable whether a government more visionary towards the Empire at this critical moment of its history could have avoided the decline. Much good will existed within the Dominions and colonies following the war in which they had played such an essential part. Thus, a true commonwealth of nations, trading within its own parameters of a free market and served by its own shipping, could have done well. Had the Government taken steps to that end immediately following the war, they might well have succeeded.

Meanwhile, Martin Hill was reporting under annual reports of the Liverpool Steam Ship Owners' Association well noted for their forthright comments:

'Over the years, the Association has consistently warned the country of the danger of being priced out of the export market. Our overseas buyers owe no duty to buy from us. They can and will go elsewhere. The consequence to us of failure to market our exports is a decreasing ability to buy our essential food and raw materials and a permanently lowered standard of living. In the ultimate extreme, it means virtual starvation or a very large reduction in the population that we may sustain in these islands.'

The Government largely ignored these warnings, as it ignored warnings against taxing shipping in a way that did not allow for its replacement. Thus, Martin Hill was repeatedly warning that shipowners did not earn a true profit until they had put aside sufficient monies for the periodic renewal of their ships. Especially, he pointed out that the Government was under a misapprehension when it calculated a taxable profit on the ship's initial cost as distinct from its renewal cost. That policy, continued by successive post war governments, was effectively to consume the nation's seed corn. It was the root cause of the catastrophic decline that later took place in the nation's merchant fleet.

Meanwhile, dispensation granted by the Law Society to the returning service men resulted in a reduction of my articles from five to two years. Thus, I had only to serve a further 193 days before being admitted as a solicitor. I returned to the London office of Hill Dickinson to receive a salary of £300 per annum increased to £400 on my qualification. On my return, I learned that one partner in the Liverpool office, Cecil Jones, had died in action following the fall of Singapore. Also that Leslie Adam, previously mentioned, had returned from a prisoner of war camp after five years confinement following his capture at Dunkirk.

Sir Norman Hill had died on the 7th January 1944 three months after the death of his wife Mary. The shipping industry had paid many tributes to his lifetime service to shipping. Sadly, a few months later, his only son, Norman Gray Hill, a Lieutenant Colonel in the Royal Army Medical Corps (Airborne Division), was shot down over Catania. The baronetcy died with him.

Following the end of the war, I had become engaged to Norah. On a blustery 3rd May 1947, we were married at Chale church on the Isle of Wight. I had a most beautiful bride who had somehow managed to find sufficient clothing coupons for the day. Motor cars were then scarce, so that my mother lent us her little prewar Austin 7 for the honeymoon. We enjoyed our fortnight at the Tors Hotel, Lynmouth, Devon. From there we explored the then remote and beautiful Lorna Doone countryside. A rewarding experience was attending a local auction sale where the auctioneer knocked down a small Elizabethan chest to us for six pounds. It has remained a prized possession.

Housing was scarce and by prewar standards very expensive. We were fortunate in finding an attractive chalet bungalow in the Chipstead valley in the lovely Surrey countryside. Norah gave up teaching to become a housewife. That was then the preferred vocation of young married women who still looked to marriage for fulfilment and the family as the essential element of society. Divorce was difficult and unusual, and the guilty party regarded with contempt. Wants were simple.

Life was peaceful without the later scourge of the mass motor car and aeroplane. To cycle was still a real pleasure that Norah and I greatly enjoyed through the many miles of quiet Surrey roads. The air was a delight to breathe. The countryside was beautiful whether in the outburst of spring or leafy summer or autumn colour or the icy tracings of winter frost.

Shopkeepers had time for a chat. Supermarkets were an abomination still to come. Domestic heating was by coal and open fire. That did cause some environmental problems and, especially, the notorious yellow pungent fogs of London. The pub remained a male prerogative and not regarded as a proper place for an unaccompanied lady. Ladies and the elderly received respect. A man failing to offer up his seat to either was a cad. Rationing and shortage of one sort or another remained for several years after the war. Little of the material goods regarded as so essential by later generations was available. Holidays, if taken at all, were spent at seaside resorts.

Much of the country remained agricultural, and village life continued as before the war. Crime was no real problem. When committed, the authorities invariably solved and properly punished it. A box around the ears by the local bobby or the cane at school deterred the prospective thug. Life remained much in this form during the 1950's. Yet that was the calm before the storm.

In 1950, I moved to Liverpool and joined the Liverpool office still at 10 Water Street. A male shorthand typist worked for the senior partner, Mr. Goffey. Otherwise, typing was by young ladies provided by Miss Foulke's establishment. She taught shorthand and typing to young ladies of middle class family background. She had a steady turn over because the young ladies regarded their position as temporary while seeking eligible husbands.

Otherwise, staff were male apart from one female telephone operator. Herbert Peever was chief summons clerk. He had a unique knowledge of court procedure acquired over his many years. He would argue many abstruse technical points of procedure before the Court. Points that solicitors if not Counsel would argue today. We rightly said at the time that we would never find another Peever.

266

The cashier wrote up the ledgers and account books daily by hand. Copying of documents was done in type with carbon copies. The typist erased and retyped minor inaccuracies. Otherwise, she needed to retype the page. Likewise, she had to retype corrected drafts. The typist took dictation in shorthand. When on board ship, the male typist took that dictation and typed it on the ship. It was not considered suitable for the young ladies to go aboard a ship except the larger passenger liner. Copy typing was voluminous especially at times of trial or acquisition. We sent much out to law stationers who conducted a thriving business.

Thus, like so many activities of the decade, the firm was labour intensive at a time when labour costs and legal costs were low. Consequently, solicitors often found themselves engaged to carry out activities of an essentially semi-clerical type.

Liverpool had suffered extensive war damage. Little repair had taken place with many derelict spaces remaining. Yet the Port and City were thriving and believed that they would continue to do so as before the war. I was crossing the river daily by ferry. I saw for myself the heavy flow of traffic inward and outward bound from the river Mersey. The firm was handling much shipping casualty work occurring on the river: both collision and salvage.

A case in which I became concerned on arrival in Liverpool was that of the wartime collision between the *Queen Mary* and the cruiser HMS *Curacao*. This had taken place on the 2nd October 1942 when the *Queen Mary* was off the Donegal coast. She was completing a voyage from New York to the Clyde carrying some ten thousand American troops. During the war, both the *Queen Mary* and the *Queen Elizabeth* had been engaged in trooping. The Germans regarded them as so important that Hitler was reputed to have offered a reward for their sinking.

In 1943, the Admiralty, as Owners of HMS *Curacao*, had issued a writ against the Cunard Company, as Owners of the *Queen Mary*. They had deferred further steps in the action because of the wartime security surrounding the *Queens*. Mr. Justice Pilcher, an outstanding admiralty judge, ultimately heard the action. He gave judgment in January 1947.

As the evidence showed, the *Queen Mary* was first escorted by a United States Flying Fortress. The cruiser *Curacao*, accompanied by six destroyers, was to meet and escort her into the Clyde. She was under strict orders to maintain her speed and a secret zig zag course known as zig zag No.8.

Zig zag No.8 consisted of four minutes on the mean course followed by four minutes each of two 25 degree variations first to port and then to starboard. Then, four minutes again on the mean course followed by four minutes each of two 25 degree variations but first to starboard and then to port. The course changes were shown on a blackboard in front of the helmsman and signalled by an automatic bell. This zig zag course was intended to defeat a submarine torpedo attack.

At 10.30 am on 2nd October 1942, HMS *Curacao* was steaming about 5 miles ahead of the *Queen Mary*. They exchanged visual signals. At 11.30 am, the *Queen Mary* signalled her course and speed as 108 degrees true course at 26½ knots. That was her mean course and speed on zig zag course No.8. At 12.20 pm, HMS *Curacao* sent the *Queen Mary* a further visual signal: 'I am doing my best speed twenty-five knots on a course of 108 degrees. When you are ahead, I will edge in astern of you.'

At 2.00 pm, the *Queen Mary* came out of the port leg of her zig zag and at 2.02 pm steadied on her mean course of 106 degrees. HMS *Curacao* was then distant about a mile forward of the starboard beam.

At 2.04 the *Queen Mary* turned onto the starboard leg of her zig zag and at 2.06 settled on that course of 131 degrees. HMS *Curacao* was then under a mile distant bearing four points on the starboard bow. The courses of the two vessels were converging at 23 degrees.

Earlier, the Master of the *Queen Mary* had instructed the Officer of the watch:

'It is important to stick to your zig zag. You need not worry about *Curacao*.These fellows are used to escorting and will keep out of your way.'

Yet, as the *Queen Mary* continued her starboard leg of the

zigzag, HMS *Curacao* failed to go to starboard. At the last moment, in the imminence of collision, the *Queen Mary* put her wheel to port but it was then too late to avoid collision.

In the words of the Captain of HMS *Curacao*:

'The *Curacao* heeled over as a result of the blow certainly to her beam ends. I thought for a moment that she would never recover. On the bridge we were hanging on. The fore part of the ship that formed the major part of the ship then righted to within a few degrees from upright. I formed an instant opinion that there was a chance to save the fore part of the ship. Very shortly after, I realised that she had no chance and that the fore part of the ship must go down. I gave orders to abandon ship. I was standing on the *Curacao* until she finally dipped and then I dipped too. The *Queen Mary* properly steamed on. I and one other Officer and ninety-nine ratings out of the four hundred on board were saved. We were picked up by two of the destroyer escort.'

In these circumstances, Mr. Justice Pilcher held that the *Queen Mary*, as the escorted convoy, was under a primary duty to keep her speed and zig zag course. He further held that HMS *Curacao*, as escort, was under the reciprocal duty to keep a close watch on the *Queen Mary* and to keep out of her way. He thus found the *Curacao* alone to blame for the collision. The Admiralty appealed.

In the Court of Appeal, Bucknill L.J. and Wrottesley L.J. held that the *Queen Mary* was one-third to blame for failure to take avoiding action until much too late. Leslie Scott L.J, dissenting, concurred in the Judgment of Pilcher J. He considered that HMS *Curacao* should have allowed the *Queen Mary* to carry out her zig zag course undisturbed and that the *Queen Mary* acted prudently in not porting earlier.

The dissenting judgments of Pilcher J. and Leslie Scott L.J. pay more attention to the wartime orders of the *Queen Mary* and to HMS *Curacao* allowing for this. Those orders were, of course, to maintain her zig zag course and speed. Severe criticism or worse would have been levelled against those navigating the *Queen Mary* had a submarine torpedoed her following a departure from her orders as happened to the *Lusitania*. Such a sinking and loss of US troops would have had appalling consequences on morale in war torn Britain and in the USA and for the second front.

Yet, the House of Lords upheld unanimously the majority decision of the Court of Appeal. Doubtless it was within their Lordships' minds that their decision would enable the dependants of those lost from the *Curacao* to recover compensation in respect of their loss. Such compensation was not then recoverable in law directly against the Crown by serving military and naval personnel. Though, it was recoverable in full against the owners and insurers of the *Queen Mary* if the Court attributed any blame to that vessel. The latter could then recover against the Admiralty in the proportion that the Court held HMS *Curacao* to blame for the collision.

Another casualty following wartime service was that of a heavy explosion in the engine room of the *Reina Del Pacifico* owned by The Pacific Steam Navigation Company. That explosion occurred on 11th September 1947 while the vessel was undergoing sea trials off Belfast following restoration from war time trooping to a luxury passenger liner serving South America. The explosion caused serious damage to the crankcases of the four main engines. It resulted in twenty-eight deaths and serious injuries to twenty-three other persons.

The Chief Office described how he had organised a rescue party to haul up the injured men and for removal of the dead and continued:

'Most of the injured in the main engine room were at the starting platform where the explosion had killed about three. Those between the engines were mostly all dead. In the auxiliary engine room, flame and blast through the door had injured four or five.'

As further described by the ship's doctor:

'I went to the engine room where I saw smoke and fumes and heard groans. One body was burning in the generator room and another between the main motors. I saw extinguishers used on these. Most of those in the main engine room were dead. I recognised Mr. Johnston, the First Engineer, lying face downwards at the starting platform. I attempted to administer morphine tablets to the injured but many could not swallow. I requested outside medical aid to include doctors and morphine suitable for injection.

'Removal of the injured was taking place by way of the escape and use of a hammock to haul them up to deck and into the second class lounge. All the serious cases were suffering from severe burns and, in addition, some had fractures and some internal injuries. The degree of burning mostly required intravenous plasma transfusions needing hospital treatment at the earliest possible moment. Ship's burn dressings were generally too small for the extensive burns.'

The technical and legal complications arising out of the casualty occupied the firm during much of the 1950's.

Following the war, Liverpool and its mercantile community looked forward to a continuing role as a major port and maritime centre. I had come to Liverpool in that belief to a then foremost legal maritime practice. Many large liners, both passenger and cargo, were sailing in and out of Liverpool. Frequently, they encountered bad weather in the Atlantic that caused shifting and damage to cargo and injury to passengers. Collision, salvage and fire aboard ship were taking place. All required investigation and appropriate action. Generally, that could be done in Liverpool or at another British or European port. Sometimes, we instructed lawyers overseas to take action. Later, development of air travel allowed journeys overseas to investigate the more serious mishaps.

The Liverpool ferry service operated a frequent service across the river departing every few minutes from Birkenhead and Wallasey. This could be hazardous in thick fog with large vessels moving or anchored in the river. Sometimes, the ferry company suspended the service. However, subsequent installation of an efficient shore radar system enabled the ferries to operate under such conditions with minimum problems. Increasingly, as radar came into general use at sea, a collision required close interrogation of those at the radar to discover what the radar had shown. Thus, I was finding my extensive knowledge of radar of increasing use.

I was doing a job that I much enjoyed in helping those at sea

271

who had the misfortune to become involved in a shipping casualty. I had the knack of being able readily to interpret and reenact the circumstances of a casualty from the chart. Sometimes, overwhelming in its effect upon those involved but open to simple interpretation. This could especially help a ship's officer in clearing his mind for a Board of Trade investigation or owner's domestic enquiry and avoiding a finding of blame. That was especially important at a time when instant dismissal could follow censure.

Firms of solicitors remained small with partnerships limited by law to not more than twenty partners. The commercial solicitor advised on all aspects of mercantile law. Besides advising on maritime law, I was acquiring an expert knowledge in pension, building and property law. Peculiarly, many commercial solicitors avoided pension law as too specialised. In fact, it was then no more than an extension of trust law and an understanding of two relevant tax acts.

My father, Martin Hill, enjoyed recognition as a pension specialist. Many shipping and industrial companies came to him for setting up a new pension scheme or a revision of their existing scheme. As earlier described, he advised on the setting up of The Merchant Navy Officers Pension Fund, which continues today as a model pension scheme. Under that scheme, a trust deed and rules appointed thirty-two trustees equally representing shipowner and officer members. The Trustees met quarterly and a general purposes subcommittee met monthly for management purposes with Martin Hill, and later myself, attending. First my father and then I provided our services for more than half a century at nominal fees to help those at sea build up adequate pensions for retirement.

Martin Hill then enjoyed the highest reputation within the maritime world for his expert legal and marine knowledge. Not only with shipowners whom he represented through the Liverpool Steam Ship Owners' Association and the General Council of British Shipping, but with those engaged in underwriting marine risks. The Maritime Insurance Company of Liverpool appointed him a non executive director of the Company.

Like his uncle Norman before him, Martin Hill had specialist

272

knowledge of the Hague Rules, the Carriage of Goods by Sea Act 1924, and limitation of shipowners' liabilities. He was a member of the British Maritime Law Association and of the Committee Maritime International (C.M.I.). He advised the UK Government at international conferences held to consider draft shipping conventions and played a large part in achieving uniformity in international shipping law.

Meanwhile, in October 1951, I became a salaried partner at an annual salary of £750 increasing to £1,000 in the second year and to £1,250 in the third year. Not that generous even by the values of the day, but in the professions seniors expected juniors to look to their ultimate prospect of succession to senior partnership. A prospect that might lie far ahead at a time when late succession and penal taxation militated against adequate savings and a pension for retirement. Consequently, senior partners continued to retain their major proprietorship and earnings within a partnership to advanced years. When they did finally retire, it generally took the form of a transfer of their interest for a lump sum payment or an annuity.

In that same year, 1951, the Law Society appointed me their examiner in the optional maritime paper offered to candidates in the Solicitors' Final Examination. Thus, I accepted an academic position that I was to continue for some twenty-five years. During that period, the Law Society was to end the optional marine paper and to appoint me their examiner in the compulsory paper on commercial law.

In 1952, the Liverpool Steam Ship Owners Association appointed me an assistant secretary of the Association. That same year, Ellerman Lines invited me and my wife, Norah, to spend a week's holiday as their guests on their steamship, the *City of Ottawa*. The vessel was on a voyage discharging and loading cargo around the North coast of Europe. We called at Le Havre, Antwerp, Rotterdam and Hamburg. An exciting trip to us as we were the only passengers and made good friends aboard. At Hamburg, we went ashore to explore and have a meal.

We saw much work of reconstruction of former war damage. After an excellent meal, we decided to walk back to the ship. Some young Germans followed us and we heard the term Englander

Swinehund. They showed a threatening attitude, and we became lost in our endeavours to throw them off. Fortunately, we came to a police station. There we sought both direction and short refuge while they went on their way. Still we were relieved to get back on board the *City of Ottawa*. This was seven years after the ending of the war.

Roy Gray Hill and Norah Olive Hill, Wedding Day

Roy Gray Hill

CHAPTER 16

A PEACEFUL DECADE

I look back to the 1950s as good years filled with hope for the future and for the continued prosperity of Liverpool and its shipping. A national merchant marine continued to contribute substantially to overseas earning. Thriving agriculture and fishing supplied much of the nation's food. Life was predominantly peaceful with little materialism or self seeking. The sacrifices of war remained fresh in mind. People were generally courteous and kind one to another. I enjoyed living in a land of peace and unspoilt beauty where the air was good to breathe.

More women were entering full time employment in a country that offered full employment. Immigrants were coming from the dominions and the colonies and, especially, from Africa, the West Indies and Pakistan. They were welcomed into the rail and road services and into the construction industries that were seeking labour. Before the war, to see a dark skin was unusual. After the war, it became the norm. A family of widespread Empire coming to the mother country, but the Empire was ending.

The River Mersey was full of ships. They included the great passenger liners that were sailing from Princes Landing Stage to all parts of the world. Birkenhead and the Cammel Laird yards continued a thriving centre of shipbuilding and ship repair. Liverpool remained much as described by my grandfather, Leonard Hill, half a century earlier.

This was well illustrated in the Liverpool shipping pavilion that formed part of the 1951 Festival of Britain. Outwardly celebrated throughout Britain to mark the centenary of the 1851 Great Exhibition, the Festival's true intention was to show recovery from the war. Liverpool shipowners exhibited a long line of ship models through the ages with their many flags and funnels. It was an impressive display that illustrated the history of the then many Liverpool ship owners and, especially, the continuing importance of Liverpool as a maritime city.

Thus, much optimism filled the early years of the decade. The country had emerged victorious from six years of disastrous war. A young queen had ascended the throne. The nation held the monarchy in high esteem and affection and as the source of its stability. Talk was of this new Elizabethan and enlightened age and the prosperity it would bring. Television was increasingly making its appearance in the home. The new material, plastic, was coming more into use within the home. Nylons had replaced silk stockings. A new wonder drug, Penicillin, was to be the cure for all ills.

Yet, during the decade, seeds of destruction were beginning to take root. Boards of directors and management were replacing the entrepreneur, but they frequently lacked real managerial skills. Bureaucracy, generally mediocre, was replacing ambition and vigour. Succession was becoming dependent upon behaviour acceptable to those at the top and awaiting to fill dead men's shoes. The nationalised industries and the many public services were profligate in their expenditure resulting in lavish government subsidies and excessive taxation.

Talk was becoming more of rights and less of duties; more of state giving and less of private responsibility; and more of being owed a living and less of earning a living. Above all loomed the spectre of penal rates of taxation like Dracula seeking to drain the life blood of individual effort and thus of the nation. Rich and the not so rich alike were questioning: Why toil for the benefit of the tax man? Some of the best brains of the country were looking to find a means of avoiding the worst excesses of taxation and others in thwarting that avoidance.

In 1950, Martin Hill was awarded the C.B.E. in recognition of his wartime services to shipping. That disappointed the Liverpool shipowners who looked upon his services as equally meritorious and deserving similar honour to Sir Norman Hill following the Great War. However, Martin Hill was not endearing himself to the Government by his outspoken attacks on their failure to take proper steps in support of the nation's merchant shipping.

Indeed, he was one of few who then recognised and spoke

out vigorously against the appalling consequences of the labour Government's taxation policies for the nation's merchant fleet. Policies continued by successive governments of consuming the seed corn for instant benefit, and thus discriminating against future national earnings and the livelihood of those serving at sea. Micawbian behaviour of a nation determined to live beyond its means without proper recognition of the need to earn those means.

These repeated attacks upon the Government for their penal taxation, profligacy, and failure to support the shipping industry may not have endeared Martin Hill to those in Government. Still, how right he was in his dire warnings, and what little attention they have received over following years. Within half-a-century, Government policies have succeeded in reducing the greatest merchant fleet owned by any nation from 25 per cent of world tonnage to a meagre half per cent.

Two quotations from the Liverpool Steam Ship Owners' annual report written by Martin Hill epitomise his views. First, the nation must earn the standard of living it seeks to enjoy. Second, the Government's taxation policies were gradually but progressively destroying British shipping in order to provide a standard of living not truly earned.

Thus, in March 1950, he wrote:

'This country must sell sufficient exports to purchase the food and other things necessary to maintain its population and to purchase the raw materials needed for manufacture of its exports. Before the first world war, contribution by the so-called invisible exports, namely overseas investments, shipping, insurance and other services, paid for 20% of imports. During the latter part of the period between the wars, cost of imports was exceeding the income derived from exports as a whole. The need to finance the last war by sale of overseas investments greatly aggravated the problem by loss of income on those investments.

'One thing remains unquestionably true. Namely, those to whom we wish to sell will not buy from us if the price is not right. Wants on our part for improved standards of living, for the amenities of the Welfare State and for better pay and more leisure will influence

277

them not at all. The nation must now fully face the unpalatable fact that its standards of living may only be those that it earns and no more. If the nation is not to face continued austerity, it must appreciate that hard work and honest endeavour will alone enable it to pay its way in the world.

'The Association has consistently maintained that no one earns a profit for taxation purposes until he has provided for the periodic replacement of the tools of the trade. Thus, in the end, the shipping Industry will be unable to carry on if it suffers taxation at penal levels. Especially, if imposed on that part of its so-called taxable profits that it necessarily retains in the business for replacement purposes. While such money so set aside for replacement is so used, the Government should not tax it as though it were profit available for distribution. Before long, the present basis of assessment of profits to taxation coupled with the rate of taxation levied will lead to a gradual but increasing reduction in our mercantile marine. This would have appalling consequences for a country that depends in peace and in war on its maritime economy.

'British shipping receives no State aid by way of subsidy or otherwise and it seeks none. Yet it does ask its own Government not so to denude it of resources that it imperils its ability to compete with increasing foreign competition. Such has been the action of government during the post war periods through the taxation it has levied and continues to levy.'

Later, under the 1955 Report, Martin Hill wrote:

'UK Shipowners may have to seek a more sympathetic regime for registration of their vessel if they are to remain in business. New competitors have come upon the scene. Governments foster and aid these competitors through various methods of flag discrimination. Some give preference to the national flag by allowing reduced port dues, pilotage, consular and other like charges. Others give preference by a law requiring a stipulated proportion of their own imports and exports carried in ships of the national flag.

'Even more invidious is the flag of convenience by which a vessel registered under such a flag obtains freedom from legislative control. Principal flags of convenience are those of Panama, Liberia and Honduras. Thus, Liberia has a population no greater than the combined population of Liverpool and Manchester with little overseas trade and no substantial port facilities. Yet, it ranks only behind the UK, USA and Norway in the tonnage of its mercantile marine.

'The motive behind this remarkable development is tax avoidance. Ships registered under the flag of convenience pay virtually no tax, while UK shipowners pay over half their taxable profit to the Inland Revenue. Cost of replacement of the prewar ship has multiplied five times and that of a ship built between 1946 and 1951 by more than twice. The excess has to be found out of taxed profits put aside for the purpose with some help this year from investment allowances.

'The Association has said and repeats that the British mercantile marine will gradually but surely decline if the earnings needed for replacement and expansion continue taken away in taxation.'

Martin Hill was repeating these warnings throughout the 1950's but to little avail no matter the political party in power. Those warnings continue to apply today to the trifling remains of a once great national fleet. If politicians continue to ignore them, then even those trifling remains will have wholly disappeared early in the next century.

In 1956, Egypt nationalised the Suez Canal, which was followed by Israel and Egyptian hostilities and Anglo-French military intervention. Russia severely criticised that intervention, and so did the United States and others who feared an extension of hostilities.

The Liverpool Steamship Owners Association reported for that year:

'The Suez Canal Company opened the Canal in 1869 and continued its administration until Egypt nationalised the Canal in July 1956. For some three months after nationalisation, Egypt kept the canal traffic moving almost normally despite withdrawal of many pilots and others on the canal company staff. Still, to avoid deterioration in the Canal, the users established the Suez Canal Users'

Association to negotiate with Egypt for the future of the canal and its administration.

'However, at the end of October 1956, hostilities flared up between Israel and Egypt. Anglo-French intervention followed. It was withdrawn at the request of the United Nations Organisation and the readiness of the Organisation to put things right. Craft sunk by the Egyptians and the blowing up of two bridges blocked the canal along its full length.'

Shortly before the Suez intervention, a meeting of the Liverpool & London War Risks Association took place. In reply to a Government enquiry, shipowners present emphasised that they would regard closure of the Suez canal as intolerable to them and thus to the nation. That thinking may or may not have contributed to the decision to intervene. In all events, closure of the Canal did result in shipping having to voyage around the Cape of Good Hope with its additional voyage time and cost.

Egypt took some six months to clear the Canal that she reopened in April 1957. With United Nations agreement, Egypt imposed a 3 per cent levy on Canal dues to meet the cost of clearance. This levy fell mostly on British shipowners as the major users of the Canal. They complained of an unfair imposition. The Government, which had accepted the levy for political reasons, agreed to make reimbursement. Following these events, the then conservative Prime Minister, Anthony Eden, resigned and Harold Macmillan succeeded him.

During the decade, Martin Hill was a member of the British Maritime Law Association and the Committee Maritime International (C.M.I.) and an adviser to the UK Government. As such, he took part in several governmental conferences considering shipping conventions. These included arrest of ships; shipowners' limitation of liability; liability as a passenger carrier; and the liability of operators of nuclear ships. All resulted in international conventions and legislation.

Martin Hill was especially interested in nuclear power and led the UK delegation at the C.M.I. conference. He believed that nuclear power offered the same golden prospects to the British Merchant Marine as steam had offered a century earlier.

Thus, the concluding paragraph of the centenary History of the Liverpool Steam Ship Owners' Association read:

'A hundred years have passed and the world overall and shipping in particular is again entering a new epoch. In 1858, it was the steam engine. Today it is nuclear power. The steam engine enabled the British Mercantile Marine to secure a dominant place in world shipping. A place that it still holds in spite of all competition. Nuclear power applied to marine propulsion may offer the same golden prospects. No other nation has greater need for its further development.'

Those golden prospects vanished with other prospects in the sad events of following years.

Martin Hill participated within the International Chamber of Commerce in maritime legal discussions that included bills of lading and the Hague Rules.

In May 1957, he attended the 16th biennial Conference of the International Chamber held in Naples in respect of which he reported:

'In discussions on international transport, Dr. L. A. Stalemaker, a vice-president of KLM, forecast a very rapid development of air transport. He estimated that within five years at least a million people would probably cross the Atlantic at twice the speed then possible and at considerably reduced fares. He calculated that a single jet aeroplane would probably carry 60,000 passengers a year.'

Martin Hill feared the effect that this would have on the great passenger liners of the day.

My mother invariably accompanied my father on his travels and played her part in the social activities of his work. She was a vivacious and attractive lady who enjoyed playing her part to the full. She well complemented my father's intellectual reserve at social events. I recall her amusement when, returning home with Lord Justice Scott, the French police met them with calls to make way for the English lord and his party. Still, those were days when the English continued in high esteem.

Grateful shipowners showed their appreciation to my mother by inviting her three times to launch their ships. The first was the Blue Funnel M.V. *Menelaus*. Unfortunately, a shipbuilding strike curtailed social activities but not the presentment of a diamond ring. The second was the Ocean Group M.V. *Menestheus* launched at Dundee in August 1957. The Owners invited the family as guests with celebrations overnight at the Gleneagles Hotel. My mother was presented with a diamond watch. A third launch was that of the Coast Lines *Wirral Coast* .

Shipowners also showed their gratitude to my father by many invitations to him and my mother to travel as guests in the luxury passenger liners of the day. They made several voyages to South America that they especially enjoyed. Yet, they were enjoying a luxurious and elegant way of life that, unbeknown to them, was approaching a sudden ending.

However, they did not foresee that in 1958 when the centenary of the Liverpool Steam Ship Owners' Association took place. To the contrary, few thought that the Association would not last to enjoy a second centenary. Many celebrations took place including the Chamber of Shipping presenting a Georgian ink stand. The Association published its history and said of Martin Hill:

'Like Sir Winston Churchill, Mr. Martin Hill does not ordinarily use his second name Spencer. It is as Martin that the shipping public know him. As well as secretary of the Association, he is joint secretary of the General Council of British Shipping and the British Liner Committee. He is manager and secretary of the Liverpool and London Steamship Protection and Indemnity Association and of the Liverpool and London War Risks Insurance Association. He is chairman of the Governing Body of the Royal Seamen's Pension Fund.

'Yet a statement of these bald facts does nothing to convey the influence - one almost said power - which Mr. Hill exercises quietly, unostentatiously, but definitely in shipping affairs. Shipowners repose in him confidence to a degree rarely to be found in any industrial organisation. Government departments too defer to his wide experience and his wise counsel. The Association owes much to the Hill family and not least to their present secretary.'

During these years, I was residing in lower Heswall then a small country village in the Wirral that looked across the River Dee to the distant Welsh hills. Such was the view from my home across open farmland and the distant railway line. The occasional steam train puffed its way between Birkenhead and West Kirby appearing more like a toy than the real thing. This was a peaceful view from a peaceful garden not overlooked.

I constructed most of this garden myself with brilliant rockeries and tiny spinneys and a scented rose garden all contained within one-eighth of an acre. There our firstborn, Elizabeth, and later our son, Martin Gray, could be left alone to play without fear of violence. Later, similarly, Elizabeth could make her way unaccompanied across the field track to her adjoining school or to meet the bus on which I was returning from Liverpool. Sadly, like many country districts, suburban development has much changed the area.

During this period, I was serving on the Sea Transport Commission of the International Chamber of Commerce. The Commission was then studying the practice of shipowners giving clean bills of lading on shipment of goods apparently damaged or inadequately packed. In return, the shipper gave the shipowner an indemnity against claims for that damage. A practice that enabled the shipper to negotiate the bill of lading through a bank, which might have otherwise rejected it. I considered the practice as illegal and probably fraudulent and that the shipowners could not legally enforce the indemnity given. The Commission accepted that view and issued a strong recommendation against continuing the practice. I also participated in various legal conferences of the Sea Transport Commission held to settle various shipping documents.

These were enjoyable events. The Commission met in Paris, which was a delightful city in the years following the war. Parisian memories of the occupation and the part that Britain had played in its liberation ensured this. Travel was by the luxurious Golden Arrow train from London to Paris either by day or by through sleeper coach. I preferred to travel by day in the elegant Pullman coaches. In France, these converted to luxurious armchairs and table at which waiters served a sumptuous six course lunch or dinner. The meal was French at its very best with the best of wines. I marvelled how they managed to achieve such cooking on a train. Still, a rough crossing following such a meal could take its toll. Unfortunately, passage of time has now consigned this elegant Pullman train to history.

In Paris, French colleagues entertained me to dinner at the Chanticleer restaurant that they followed with an evening at the Lido. The Chanticleer was in the market area and was unpretentious in appearance. It offered the best of French food at reasonable prices. The Lido was far from unpretentious and charged outrageous prices. It comprised a Parisian cocktail of sensual music and lavish tabloids consisting of dancing girls in various stages of nudity, though they did confine entire nudity to still posture. Nevertheless, that was then an unusual performance to the visitor from England where decorum still prevailed.

In May 1956, I visited Sicily concerning proceedings taken there against the Cunard Steam Ship Company. The proceedings raised a difficult question regarding English law and the application of the Hague Rules on which the Palermo Court sought my opinion. I was intending first to visit Paris for a meeting of the Sea Transport Commission and then Genoa in relation to another Cunard case. The opportunity for a holiday in Sicily proved too good to miss.

Accordingly, I and my wife, Norah, departed on the Golden Arrow train for Paris. We then went on to Genoa where we stayed two nights before a twenty-four hour journey via Rome and Naples to Palermo. There the Cunard agents and our Sicilian lawyer, Professor Catinella, with his wife met us on arrival. In those days, Cunard was all but synonymous with the British flag that assured prestigious treatment wherever one went.

We had arranged to stay a week in Palermo. The first day there we visited the Cathedral. Unhappily, we found that, during their wartime occupation, the Germans had despoiled this wondrous building by stripping out the gold leaf. The Sicilians have since restored it to its former magnificence.

The second day, I expressed my opinion before the Court

and was warmly received. Later, Professor Catinella told me that my testimony had carried much weight with the three judges who decided the case in favour of Cunard.

Professor Catinella and his wife invited us on a drive into the wild Sicilian hinterland. However, before setting off, they advised us to leave behind all of value in case Mafia bandits should stop us. We set off with some qualms, but it proved a delightful day with picnicking in the country and visits to many scenic places. Fortunately, we did not come across any bandits.

I envied Professor Catinella's way of life. He arose at 5.00 a.m. and worked until 8.00 a.m. when he breakfasted. Then he took a swim or a trip into the country or similar leisure activity. He would resume work at 4.00 p.m. until 8.00 p.m. when he had dinner. Besides having a large legal practice, he was a judge of the Supreme Court of Rome and had a flat in Rome. Myself an early riser, I would have liked to follow his way of life back home.

After a week in Palermo and much entertaining by the Catinellas, we moved on to Taormina to stay a week in the Hotel Timeo there. Our hotel had a magnificent balcony overlooking the smoking Mount Etna. We took breakfast on this balcony in the cool of the morning. Later, we had the shelter of a lemon tree. A steep walk down the cliff side led to the shore below and the delightful bathing beaches. We could take a bus, but we preferred to walk. Once, when we were making our way back up the cliff path, we got into conversation with a charming and handsome Sicilian. He had deviated on his motor bike from the adjoining roadway to admire the view. Sensibly, he equally admired Norah. However, he disappeared on his motor bike in a cloud of dust.

Our seven days in Taormina passed all too swiftly. In those days of absence of air travel, few tourists were about. The colourful costumes and music in the evening were genuine. I still hear the sounds of the tambourines ringing in my ears. I see the crowd of young urchins gathered around us seeking liras. Their plight touched me, and I was foolish enough to take out my wallet to distribute largesse. We had to make a hasty retreat to avoid being overwhelmed. I regard myself as fortunate in having visited Taormina so unspoilt.

In 1957, I took part in an intergovernmental conference held in Geneva. The object was to examine the law of the sea in its legal, technical, biological, economic and political terms and to embody the results in suitable conventions. In truth, it was an attempt to sort out a whole variety of matters left over following the war. In particular, territorial waters and their width were very important to the nation's then substantial shipping and fishing interests. Especially, the control that differing national governments might seek to exercise over those waters for purely national purposes.

In 1960, I acted as an adviser to the United Kingdom goverment delegation attending the International Conference on Safety of Life at Sea held in London. Discussions covered proposed revised Collision Regulations and guidance for using radar as an aid to navigation. It was still early days in the use of radar at sea, and I was pleased to see my views adopted into that guidance.

During the Conference, I came to know one of the Russian delegation. I would have much liked to entertain him to dinner, but he made it clear that this would not be wise. As he put it to me, socialising with foreigners would not be well regarded back home.

In May 1961, I attended the eighteenth Conference of the International Chamber of Commerce held in Copenhagen. The agenda included a report that especially interested me. Namely, a proposed warning to shipowners against issuing bills of lading that did not draw proper attention to known inadequacies of cargo.

Roads in England and especially on the Continent were then still free of heavy traffic. I decided to go by car and to take the family. On the way, we passed through Arnhem and the wartime battle area. Remembering that peaceful and sunny morning that this had been a place of death to so many brave young men was a poignant reminder of desperate years passing into history. That reminder remained with us during the next night spent in the fascinating German city of Luberg that the war had left much damaged.

In Copenhagen, we stayed at a quiet Scandinavian hotel. There, our children could be safely left while we participated in the evening social activities. These included a banquet held in the Tivoli Gardens, a visit to the theatre and a Mozart opera. The King and Queen of Denmark gave an afternoon garden party at the Palace where they mingled freely with their guests.

In 1962, The Pacific Steam Navigation Company invited me and Norah to take passage as their guests in their luxury passenger liner the *Reina Del Mar*. The vessel voyaged between Liverpool and South America at a time when travel by air as the norm was still to come. We were to disembark at Vigo North Spain. The invitation included both children. It also included our drop head Ford Consul to enable us to drive back along the North Coast of Spain and up through France. Our voyage was to last four days.

We sailed from the Princes Landing Stage Liverpool on a lovely summer evening. It was a most romantic occasion. We slowly drew away from the quay with the Royal Marine band playing there to the departing vessel and the waving of goodbyes from the shore. The vessel headed down river into the setting sun that gradually disappeared in a red glow below New Brighton. As dusk fell, we went below to the restaurant for dinner. We chose from an extensive menu of the finest calibre.

The voyage continued in that same elegant manner. Every choice was available on a movement of the hand. It was all bliss around the pool as we voyaged through brilliant sunshine. Most of the passengers were in commerce or in public or diplomatic service in South America. Some were from the British Council. All were enjoying a leisurely voyage before returning to their duties or taking up a new post. For us arrival at Vigo came all too soon. We disembarked little realising that the days of this elegant ship and her way of life were numbered.

During the 50s, we had developed a love for the open air existence and the peace provided by the touring caravan. In today's circumstances of noise and dirt, I have difficulty in expressing the peace of those earlier days. No motorways nor mass movement of traffic spoilt the environment. Little hindrance stood in the way of camping whether by regulation or from fear of violence.

Travelling and camping was even more peaceful in France.

There the French still regarded British visitors as their saviours from German tyranny. We visited Lake Geneva, the Pyrenees and the Forest des Landes. We even obtained permission to camp overnight outside the gates to the Palace of Versailles. Later, we discovered the then remote village of St. Gingolph on the Rhuys peninsular in Brittany. It had a delightful space for the caravan on the cliff top directly overlooking the sea with its fine bathing beach and cliff walks. We returned there often. Today, on a visit to the past, we find it much developed with many villas on the cliff top where we had previously camped in such peace and delightful scenery.

Meanwhile, in 1958, we had moved from Lower Heswall to Caldy because of an intended development of the fields surrounding our former home. I was adopting my advice to clients 'buy the most expensive house you cannot possibly afford.' I envisaged currency problems with possible devaluation of sterling. Moreover, I regarded property as essentially cheap. I purchased for £6,750 a large four bedroom house and an acre of garden within the local beauty spot of Thurstaston Hill. Later, I added a sun room with full picture windows opening onto the scenic views and a Nordic log cabin containing a small indoor swimming pool and sauna. This with my large garden has enabled me fully to indulge my passion for hard physical exercise.

During the decade Leslie Adam, my previously mentioned partner, had achieved a reputation as an eminent company lawyer whose opinions clients much respected.

He later wrote of the decade:

'The fashions that effect the law have always fascinated me. After the war, fashions in company law and taxation followed each other thick and fast. An amendment of debentures reduced the rate of interest from 5% to 3½% per annum. These were the days of cheap money and 2½% Daltons named after the Chancellor of the Exchequer who even imposed a tax on bonus issues. The Companies Act 1948 brought a spate of new Articles of Association. Pensions became fashionable and required amendment of Company Memoranda of Association. That is until the Inland Revenue accepted that no express power to pay pensions was necessary.

'Take over bids became the fashion and, particularly, the taking over of shell companies to obtain their quotations on the Stock Exchange. Property developer became the new in title to describe those who had obtained planning permission to develop office sites bought at low prices during and immediately following the war. Mergers and group accounting came in. Dividend limitation made rich men richer. Floating companies on the Stock Exchange by means of a placing provided new companies for take over. Groups of companies led to the complexities of group accounts.

'Tax changes came and went. They caused extraordinary agreements and service companies to subvert the imposition of tax. Payments of compensation for loss of office or golden handshakes became a favourite device for tax avoidance. Many aspects of life became the subject of tax planning. These included all manner of tax avoidance schemes devised and altered in a continual battle between the Inland Revenue and commercial interests and their lawyers.'

The final paragraph of the Liverpool Steam Ship Owners' Association centenary history illustrates the general optimism prevailing into the 60s for the continued prosperity of British shipping:

'The world and shipping in particular are entering a new epoch of nuclear power, which applied to marine propulsion may offer the same golden prospects as steam in 1858.'

So, Liverpool entered the 60's decade with much optimism in a future linked to the prosperity of its shipping.

CHAPTER 17

VICTORIAN ROOTS

As earlier described my grandfather, Sir Leonard Hill, and his wife, Janet, had six children: four boys and two girls. The four boys in order of age comprised my father, Martin, and my uncles, Brian, Austin Bradford (Tony) and Maurice. My grandparents brought them up within a devoted and lively family atmosphere as the Victorian era ended. Great Britain was then prosperous and headed a great Empire on which its people proudly said the sun never set. The nation owned half the world's shipping and Britannia ruled the waves. The British people regarded their position as secure and continuing for generations to come. It would have appeared to my grandparents a good time for their children to be born with Queen Victoria celebrating her diamond Jubilee in 1897. Yet, during the next fifty years, two world wars were to cause dreadful injury and loss of life and all but bring the nation to its knees.

Martin, my father and the eldest of the four boys, was born in 1893. He is already a central figure under these pages.

Brian, the second son, followed three years later born in 1896. His description of early years at Hampstead and later the family's move to Loughton appears under earlier pages. He qualified as an accountant, joined the gas industry and invented Mr Therm. Older readers will remember Mr. Therm as an appealing little figure appearing under past gas advertising. Yet Brian's most notable claim to fame was that of a writer.

In his earlier days, he wrote several novels under the pen name of Marcus Magill. In my youth, I enjoyed his novel *Hide and I'll Find You*. The tale was of a young man wagering a press baron that he could remain in hiding undetected for seven days. Then deliver a letter directly into the hands of the press baron. If he lost, he forfeited the girl he loved. Of course, after many escapades, he delivers the letter as a telegram undetected in the guise of a telegraph boy. Hollywood produced the tale as a romantic film, which again I much enjoyed.

In later years, Brian compiled several anthologies. Especially, I liked *Such Stuff as Dreams* published in 1967. It comprised two hundred and fifty dreams of notable persons over the centuries.

Many are poignant, but none more so than that of Abraham Lincoln prophesying his own assassination:

'.....''Who is dead in the White House?'' I asked a soldier.

''The President'' was his answer. ''An assassin killed him!'' Then came a loud burst of grief from the crowd, which awoke me from my dream. I slept no more that night.'

An earlier anthology *The Greedy Book* consisted of more than three hundred extracts on the subject of eating. He followed these and other anthologies in 1973 by his life of Julia Margaret Cameron entitled *A Victorian Family Portrait*.

Julia was one of the earliest photographers and her work highly regarded as of much ability. In 1860, she bought the house Dimbola overlooking Freshwater Bay on the Isle of Wight to be close to her friends the poet, Tennyson, and his wife, Emily. They had moved in 1853 to Farringford bordering Freshwater Downs. Brian describes how Emily Tennyson wrote enthusiastically to Julia Cameron about their new home. 'The elms make a golden girdle around us now. The dark purple hills of England behind are a glorious picture in the morning when the sun shines on them and the elm trees.'

Julia's portraits included many notable characters such as Darwin, Carlyle, Browning, Longfellow and other great Victorians. Today, collectors highly prize her photographs. During the 1980's, public subscription succeeded in purchasing and preserving Dimbola as a memorial to Julia and as a museum of her work. To learn more about this remarkable lady read *A Victorian Family Portrait* published by Peter Owen Limited.

Austin Bradford (Tony) the third son born in 1897, was outstanding. During the first world war, he joined the Royal Naval Air Service from school. He crashed three aircraft, including one

291

into a reservoir, but without injury to himself.

Sadly, while serving in the Aegean, he collapsed with advanced pulmonary tuberculosis that his medical officer failed to diagnose and mistreated. The navy brought him home by hospital ship with little hope of survival. They awarded him a full disability pension for life that they thought could not be for long. His father had the sad task of telling the girl he wished to marry that he could never hope to support her. She met him with a brave response for those days: "Then, I must support us both."

Happily, events confounded that gloomy prognosis and he did recover. Though only after he had remained in bed for two years with an artificial pneumothorax and a complicated lung abscess followed by a further two years' convalescence. During this period, he occupied his time in mental arithmetic performing various calculations and in teaching himself embroidery that became a lifetime hobby.

He was no longer able to achieve his wish and that of his father of becoming a doctor. Instead, while convalescing, he studied for and obtained an external honours degree in economics from the London University. That degree and a keen and analytical mind enabled Tony to employ his undoubted talents in medical statistics and the then new emergent science of epidemiology. He contributed much to the understanding of occupational health and the causes of occupational disease and mortality.

However, first, having obtained his degree, he took up a one year post with the Industrial Fatigue Research Board set up by the Medical Research Council. On the strength of that appointment and with no certainty of its renewal, he married his beloved Q. That was his abbreviation of her longstanding nickname, Queenie, bestowed because of her regal bearing. Throughout her life, she continued one of the most elegant of women. Fortunately for Tony, the post proved permanent. In 1933, he moved to the then recently founded London School of Hygiene that later became the London School of Tropical Medicine.

During the 1939-45 war, Tony served, first, with the Ministry of Home Security and, later, with the Air Ministry working on medical

292

statistical problems. These problems included night vision for air crews and stresses suffered by bomber crews. Following the ending war of the war in 1945, the London School of Hygiene and Tropical Medicine appointed Tony emeritus professor of medical statistics. He took part in many clinical trials that included streptomycin for tuberculosis meningitis, aspirin and cortisone for rheumatoid arthritis, and the introduction of whooping cough vaccine.

However, undoubtedly, Tony's greatest contribution to medical thinking was his research into smoking and detection of the connection between smoking and lung and other cancers and circulatory and heart diseases. From 1950, with his then research student Richard Doll, he showed in a series of papers the central aetiological importance of tobacco in increasing lung cancer. An hour spent with Tony would dissuade the most hardened smoker from his vile habit.

Today, it may seem surprising that in the past they looked upon tobacco as manly if not healthy and of social merit. Thus, during the war, the Government reduced the duty payable on tobacco issued to serving personnel. For many years after the war, trains carried only a few nonsmoking compartments and theatres, restaurants and other public places allowed unrestricted smoking.

Tony received many honours both national and international including the CBE in 1951 and a knighthood in 1961. The Royal Statistical Society appointed him their President 1950-2 and he was a member of the Medical Research Council. Many leading medical and other learned societies appointed him an honorary member. He was in great demand as a lecturer both at home and overseas and as a committee member and chairman.

Following his retirement, Tony travelled extensively in the United States on an annual lecture tour. He loved the social life of the transatlantic liners and hated their replacement by jet aircraft. During the 1960s, I arranged several times for him and his wife, Q, to enjoy the best of the comforts and social life offered by the transatlantic liners. Although in their seventies, they would dance until the early hours. He would tell me with his puckish grin how the Nevada State appointed him an honorary admiral of its landlocked navy.

Tony had a refreshing humility and much humanity towards others. His keen and analytical mind remained untarnished until the day of his death in April 1991 aged ninety-three. His legacy to me of the cocktail cabinet presented on his retirement by the London School of Hygiene and Tropical Medicine is a happy reminder of good times now past. From this we shared many a convivial drink.

Thus, in spite of only one lung, Tony lived to the age of ninety-three years and achieved his ambition of becoming the longest lived of his kin. He was puckish in his glee at having enjoyed a full disability pension for more than seventy years tax free, which he described as his hero's pension.

I leave the last word to an extract from Tony's obituary contained under the British Medical Journal. Saying that, initially, doctors were ignorant or felt threatened by the new concepts of epidemology, it continued that Hill was an inspiring writer, teacher and proselytiser and made many converts. Especially, recognition of his pioneering role in establishing the connection between cigarette smoking and lung cancer puts him among the greatest physicians of the twentieth century. Yet he had only honorary medical degrees.

The obituary concluded:

'Hill will go down as yet another occupant of the 41st Chair. The term used for the distinguished who fail to be elected to the French Academy, such as Descartes, Moliere and Proust. For if anybody deserved a Nobel prize, it was Bradford (Tony) Hill.'

Maurice, born 1905 the fourth son of Sir Leonard Hill, first qualified as a barrister. He practised for a few years, but found this unrewarding and gave up the bar to become a solicitor. He joined with a Mr R.A.H. Clyde who had established a practice under his own name in London.

During 1937, Lloyds' Recoveries Department approached Martin Hill enquiring whether he would take on the legal work of recovery of marine claims paid by Lloyds Underwriters. He declined because of a conflict of interest in circumstances where he acted for so many shipowners against whom Lloyds would make such claims. Instead, he recommended his younger brother, Maurice. Lloyd's Recoveries accepted the recommendation, so giving to Maurice Hill and this new firm a valuable connection into marine insurance.

However, the war soon interrupted these activities. Maurice joined the RAF and became a squadron leader in intelligence. Mr. Clyde, being the older, remained to carry on Clyde & Co. Maurice rejoined him after the ending of the war and his demobilization. Yet, Mr Clyde did not remain for long. He retired to become an arbitrator. Maurice carried on the firm of Clyde & Co under that name with three younger partners.

Under Maurice Hill, Clyde & Co prospered. He was a jovial man completely without arrogance. Moreover, he had the talent of getting on well with people and making even the most junior feel important. This approach was one that earned him many friends.

Perhaps, he showed his character in his love of the turf that led him to open a book in which he was equally successful. Others may have coupled the roles of a leading commercial lawyer with that of a bookmaker but, if so, I am not aware of them. In all events, under his leadership, the firm of Messrs Clyde & Co. prospered. It is today one of the major international legal firms specialising in commercial litigation and marine and insurance law.

Sadly, in 1971, Maurice died of a heart attack at the comparatively early age of sixty-six. Still, by then he had set Clyde & Co on course to become what it is today.

Rosalind Mary Theodosia Hill. A description of those of Victorian roots would not be complete without the inclusion of Rosalind Hill, namely the daughter of Sir Norman and Mary Hill and cousin of those earlier portrayed. Although of the same generation as her cousins, she was born in November 1908 and thus more accurately described as of Edwardian roots. I recall as a child accompanying my parents on several visits to Sir Norman at Green Place, Stockbridge. There I met this beautiful and willowy young woman in her early twenties, introduced as cousin Rosalind. Then, unbeknown to me, she was reading history at St. Hilda's

College, Oxford and, after graduating, she obtained a B. Litt.

In 1935, Rosalind and her brother, Gray, were clearing ground in the manorial estate when they discovered what they knew to be a grave site of executed Saxon felons. They excavated and found a number of skeletons including one with a linen bag secreted between arm and ribs. This contained six silver pennies of the reign of Edward the Confessor, from which they gauged the date of execution as about Christmas 1065. The coins are now in the British Museum.

After graduating from Oxford, Rosalind first taught history at University College, Leicester. In 1937, she joined Westfield College as a lecturer in history and, in 1955, the University appointed her as Reader and, in 1971, as Professor of History. She occupied the Chair until her retirement in 1976. Her particular speciality was mediaeval history and, of particular interest, the crusades and the English Church in the thirteenth century.

In 1962, Rosalind published with R.A.B. Mynors a fine edition of one of the more important documents to come out of the Crusades. This was an account of the first crusade written by an Apulian Norman soldier who had served under Bohemund of Taranto entitled *Gesta Francorum et aliorum Hierosolimit anorum* (The Deeds of the Franks and other pilgrims to Jerusalem). A work in which she brilliantly captured the spirit and detail of the crusade. Another of her published works, adding to general knowledge of the early English Church, comprised an eight-volume edition of *The Rolls and Register of Bishop Oliver Sutton, 1280 - 1299.* A little book entitled *Both Small and Great Beasts,* published in 1953 (with Fougassel), comprised an intriguing study of heraldic beasts.

Rosalind had all the attributes of a great teacher. She was kind and humorous and knew how to instill student interest in her subject. She took particular interest in adapting her original works into lectures and seminars that would stimulate enthusiasm in her students for discovering how people lived in days long past. When she came to retire in 1976, her students petitioned for her to continue her teaching. Such was her love of Westfield that she continued to do so in her retirement and was still giving occasional classes as

296

late as 1992.

Towards the end of the war, Rosalind suffered the saddest period of her life when both her parents died within three months. She was particularly fond of her father and his passing was great loss to her. However, her parents were elderly and their deaths not unexpected. Her great tragedy was the loss shortly afterwards of her much loved brother, Gray. A lieutenant colonel in the Royal Army Medical Corps (Airborne Division), he was shot down over Catania without learning that he had become the second baronet. Disgracefully, the social order did not allow the title to pass to the female line and thus to Rosalind, so it lapsed. However, she did inherit the title of Lady of the Manor of Stockbridge and was most punctilious in the performance of her duties. These included presiding over her seigneurial court held annually in March.

Rosalind lived in Hampstead where she acquired a love of gardening. On her retirement, she moved to Radlett, Hertfordshire up a small lane where she shared a peaceful house and garden with two old friends.

Throughout her life and in her final days, Rosalind continued a keen walker, especially in the mountains and lakes of the Lake District and Austria. In later years, she accompanied a strenuous expedition to the Himalaya foothills. On being asked on her return how she fared, she replied in her usual unassuming way: "Well, some young ones seemed to find it rather taxing."

Rosalind died in January 1997 having lived her life to the full.

CHAPTER 18

END OF AN ERA

The 1960's and the 1970's were horrendous times for Liverpool. As the city once led the nation in shipping and industrial development, it led the nation in its decline and collapse of traditional values. Yet, the 1960's dawned with continuing optimism for the commercial and shipping future of Liverpool where they were saying: "Liverpool does today what London thinks tomorrow." This was perhaps an arrogant remark, but it displayed the continuing commercial confidence in Liverpool.

There were gathering clouds. The closing of the Cotton Exchange by the Labour Government after the war had done much irreparable harm. Passengers were deserting the great passenger liners to travel by air. The container ship was replacing the traditional cargo liner. Much war damage remained. The City Counsel was slow to act. There appeared a growing tendency to rest on laurels and to believe in an entitlement to a comfortable life as distinct from earning that life. Management both public and private were becoming more bureaucratic and lacking in enterprise intensified by penal rates of taxation. Ridicule of working and risking capital for the benefit of the tax man was increasing. The common interests of management and labour were little recognised with too much talk of we and they. Strikes were becoming more common with the one nation spirit and joint effort fostered during the war in decline. The ending of National Service aggravated a loosening of discipline.

Yet, as the decade opened, confidence abounded. The Prime Minister, Mr. Macmillan, was saying: "You have never had it so good." Rightly in the sense of the full employment of the time producing ever more motor cars, refrigerators, washing machines, television and hi-fi apparatus. More goods were appearing in the shops including the new colour television. These goods still largely consisted of high quality home manufacture as British industry struggled to resume its prewar eminence. The standard of living of all was improving.

Yet, the nation failed to recognise that a once great power and empire were in decline and the consequences of that decline. For Liverpool this meant a declining importance as the European gateway, and its replacement by Rotterdam with its modern port and efficient labour facilities. A time, like the war, when the nation should have been working as one to avoid catastrophe.

Instead, those engaged in the dock industry of Liverpool and elsewhere were burying their heads in the sand. Management was inefficient, hidebound and at loggerheads with labour. The industry was we and they at its worst. The two sides of this still great dock industry of Liverpool did not try to organise let alone plan for the future. Strikes and rumours of strikes were becoming the order of the day. Liverpool docks were to become synonymous with all that was rotten in labour relations. Idleness, go-slow and obstruction with their resultant delay to ships visiting the port were replacing the scenes of activity described by my grandfather eighty years earlier.

Martin Hill was repeatedly warning under the Liverpool Steamship Owners' Association annual reports:

'Delays in port continue to hamper the efficient conduct of the carrying trade. The waste of carrying space from these delays is disastrous. In the principal ports of this country, the turn-round of ships is far from satisfactory in comparison with prewar. Unofficial and totally unjustifiable strikes contribute to defeat the endeavours of the shipping industry to use its ships in the best way. Traders fail to take delivery of their goods in due time, which they allow to block up the quays. There seems no knowledge or sense of urgency of the economic perils that lie so near ahead. Moreover, there appears no appreciation of the intense endeavours needed to avoid them and the threat of national bankruptcy that they entail.'

Conditions worsened as the decade progressed. In Liverpool and throughout the nation strikes of one sort or another were the order of the day. They were spreading from the mining, dock and ship building and repairing industries, and later the motor industry. The nation was replacing its wartime cohesion of discipline and effort by the term of the day - I'm all right Jack-damn you. Successive governments were paying little more than lip service to the repeated warnings of Martin Hill as he stressed the parlous effect of government policies on the British merchant marine.

Throughout the 1960 and 1970's, shipping companies were moving from Liverpool to London and amalgamating. In 1963, the Government was calling for a single representation of shipowners with whom to speak. That representation was to be the Chamber of Shipping. In October 1963, the Liverpool Steamship Owners' Association became affiliated to and its members joined the Chamber of Shipping. That ended the Association as a national organisation, although it continued in a minor role as a local association for some years to come.

Martin Hill retired. In recognition of his unique services to shipping, the Council of the Chamber of Shipping singularly honoured him by an unprecedented appointment to their body. I resigned as assistant secretary and took over the management of the Liverpool & London War Risks Association. This all came as a great shock to Martin Hill. Despite his many warnings, he had never envisaged so sudden an ending to the Association and to Liverpool as a national centre of shipping.

Liverpool was then losing not only its former renown and elegance as a great commercial and intellectual centre. Instead, it was getting an international reputation of being work shy and a centre of strikes. A city said to lack moral fibre due to sexual laxity, drug abuse and violence and gone crazy over football, pop idols and false ideals. That reputation was increasing the problems of Liverpool and those seeking to turn its talents in new directions.

The country as a whole was facing decline. The adverse balance of payments warned by Martin Hill and largely ignored haunted these two decades. Thus, in 1967, a balance of payment's deficit of two hundred and fifty million pounds caused a run on sterling and required assistance from the International Monetary Fund. The Fund only gave that assistance against undertakings for improvement. Nevertheless, trade deficits continued. During 1976, they entailed a further loan from the Monetary Fund of three billion nine million dollars coupled with undertakings to curb expenditure. Value of sterling was spiralling downwards and was to fall to one-tenth of its 1960 value over the next thirty years. Talk everywhere was of the English disease of bad labour relations with its associated very low productivity and of declining monetary and moral values.

Martin Hill was in declining health and died in January 1968. In truth, he could not face the vicious decline of Liverpool and its shipping and, especially, the end of the Liverpool Steam Ship Owners' Association. Two letters that followed his death best sum up his life's work.

First, from the President of the Chamber of Shipping:

'Mr. Martin Hill held a unique position in the shipping Industry for many years. Shipowners, and especially those in the liner sphere, regarded him as a very wise counsellor. He will long be remembered. Perhaps, especially, for the contribution he made for the benefit of the Industry during the war, and as one of the most knowledgeable people connected with maritime law. The fact that he was a co-opted member of the Council of the Chamber was a measure of the respect felt for him throughout the Industry.'

The second letter came from the Secretary of the Merchant Navy and Airline Officers' Association:

'The death of Martin Hill is a great loss to the shipping Industry. In my own long association with the Industry, he is one who is indelibly imprinted on my memory. The longer I knew him, the greater grew my respect and admiration for him. As for seafarers, they owe him a greater debt than many realise, not least for his contribution to the development of the Merchant Navy Officers Pension Fund. That must have brought him very much satisfaction.'

These two letters show the character of Martin Hill as he passed into history. Namely, one who appreciated that we were one people and should behave as such. If others of the time on both sides of the political divide had been of similar vision, then prospects for the nation could have been very different.

In November 1969, Hill Dickinson & Co. moved from Water Street to Castle Street. This was not only a move after 100 years from a building that had many maritime connotations at a time when

Liverpool was fast losing its maritime importance. It was also the beginning of a great change in the legal profession and the tools by which the profession conducted its business.

The dictating machine and the photocopier were replacing shorthand and copy typists. Telex and in turn faxes were replacing the telegram and cable. Electronic accounting and computers were making an appearance. Yet to come, were the personal computer and the many associated electronic devices for the storage and retrieval of every manner of information. Women were entering the professions and, especially, the legal profession in ever increasing numbers.

Meanwhile, I and my partner, Leslie Adam, continued the firm's close relationship with Cunard for over a century. Leslie was advising on the corporate side and I on the marine side. Earlier, in 1955, Leslie had advised the Cunard regarding their acquisition of the independent airline, Eagle Airways. Cunard recognised that the future lay in air transport, and they intended to be part of that future by offering transatlantic passengers the alternative of air flight. In 1962, Cunard purchased a 30% interest in British Overseas Airways Corporation (now British Airways) at a price of eight million five hundred thousand pounds. Cunard was looking to establish a pattern of one way travel by sea and the other by air.

In 1963, following long drawn out negotiations, Cunard contracted with John Brown Clydebank for the latter to build the *Queen Elizabeth 2* at a price of £25,447,200. A Government loan raised £17,500,000 at 4½% per annum. After serious delays, the *Queen Elizabeth 2* came into service in 1969 but suffered a series of turbine breakdowns and other problems.

In 1965, management consultants warned Cunard that without major reorganisation the company faced serious financial losses. Resultant upon that advice, Cunard transferred its passenger management from Liverpool to Southampton and sold its luxury transatlantic ships, *Mauritania*, the *Queen Mary* and the *Queen Elizabeth* with several Cunard buildings. The company rightly envisaged that the growing transfer to air would continue and that the Company was right to maintain its expansion there.

Regrettably, a strike of the National Union of Seamen caused heavy losses in 1966. Those losses coupled with an increasing demand by British Overseas Airways Corporation for development funds led to Cunard withdrawing from the air and selling its interests in the Corporation. An unfortunate decision forced upon Cunard by the readiness of the time to allow labour disputes to result in strikes despite the ultimate consequences to all.

By 1970, Cunard's financial position had worsened again with its accountants warning of a two million pound operational loss. The following year saw what earlier the nation would have regarded as unbelievable. Namely, the emergent property company, Trafalgar House, acquiring Cunard for a mere twenty-six million pounds. Thus, Cunard ceased to be an independent company, so ending a century of close relationship between it and Hill Dickinson & Co. Nevertheless, Cunard continued to instruct me in relation to its marine affairs. These included a number of casualties during the 1960's.

The most newsworthy was the *Carmania*. She grounded on a reef off the Island of Salvador when navigating close into the Island to allow passengers a view. The vessel had managed to refloat, but only after she had sustained bottom damage. I immediately flew out to the vessel that was then in dry dock in Newport News USA undergoing repairs. I found the ship's officers shocked and confused by what had occurred. Careful plotting and rechecking on the chart from earlier fixed positions established what could only have been an uncharted reef.

The Board of Trade surveyor, who had followed me out to the vessel, agreed with that explanation and accepted that the ship's officers were without blame. The hydrographic office subsequently accepted the explanation and revised the chart to show the reef. Still, a new cocktail, Carmania on the Rocks, came into vogue on other Cunard cruise vessels.

In 1969, I was back again on the *Carmania*. She had collided with the Russian freighter *Frunze* off Gibraltar. There I joined her on the homeward leg of her Mediterranean cruise. That voyage showed the changing standards of Cunard that had deteriorated from vessels of great elegance and luxury to vessels employed in

303

mass holiday travel and entertainment.

In 1974, fire caused the loss of the Cunard *Ambassador* while on passage to pick up passengers off Key West. She was a beautiful ship built two years earlier for the American cruise market and carried 650 passengers in every comfort. Like so many tragic incidents, the origins of the fire were simple. A faulty fuel pipe leaking on a hot surface caused fuel to ignite and fire to spread rapidly to engulf the engine room. Fortunately, no loss of life occurred. A similar incident occurred on board the *Queen Elizabeth 2* in 1976. Then, the engine room staff contained and extinguished the fire within ten minutes with little damage done.

I made several visits to the Caribbean to Cunard cruise vessels that had been in collision. This entailed my travel on the vessel while she visited various Caribbean islands during her cruise and my staying on a Caribbean island before returning home. This gave opportunities to view a beautiful part of the world before it became despoiled by tourism and development. The vessels were engaged in the American market in which love of mass entertainment and change from the Cunard's elegant past was most striking. What would the prewar gentleman taking dinner in his elegant evening attire make of his modern counterpart? He was also at dinner but in shirt sleeves and braces wearing a party hat with the inscription *Kiss me Kate*?

During the 1970s, I was mostly engaged in marine activities for British shipowners. In 1976, I visited Tokyo for some ten days concerning a tanker that had destroyed an oil jetty and the need to settle claims for the damage done. While high up in the offices of the ship's agents, the building appeared to sway back and forth. I put this down to jet lag. That is until I observed those around me diving under their desks. By then the earthquake was over. Fortunately, it caused little damage. I enjoyed the return journey home over the North Pole with all the freezing waste below. Yet in perfect relaxation enjoying Japanese food and drink as I contemplated upon the extraordinary developments that had taken place in my then fifty years.

An interesting case that I handled for the Merchant Navy Officers Pension Fund was the *Halcyon Skies* owned by Court line Ltd. This well known shipping company had gone into liquidation in the early 1970's owing substantial arrears of contributions to the Merchant Navy Officers Pension Fund. These arrears included both employer contributions and officer contributions deducted from wages but not paid over to the Pension Fund.

We took action against the Liquidator for recovery of these arrears. We did so on the basis that the contributions were arrears of wages owing in respect of each individual officer. If the Court accepted that argument, it followed that the arrears of wages gave rise to a maritime lien. Namely, a lien enforceable by the officer as an overriding and continuing charge against the particular ship in respect of which the arrears had accrued due.

The Court held that the arrears of contributions deducted from pay retained the characteristic of pay and that the employer's contributions effectively formed part of pay. So the maritime lien was enforceable to recover both the employees' and the employers' contributions. The Pension Fund made a full recovery in respect of all outstanding contributions.

Meanwhile, in June 1967, hostilities had again broken out between Israel and Egypt. The latter had again blocked the Suez Canal entrapping the vessels *Melampus* and the *Agapenor*. The owners had maintained skeleton crews and readiness to sail on both vessels in hopes of an early release, but they did not realise these hopes. Each owner had entered its vessel in the Liverpool and London War Risks Association. On 19th February 1969, the Association accepted a total loss of both vessels and made payment of the insured values: namely £1,162,000 for the *Melampus* and £559,000 for the *Agapenor*. The Egyptians did not release the vessels until 1974. They then realised mere scrap value.

At the time of acceptance of the loss, a press reporter telephoned me as manager of the Association. He asked whether the vessels might have an increased value on release. I replied that this was extremely unlikely. However, in answer to his further questioning, I did agree that, in case of very high levels of inflation, this was perhaps a remote possibility. Resultant front page headlines that the Association hoped to make a profit out of the entrapment

305

confirmed my view that the media invariably exaggerates and is always suspect. Since then the behaviour of the media has much worsened, so that today little is trustworthy.

The late 1960's and the 1970's were a time of traditional values of morality and loyalty turned on their head. The nation had entered a new era of half truths, mistrust and downright dishonesty. Greed and selfishness were rampant combined with materialism and the vulgar display of self. A new golden calf of the day took the form of the newest and the biggest motor car driven without courtesy or regard for others. The tradition that the Englishman's word was his bond no longer held good even within the confines of the legal profession. Instead, the verbal agreement needed always to be confirmed in writing.

A malaise had spread throughout the nation nurtured by penal rates of taxation, unrestricted subsidies and welfare benefits. Symptoms comprised doing ever less for ever more while seeking every means of avoiding tax and obtaining welfare benefits. The consequences were continuous strikes, very low productivity and high inflation coupled with an objection to working for the tax man to subsidise those regarded as shirkers. A vicious circle fed this malaise as low productivity and high inflation coupled with penal taxation led to ever increasing demands of more for me.

Internationally, they knew this malaise as the English disease and they scorned the British for it. The malaise reached its crisis in 1978 in what became known as the winter of discontent. Those with industrial muscle sought to impose their will and demands for more upon others by withdrawing their essential labour or services. Perhaps, the most disgraceful were refusing heat and light in winter months even to the elderly and allowing refuse to collect and rot in city streets. The ultimate degradation was a refusal to bury the dead. To their credit, the medical and associated professions never failed to recognise their duties to humanity.

In retrospect, how could a people who had stood alone in a combination of courage, humility and selflessness have come to such a pass? Ineffectual leadership must surely be the root cause. Yet continuing excessive rates of taxation and uncontrolled public spending and subsidies were the trigger. Introduced by the labour Government directly following the war, they had been little altered by successive governments despite the vast changes that had taken place in social conditions. They, at least, required the pruning knife that was then long overdue.

The 1980's opened with a new government under the premiership of Margaret Thatcher. Popularly elected to restore sanity to labour relations and to find a cure to the English disease, it appeared that the nation was drawing back from a complete catastrophe. She was to remain in office for over a decade during which she was to transform the economic and social structure of the nation.

Earlier so full of ships, the River Mersey was then little more than a ferry crossing between Liverpool and Birkenhead and Wallasey. Such shipping as remained was a mere shadow of former substance. Bereft of its shipping and deserted by much of its former commerce, Liverpool, was in severe depression and at the nadir of its commercial collapse. Its reputation for every misbehaviour and irresponsibility, including rioting in Toxteth, did not help. The Government took steps to invigorate the area. They established the Mersey Development Corporation with Government funds. Housing, offices and shops replaced the defunct dock area. Liverpool was beginning to look to its very survival as a place of business.

On 1st April 1982, Argentina invaded the Falkland Islands and took unlawful possession of those islands. The Prime Minister, Margaret Thatcher, and her government assembled a task force of ships for transporting troops and their equipment out to the Falklands. These ships were to act as stand by vessels in case of resulting hostilities. Fortunately, sufficient British flag vessels remained available to make up that task force and sufficient volunteers from seamen ready to man the task force.

The Liverpool & London War Risks Association managed by myself and other war risk associations were much involved. The Government agreed to reinsure the associations fully against war losses of ships comprising the task force. Sadly, during operations, the Cunard vessel, *Atlantic Conveyor*, was the subject of an air attack. She was sunk with the loss of her Master, five members of her crew, and three Royal Navy and three Royal Fleet Auxiliary personnel. The Liverpool Cathedral held a remembrance service on 1st July 1982. It was a sad and moving occasion.

This was probably the last occasion on which Britain would possess sufficient merchant ships to support the nation in an emergency. For the worst fears expressed by Martin Hill twenty-five years earlier were coming to their ultimate fruition. Government policies pursued by both political parties since then had decimated the number of ships of more than 500 gross tons owned and registered in the United Kingdom. The nation's proportion of world tonnage had declined dramatically.

Thus, in the 1950's, the proportion was 25%. By 1975, it had reduced to 8.8% or 1,614 ships and, by 1980, to 5.3% or 1,143 ships. The rate of decline accelerated during the Thatcher years from a halving of the proportion every five years to near halving every three years. Thus, by 1985, the proportion had declined to 2.5% or 627 ships, by 1988, to 1.4% or 350 ships and, by 1993, to 0.5% or 274 ships. A similar decline had taken place in the number of British seafarers at sea and cadets training for officer rank.

Looking back over the last half century, Martin Hill was so right in his forecast of the ultimate effect of taxing monies put aside for replacement of ships. Yet, he never envisaged rates of inflation of up to 20% per annum. Such inflation made crucial Government support if shipping was to survive. It is quite extraordinary that governments over the years and, especially, that of Mrs Thatcher did not recognise this. For shipping had been a substantial earner of overseas currency. Apart from which, it had served the nation so well as its fourth arm of defence in the two world wars and in the Falklands.

It is fair to add that for a time during the 70s Government appeared to recognise this. Tax provisions allowed depreciation of the full cost of a new vessel against profits earned during the year of purchase and the preceding three years and future years. That relief went some way towards meeting Martin Hill's earlier premise that the State should not tax money put aside for replacement of ships. The result was to put some prosperity back into shipping.

However, in 1984, that limited recognition ended with shipping treated similarly to industry generally. Surprisingly, so soon after the Falklands' success, the Thatcher government reduced the allowed rate of depreciation to 25% per annum on initial cost as already depreciated. Special dispensation in favour of shipping did allow this limited depreciation to be carried back against profits earned over the three preceding years. That dispensation had some limited value, but the accelerating decline speaks for itself.

In 1983, the three associations then representing merchant navy officers approached me. They comprised the Merchant Navy & Airlines Officers Association (MNAOA), the Mercantile Marine Services Association (MMSA) and the Radio & Electronic Officers Union (REOU). We knew each other well because of my position as legal adviser to the Merchant Navy Officers Pension Fund. They sought my help in amalgamating the three Associations that combined to form the National Union of Marine Aviation & Shipping Transport Officers (NUMAST). That organisation now represents all merchant navy officers. I agreed to serve as a trustee and subsequently as chairman of the trustee company set up to hold the assets of NUMAST.

Those assets include the former MMSA trusts and charitable estates at Mariner's Park, Wallasey. They comprise residential property, widows' flats and an infirmary that provide peaceful accommodation overlooking the river Mersey for retired seamen and their widows. They are a place of tranquillity in a troubled, selfish and sometimes violent time for the elderly. Additionally, the MMSA trusts include funds for the provision of grants and pensions to seamen who are in need and their dependants.

Mariner's Park is a testament of past humanity provided by those who had earlier profited out of the sea and wished to benefit those who had served them. Thus, at the end of the 19th century, Liverpool shipowners purchased and donated the original park. In 1906, a Liverpool shipowner and philanthropist, Andrew Gibson, built Gibson House. He did so, recognising the need of seafarers' widows for flat accommodation into which they could bring their own furniture and personal belongings. In 1937, Annette Davies donated the John Davies Memorial Infirmary to the memory of her husband, John Davies, underwriter of Liverpool. It serves the sick and infirm of Mariner's Park.

As the decade progressed, strikes that had so bedevilled the 1960s and the 1970s abated. However, greed, disloyalty and demands for self began to appear in others who were already earning well. They were demanding and receiving ever more in increased salaries, bonuses and fees. Worst offenders included top executives of leading industrial and commercial organisations with their incestuous arrangements for ratifying each other's earnings. The expressions fat cats and cream came into vogue to describe them and what appeared as an obscene total package of earnings.

Traditional relationships including those of the family were breaking down. Divorce was becoming ever more common without regard to its effect upon children and the next generation. Sexual laxity and deviation were rife. The word gay, despite its true meaning, came to mean sexual activities between those of the same sex. Partner described all those cohabiting of whatever sex. Unmarried mothers were increasing in number encouraged by the prospect of welfare benefits. Fears of violence and burglary and other thefts were common. Discipline was lacking and punishment hopelessly inadequate for purposes of a proper deterrent.

During this period, my daughter, Elizabeth Ann Hill, had studied biological sciences and had obtained a doctorate followed by an MBA from the Cranfield Business School. After serving in the pharmaceutical industry, she became a business consultant. She brings to her clients problems that same analytical and intellectual approach that has done so much within the realms of law and medicine.

Passing out of the 80's into the 90's, the London end of Hill Dickinson & Co. broke away with the Liverpool end retaining the name. My son, Martin Gray, was then a partner in the firm and an acknowledged specialist in marine insurance. He inherits the family characteristics of memory and an analytical approach to his clients' problems.

We received an approach with a view to a merger with another Liverpool firm. Martin Gray sought to reject the approach believing that the two practices were unsuited. I shared that view. All other partners sought the merger. They persuaded Martin Gray to give way much against his better judgement. The merger took place. I agreed to act as Chairman of the merged practice in hope of preserving past values.

Differences were overwhelming. On the one hand, were the analysis and handling of major marine and insurance affairs. On the other hand, were the defence and administration of a mass of small injury claims and like work carried out for maximum profit. Contrasting attitudes of a personal approach and a regulatory regime exacerbated those differences. Martin Gray especially disliked what he regarded as an avaricious policy of continuous pressure to increase profits. The merger continued for five years but unhappily with many differences and much friction. Then, Martin Gray left to join the national and international legal practice of Alsop Wilkinson. I resigned as Chairman.

Thus, the unique values of Hill Dickinson & Co. are no more. Others now use the name but not as the Hill family served British shipping for over a century. A time when British shipping prospered as the lifeline of the British Empire and the fourth arm of the nation's defence. Now, like the mirages seen by Gray Hill in the desert, all gone squandered away by incompetent governments subsidising a way of life not earned. To repeat the words of Martin Hill half a century ago but that remain equally applicable today:

'One thing remains unquestionably true. Namely, those to whom we wish to sell will not buy from us if the price is not right. Wants on our part for improved standards of living, for the amenities of the Welfare State and for better pay and more leisure will influence them not at all. The nation must now fully face the unpalatable fact that its standards of living may only be those that it earns and no more. If the nation is not to face continued austerity, it must appreciate that hard work and honest endeavour will alone enable it to pay its way in the world.'

Today, the nation again looks to its future with a new government in power.

311

CHAPTER 19

SO IT WILL HAPPEN

Looking back to the days of Tom Hill, the rate of change has been phenomenal. Yet much of that change has taken place during the successive lives of myself and my father. When he was born, transport was horse drawn or by steam train or steamship. The telephone, radio, television and most household electrical appliances were still to come. Families were large and early deaths common within the family. Those of the times would have regarded as fictitious fantasy a forecast of what was to happen over the next century.

At my birth, Britain was the centre of a great empire still served by a large shipping fleet. Major industries still comprised shipbuilding, coal, steel, chemicals and textiles. Major employment was in agriculture, seafaring and fishing. Britain continued, as described by Napoleon, a nation of shopkeepers. Radio, electronics, air travel, and the motor car were all in their infancy.

What has since happened surpasses the imagination of the science fiction writers of my early years. Moreover, the rate of change is accelerating far beyond their vision and that of ourselves. Most of what is imaginable and much of what is yet unimaginable will happen. We have opened Pandora's box, but with little understanding of what it really contains. Our children's children and their grand children and descendants could inherit a wondrous life, but only if the human race can overcome the grave perils that may lie ahead.

Nature or God or as preferred has little interest in preserving individual life. That is as distinct from self perpetuation and evolution of a species. Two major wars and, to a lesser extent, the *Titanic* and like tragedies teach me that. Nature herself is especially cruel in that one species devours another, so that only the strong and cunning survive. Yet man has now attained such intellect and knowledge that he will cause the next stage of his own evolution whether for good or evil. As a result, I believe that change will now be rapid and profound and more differing in effect to anything before. Indeed, without such intervention, further evolution of the human species may not be possible.

I base that thinking on three premises. First, on what has happened over the last two hundred and fifty years compared with what happened over the previous ten thousand years. Both are of short duration in cosmic terms. Secondly, that man is accelerating in his acquisition of knowledge, especially, in his understanding of the science of life and of electronics. Thirdly, what is likely to happen over the next period of five hundred years and then ten thousand years.

Looking first at the next one hundred years, major developments will take place in computers and electronic controlling mechanisms. Especially, the computer and its associated robot machinery will come to dominate our lives, perhaps, more than presently realised. I anticipate programmes enabling automation of construction, manufacturing and office industries and most domestic tasks such as cleaning, cooking and general maintenance. Particularly, the professions may expect transformation where much of the work they do and the advice they give conforms to the analytical powers of the computer.

Thus, the legal profession is ripe for transformation. It is only a matter of time, and I surmise not much time, before the present system of establishing guilt and liability ceases as an expensive relic of the past. That system presently comprises opposing teams of highly qualified lawyers. They each submit and argue their case before an even more highly qualified judge with or without a jury. Many witnesses appear and give much conflicting testimony under examination and cross examination. After they have heard the evidence, judge and jury must decide the truth and the extent of guilt or liability according to that truth and the law. Thus, the system remains much as it was when Rowland Hill visited the Shrewsbury assizes at the turn of the eighteenth into the nineteenth century.

I envisage that computers will replace much of that system. A computer is not yet able to judge the truth out of conflicting evidence. Still, we are at an early stage of machines and drugs that determine the truth. Once these are perfected, they will decide the issues that presently occupy the lawyers for such lengthy periods. Further, I envisage that, during the twenty-first century, computers will be capable of showing the thought processes and thinking of an individual. Other legal activities are equally suitable for the computer, which already does much including settling a multiplicity of agreements and other documents and testamentary and company work.

The work of the accountancy profession is primarily that of analysing figures and interpreting the consequences of that analysis and advising upon the appropriate action. Computers already do much of the work. I envisage that will extend to include most, if not all, accountancy activities. A network will link computers one to another, so that they will automatically carry out audits and similar accountancy operations and pass the results through to the business centre. The same applies to banking, insurance, and the finance industry generally.

I envisage an end to the doctor's surgery that today occupies much medical time. The home computer will appraise and pass on the patient's symptoms to the local medical computer that will put any appropriate enquiries to the patient. Advice from the computer or, alternatively, a video consultation with a medical specialist will follow. Ultimately, I envisage that computers or computer controlled robot mechanisms will do much routine medical work including that of surgery. Looking further ahead, I believe our descendants will find the means of eliminating all disease or its cure by simple purging.

Electric propulsion will replace the petrol engine and its environmental problems. It will contain a fuel unit that will be permanent or replaceable. Driving will be automatic and controlled throughout the journey to avoid accidents. I anticipate that similar but larger units will also propel ships at high speeds under automatic control from a shore base. Generally ships will be large and employed in the carriage of cargo.

A more advanced form of what we now call virtual reality will replace television. This will be three-dimensional and allow participation of the viewer as if within and forming part of the activity.

The viewer will also use this equipment to call up family friends, banks, shops and his medical and other advisers as though meeting directly with them. The scope for education is endless. Meetings will take place over great distances as if the participants were placed together in the same room. That will avoid much business travel of the future. Any required travel will be by rocket propelled aircraft reducing the travelling time from London to New York to less than three hours and not much longer to Tokyo.

Similarly, video recordings will put the viewer back into the recorded scene as it was at the time of its recording. Other video apparatus will enable the viewer to explore most parts of the world and to move about within his chosen area. More interestingly, I envisage that it will allow similar planetary exploration and, later, exploration into outer space. Colonisation of habitable planets and their moons will follow and provide a launch pad to more distant parts of the universe. I envisage later colonisation and habitation of celestial bodies and endless exploration out into the universe.

Meanwhile, our descendants will have discovered the means of controlling both the weather and the environment and repairing the damage done by earlier generations. They will look to a means of making the planets and other celestial places habitable to them. Thus, I believe that we now see the first tentative steps to conquer space as I, in my infancy, saw the earlier steps that led to conquest of the air.

I anticipate that the computer will interpret the thinking of individuals by an electronic reading of the thought processes originating within the brain. Similar experiments on animals, birds and fish will interpret their thought processes and levels of thinking and memory. This will lead to some interesting research and possible forms of communication with other species. That, in turn, will lead to research into possible conversations with other beings that may be contacted in other parts of the universe. Remotely, it might prove possible to copy or transfer the entire thinking processes and memory of the individual. That conjures up to the imagination thoughts of an extension of being outside the body.

Developments in the life sciences lead to further intriguing thoughts of the future. Already, we see the initial stages of genetic engineering and what this may come to offer. First, some adjustment of the genes carried out to avoid hereditary diseases. Later, after objections against interfering with the laws of nature or of God, adjustment of genes that avoids hereditary defects of character or increases intelligence or physical capabilities. Later still, adjustment of DNA and genetic material will reshape the physical and mental characteristics of man including his life span.

Already, we see the initial stages of manufacture of human tissue. I envisage, before long, we shall see the creation of human parts of the body allowing replacement of diseased and defective parts either by surgery or by new growth. Also, we already see the fertilised human egg growing to birth in the womb of the surrogate mother. I foresee such growth outside the womb under conditions created similarly to those of the womb.

The human life span will no longer be limited to three score years and ten with each additional year regarded as a bonus. Initially, medical progression will extend life by overcoming disease and replacing organs. Ultimately, alteration of genetic and chemical makeup will slow the life clock and prolong life and youth. It is still for the imagination whether a transfer of being to a clone or newly created body might follow. Associated questions relate to necessary birth control and a possible ending of sexual reproduction as the means of perpetuating the human species.

This is, perhaps, the optimistic assessment of human involvement in its own evolution that in cosmic terms will now be rapid. Whatever now happens, life will never be the same as that described under earlier pages. Anything that is now imaginable may happen and much of what is yet unimaginable will come about. Evolutionary change could lead to paradise on earth. Grievously, it could also lead to the horrifying alternative of the extinction of the human race as it now exists or putting it back many thousands of years.

That will happen if humanity as a whole is unable to live in peace. The planet is now too small to permit of tribal or religious wars exaggerated into global wars. Yet tribal loyalties and primeval instincts remain dominant in too many parts of the world. They are flash points that could trigger a world war. They ought to be policed but how?

The United Nations has neither the authority nor the power. Too many individual nations are looking to their own best interests or, worse, the best interests of some despot. National aspirations must give way to cooperation if humankind is to avoid a catastrophe. In that regard, I look back to the British Commonwealth. It could have taken the lead in bringing together the major nations with a view to establishing, first, a loose federation and, subsequently, a world federation with an elected parliament. Guidelines for behaviour between nations could then be drawn up and enforced by a world police force under the charge of the United Nations.

In all events, catastrophe is too horrible to contemplate. World war already means atomic weapons of fearful force guided by laser beam of great accuracy and under automated control. These weapons would continue operating long after they had destroyed the combatants. Those not killed in atomic explosions would suffer death or severe injury by radiation.

I do not believe that atomic weapons would destroy the planet as such. Moreover, some life would survive including human life but much mutated. That would lead to alternative forms of evolution probably halting or postponing human development for thousands of years and leading to new forms of life.

Undoubtedly, the next stage in evolution lies in human hands whether for good or for evil. Moreover, come what may, those who inhabit this planet ten thousand years in the future will differ as much from ourselves as we differ from earliest man. Indeed, ultimately, they will differ as much from ourselves as we differ from the dinosaurs that once roamed the world.

Yet, I see nothing in this vision of the future as contrary to the vision of God as earlier expressed by my grandfather or as appears under biblical writings. To my mind the same goes for the acquisition of all scientific knowledge. I think of my young granddaughter, Elizabeth, who should enjoy a good life, perhaps, extending beyond the twenty first century. She will see much of what I forecast and some of that not yet imagined.

317

INDEX

Adam, Leslie, 239-240, 265, 288-289, 302

Admiralty Court, 102

Aeroplane, first flight, 241

Alston, 19th century lunacy, 91-92

American Chamber of Commerce, 107, 118

Arcadia, early Cunard steamship, 105

Arnold Dr., headmaster Rugby, 35

Arthur Hill Lifeboat, 77, 111-112

Arthur Hughes, Artist, 114-115, 164, 172-175, 185

Atlantic Transport Company, 125, 126

Benson F. R, Shakespearian actor, 178

Bevan, Captain *Thesius*, 206-207

Birkenhead, 124, 129-130, 275

Birmingham, 13-14, 16, 44, 53, 58, 70, 71, 81

Blundell family of Great Crosby, 98

Board of Trade, 104, 126, 184, 182 188, 219, 272, 303

Booth, the forger, 21

Bootle, 47

Boston, 105

Boswell's Dr. Johnson, new edition, 114

Boys,Goverment and Liberal Instruction of 1822, 34, 36

Brighton Railway Company, 64

Britannia, first Cunard steamship, 105

British Empire, 80,104,118, 165, 255, 264, 275, 290, 299,
   311, 312, 317

British Fleet 1913, size of, 205

British Maritime Law Association, 238, 273, 280,

British Overseas Airways, Cunard investment, 302

British Shipping ultimate decline, 7-8, 264, 276-279, 298-303, 307-309, 311

Bruce Castle School, 38, 39, 60, 75, 110, 111, 112, 113, 116, 162

Burns, George, 104, 118

Burns, J. O., 119

Burns, John, 119

C. & D. MacIver, 120-121, 128

Caledonia, early Cunard steamship, 105-106

Carlyle, Walter, emigrated to British America, 91

Carmania, grounding off Salvadore, 303-304

City of Glasgow, first Inman emigrant ship, 121, 122

City of Rome, 123, 124

Chamber of Shipping, 237, 301

Charterhouse School, its cruel system, 36
Chas Carrol, early collision, evidence, 102
Chester Cathedral & choir delights Rowland Hill, 47
Chigwell School, 247-248, 250
City of London, freedom to Rowland Hill, 70
Clyde & Co. marine solicitors, 238, 294-295
Cockburn, Andrew, *Lusitania* 2nd Engineer, 212
Colchester & Norwich school, cruelty of Head, Parr, 35
Columbia, early Cunard steamship, 105
Committee Maritime International, 238, 273, 280,
Copyhold land, 93
Corton, 242-244
Cowan, James, 19th century social conditions, 90-91
Crawford, Alfred, *Titanic* steward, 192-193
Cunard Ambassador, loss by fire, 304
Cunard Steam-Ship Company, 105-107, 117-120, 124, 207-221
   (*Lusitania*), 238, 249-250, 267-270, 284, 302-304, 307-308
Cunard, Samuel, 104-105, 107
Cunard, William, 119

Dickinson, John, 116
Dillon, Thomas Patrick, *Titanic* engineer, 195-196
Duff Gordon, Sir Cosmo, *Titanic* passenger, 197-198, 200

Eagle Airways, Cunard purchase of, 302
Edward VIII, abdication of, 250
Electricity, 1815 lectures on, 27
Electronics, coming of, 241-249
English disease, 305-306
Entailed land, 94
Eton, cruelty of Headmaster Keats, 24, 35
Europa & *Charles Bartlett*, early Cunard collision, 106-108

Falkland hostilities, 307-308
Finlay, Sir Robert Q.C. counsel for *Titanic*, 188, 200, 199
Freeman, John, *Lusitania* passenger, 214-215
Fry, Elizabeth and capital punishment, 73-74

General strike 1926 and Great Depression, 237
Gladstone, William, Chancellor of Exchequer, 67-69, 113
Gold coins, chipping of, 93
Gordon of Khartoum, 113-114
Gun, *Studies in Heredity*, 8, 10-11

319

Hague Rules, 231-232, 271-273, 281, 284
Halifax, Nova Scotia, 104,105
Hazelwood School and fire, 30-38, 60
Hendrickson, Charles, *Titanic* fireman, 196
Hilltop School and its constitution, 24-30
Hill, Lady, Caroline née Pearson, 38, 71
Hill, Annie née Scott, 111, 115,161,163, 167, 175
Hill, Arthur, 3, 17, 28, 40, 49-52, 59, 75-78, 110, 111-112, 113
Hill, Sir Austin Bradford, 5, 169, 291-294,
Hill, Betty Doreen married John David Gregson, 244
Hill, Brian, 169-171, 290-291
Hill, Lady, Caroline née Hardy, 116, 117, 127-128, 130, 131, 133-160
 (*With the Beduins*), 164, 176, 233-235
Hill, Caroline married Clark & emigrated to Adelaide, 22
Hill, Constance, 75
Hill, Edwin, 3, 16, 19, 26, 28, 33, 39, 55, 65, 58-60,
Hill, Dr., Elizabeth Ann, 283, 286, 310
Hill, Elizabeth Louise, 1, 317
Hill, Ellen, 75
Hill, Lady, Florence née Salmon, 292, 293
Hill, Frederic, 3, 7, 37, 65, 71-75
Hill, Geo. Birkbeck, 5, 8, 9, 10, 12, 13, 18, 21, 22, 24, 41, 70-71, 76,
 77-78, 110-115, 167, 172
Hill, Gray MD, 265, 296, 297,
Hill, Howard, 17, 37, 39
Hill, James, 8, 9, 10, 11, 12
Hill, Lady, Janet née Alexander, 168-169, 246
Hill, John, 10
Hill, Sir John Gray, 3-4, 76, 77-78, 109, 110, 115-132, 133-160
 (*With the Beduins*), 161-162, 166-167, 176-183
Hill, Sir Leonard, 4, 115, 161, 167-173, 225-223, 236, 242-243, 245,
 246-247, 253, 275, 290, 291-292, 294
Hill, Leonora, married Sir John Scott, 111
Hill, Lewin, 110
Hill, Margaret, married Sir William Ashley, 115
Hill, Martin Gray, 283, 286, 310-311
Hill, Martin Spencer, 4-5, 169, 236-239, 241-245, 249-250, 252-254,
 258, 259, 264, 272-273, 276-283, 290, 294, 299-304
Hill, Mary, née Danson, 162-165, 188, 235, 265
Hill, Matthew Davenport, 3, 15, 16, 18-19, 26, 28, 31, 34, 40, 41, 44, 53-58, 71
Hill, Sir Maurice J., 4, 8, 115, 161, 167,188, 206
Hill, Maurice, 238, 294-295
Hill, Norah Olive, née Parker, 257, 260, 265-266, 273-274, 284-288

Hill, Sir Norman, 4, 161-167, 173-174, 177, 181, 184-204, 205-223, 226-236, 265
Hill, Sir Rowland, 26-40 schoolmaster; 41-52 early travels;
   60-61 Australasia colonisation secretary; 61-71 penny postage &
   modernising Post Office.
Hill, Roy Gray, 5, 241-251 boyhood; 252-262 war service;
   263-274 admiralty practitioner; 275-289 the enjoyable
   50s; 298-311 the decline; 312-317 the future.
Hill, Sarah, née Symonds, 10-13, 56
Hill, Sarah, née Lee, 3-17, 18-19, 22-23, 24, 40, 43
Hill, Thomas Wright, 3, 11-19, 22-23, 24-27, 35, 40, 47-48, 75-76
Hill, Vena, née Lancaster, 241-244, 249, 281-282,
Hill, Rosalind, Professsor mediaeval history, 295-297
Hill Dickinson & Co., 2, 5, 116, 188, 203, 207, 237, 239, 265, 301, 303, 310-311
Hughes, Arthur, 114, 164, 172-175, 185

Isle of Wight, 7, 48, 51-52, 255-257, 259-260, 262
Inman Steam Ship Company, 3, 118, 121-125
Inman, William, 121-123, 125
Inman, Ernest, 123-125
International Chamber of Commerce, (I C I), 281, 283
Ismay, Bruce, 186, 198-200, 206, 240

Jenkins, Francis, *Lusitania* passenger, 216-217
Johnson, Hugh, *Lusitania* quartermaster, 211
Jones, Arthur Roland, *Lusitania* first officer, 212-214
Joughin, Charles, *Titanic* chief baker, 193-94

Kidderminster, 7, 8, 16, 17, 70
King George II & Bonny Prince Charles, 10, 7

Lancashire & Sea Training home for Poor Boys, 180, 181-182
Law Guarantee & Trust Society Limited, 166, 180-181
Leith, Robert, *Lusitania* wireless operator, 212
Leyland, 125, 126
Leyland, Frederick R., 126-127
Leyland, Fred, 126
Leyland, Geoffrey, 226
Life of Sir Rowland Hill by Geo. Birkbeck Hill, 5, 8,12, 35, 40
Light dues, 184
Lighttoller, Charles H, *Titanic* 2nd officer, 194-195
Lines, Alice, *Lusitania* passenger, 216
Liscard, 92
Litchfield, Earl of, Post Master General, 62

Liverpool, 3, 6, 47, 70, 78; emergence of 79-97; arrival of railway 97-100; coming of steamship 101-109; prestigious years116-130, 165-166, 168, 174, 178-9, 231, 205, 207, 231; hopeful years 266-267, 271-276, 287, 289; decline 298-302, 307-308; Mariners Park 309

Liverpool Bread Bakers, 95-96

Liverpool & London Steamship P. & I.Association, 118, 166

Liverpool & Southport railway, construction of, 97-100

Liverpool Cotton Exchange, closure of, 263, 298

Liverpool Sailing Ship Owners Mutual Association, 118, 166

Liverpool Steam Ship Owners Association, 3, 5, 109 , 116, 117-118, 122-123, 167, 177, 184-5, 205, 221-222, 232, 237, 264-265, 272, 273, 277-280, 281, 282-283, 289, 299-301

Lloyd George, David, Prime Minister, 230

Load Line, 122-123, 184

Lushington, Dr., Admiralty Judge, 102, 106-107

Lusitania, 207-220 evidence; 217-220 findings; 220-221 mystery of rapid sinking

Lusquehanna, contributory fault, 102-103

Mabeddy, George, dragoman *With the Beduins*, 131-160, 183

Maberley, Colonel, Secretary Post Office, 64

MacArthur, Captain imprisoned for custom's fine, 89-90

MacIver, Charles, 119-121, 122-123, 125

MacIver, David, 105, 118-119

MacIver, David junior, 120-121

Manchester Ship Canal, 165

Manchester, 49, 165

Marconi, Gugliemo, invented wireless *Titanic* expert, 201-202

Marine Insurance Act 1906, 184

Mariner's Park Wallasey, 309-310

Married Women, 74, 83-84,174

Marshall, Lucy, 85-87

Melbourne, Viscount, Prime Minister, 62-63

Merchant Navy Officers Pension Fund, 238, 250, 304-305, 309

Merchant Shipping Acts, 125-126, 184, 250, 272,

Merchant Shipping Advisory Committee, 184, 200-201

Mere Hall, 130, 181, 233

Mersey Railway Tunnel, 165

Mersey, Lord, *Titanic* 188-202 & *Lusitania* 207-220

Moreton, Leslie, *Lusitania* AB, 208-210,

Napoleonic wars, 14-15, 17, 19-20

Navigation Laws, repeal of, 108-109

Noranmore, foundering of, 177-178
NUMAST, 1, 309-310

Oceanic, early White Star luxury liner, 165
Orion & the Brig *Revere*, early collision, 108

Palmerston, Viscount, Prime Minister, 68
Pearson, Joseph, 38
Penny postage, introduction of, 61-64
Phelps, R. W, 85-87
Philadelphia Line of sailing packets, 101
Postage, cost of prior to 1840, 25-26, 61-62

Queen Elizabeth 2, Cunard luxury liner, 302
Queen Elizabeth, Cunard luxury liner, 105, 302
Queen Mary, Cunard luxury liner, 105, 249, 267-270, 302
Queen Mary and *Curacoa*, wartime collision, 267-270
Queen Victoria, 71

Ras Aba Kharoub (Gray Hill's Mount of Olives home), 159, 167, 176, 233-234
Rebecca and her Daughters, 54
Register of Seamen, 103-104
Reina del Mar, 287
Reine del Pacifico, engine room explosion, 270-271
Richardson, Joseph, 1840 vesting of property on death, 90
Robinson, Annie, *Titanic* stewardess, 193
Rosebery, Earl of, 117
Rossetti, Dante Gabriel, 111, 114-115
Rothesay Castle, early steamer over 100 lost, 101
Royal William, first steamer to cross Atlantic direct, 101
Royd, Mabel Leigh, *Lusitania* passenger, 215
Russell, Lord John, Home Secretary 1835, 72

Savannah, first steamer to cross Atlantic, 101
Scott, Sir John, 111
Scott, Sir Leslie Q.C. later Lord Justice Scott, 8,111, 179
Sea Nymph & *Port Runcorn*, evidential difficulties,103
Second World War, 252-262
Shackleton, Sir Ernest, *Titanic* expert witness on ice, 202
Ship Masters Association of Liverpool, 103-104
Shrewsbury Assizes, 41-43
Slavery, 22, 80, 88-89
Smoke jacks (steamships), 44-45

Snaith Dr., acquittal, 54-55
Social problems 18th & 19th centuries,
Society for diffusion of Useful knowledge, 55-56, 62
Solicitor's Articles, premium & stamp duty 1888, 162
Squarey, Andrew, 109, 116, 117
Stanley of Alderley, Lord, Post Master General, 66
Steamship, coming of, 101-109
Stephenson, George Robert, 99
Stockbridge manorial rights, 235-236, 297
Stonehenge, contrast between 1817 & 1860, 48-49
Suez Canal closure 1956, 279-280; 1967, 305-306
Swinburne, 110-111
Symond connection, 10-11
Symons, George, *Titanic* fireman, 196-197

Thornton, Silvestor, deported to Australia, 88
Titanic, description 186-187 & wireless 201-202;
  Lord Mersey's investigation 188 - 202; speed 190, 191, 202-203;
  disaster fund 203-204;
Tootal, Frederick, *Lusitania* passenger, 215-216
Toxteth, 92, 307
Turner, Thomas, *Lusitania* Master, 210-211, 220

University College of Bloomsbury (London University), 56
Upton Manor, home of William Inman, 124
USA, Declaration of Independence adopts English law, 94
Usury, penalty for in 1840, 93-94

Wallasey, danger of gun powder magazine, 95
Wallop School, 247
War, Great 1914-18, the submarine menace 221-223;
  nation's health & diet 223; trench dugout ventilation 223;
  difficult social conditions following 226-230
War, Second World 1939-1945, battles Britain & London 423-254;
  Royal Air Force 253-262: radar & the magnetron 256-261;
  battle of Atlantic 258: V1 & V2 rockets 259; V.E. & V.J. days 260-261
Watt, James, inventor of electricity, 27, 70
White Star Line,125, 126, 165, 186,186-204 (*Titanic*)
With the Beduins, to east of the Jordan including an attack at Umbers and
  fears for Carrie at El Husn 133-142; to Palmyra across fifty miles of
  waterless desert 142-148; adventures south and east of the Dead Sea
  including kidnap & ransoming by Sheiks Saleh & Khalil of Kerak 142-148